MW01258432

CHURCH PLANTING

HOW TO PLANT A DYNAMIC CHURCH

DR. HENDRIK J VORSTER

FOREWORD BY: DR. YONGGI CHO

CHURCH PLANTING
(How to plant a dynamic church)

A practical guidebook to plant a Disciple-making Church

This book explores multiple aspects to consider prior to planting a new church as well
as the phases to consider when implementing essential systems in the newly pioneered
work.

www.churchplantingdoctor.com
resources@churchplantingdoctor.com
Or
www.churchplantinginstitute.com
resources@churchplantinginstitute.com

Copyright © Churchplantingdoctor.com 2021
All rights reserved.

No part of this publication may be reproduced, stored in a retrieval
system, or transmitted in any form or by any means, electronic, mechanical,
photocopying, recording or otherwise, without written permission from
Hendrik J. Vorster, also known as the Church Planting Doctor.
Church Planting Doctor is a Registered Ministry in Australia. Any profits from the sale
of this course will be used to promote church planting around the world.
Scripture taken from the HOLY BIBLE, NEW INTERNATIONAL VERSION®.
Copyright © 1973, 1978, 1984, 2011 Biblica. Used by permission of Zondervan.

ISBN: 978-1-7199398-1-2

TABLE OF CONTENTS

EXPANDED TABLE OF CONTENTS

Expanded Table of Contents

4. **Holy Spirit** - The primary person and partner for successful Church Planting.
5. **Signs and Wonders** - Our openness and willingness to the supernatural will unlock the Power of God.
6. **Apostolic and Missional** - Embracing the apostolic and being an apostolic people.
7. **Prophetic** - The Prophetic Word is present in every successful Church plant.
8. **Pastoral** - Caring for the harvest is as important as reaching them.
9. **Evangelistic** - The lifeblood of every work is her successful reaching and assimilating lost people.
10. **Discipleship** - Discipleship stands central to bringing people to maturity and fruitfulness.
11. **Servanthood** - Serving the poor, orphans, elderly and widows validates our faith.
12. **Biblical structures** - Organizational structures provide stability to growing church movements, not for lording it over but for smooth fulfillment of the purpose of God.

Chapter Six - Church Planting Terminology

Chapter Seven - Phase Two in Church Planting – Discipleship

1. Evangelising and preaching the Word of God.
2. Finding "**Worthy men**" to disciple.
3. Discipling the "**worthy men**." Discipleship process overview. (Specifics in Process of Discipleship chapter.)
4. Gather the "Worthy men" into groups.

Chapter Eight - The Process of Discipleship. Phase One in Discipleship – Salvation.

1. Repentance from dead works.
2. Faith in God.
3. Baptisms.

4. Laying on of Hands.
5. The resurrection of the dead.
6. Eternal Judgment.

Phase Two in Discipleship – Putting down roots in the Values of the Kingdom of God, and developing Spiritual disciplines.

Values

1. **Humility.** Humility is the quality of having a modest or subjected view of one's own importance.
2. **Penitence.** Penitence is the value of being meek and to practice reflective living.
3. **Meekness.** Meekness is the consistent characteristic of submissiveness.
4. **Spiritual Passion.** Spiritual passion is the value of giving, and expressing oneself fully in one's faith.
5. **Merciful.** To be Merciful is to be filled with grace towards all people, being constantly mindful of how much we've been forgiven of.
6. **Purity.** Purity is characterised by freedom from immorality, adultery and sinful contamination, and is a value of the Kingdom of God.
7. **Peacemakers.** A peacemaker is someone who actively steps up in every adversarial situation to work towards a peaceful outcome.
8. **Patient endurance under suffering.** It is the ability to endure through unjust treatment because of your faith, and even go beyond the expected response to such attacks by acting in a non-retaliatory way.
9. **Custodian.** A custodian is a keeper, preserver and defender of the Word of God and seeks in earnest to uphold the Word of God in every situation and circumstance. A Custodian is an upholder and advocate for the moral guidelines God set for His people.
10. **Reconciliatory.** We value reconciliation when we take the

someone, and expressed by showing them kindness, mercy, sympathy or tenderness.

36. **Caring.** Caring is being thoughtful and sympathetic towards others, especially considering their cares, burdens and concerns.

37. **Confident.** Confidence is the trust and faith you have in someone or something. It is a strong belief and feeling of certainty with which you do things.

38. **Steadfastness.** Steadfastness is the inner assertiveness to be firmly fixed and focused on doing what you purposed to do. It is the ability to be constant and unchanging in your course of faith.

39. **Contentment.** Contentment is the pre-positioning of being satisfied and pleased regardless of the circumstances in which you might find yourself in.

40. **Transforming.** Transformation is the process of being changed in condition, character, form or appearance. Only a commitment to being renewed in the spirit of your mind will ensure a lifetime of transformation.

41. **Deferent.** It is the considered and thoughtful action of living an exemplary life with the expressed purpose of pointing others to Christ through our way of living.

42. **Diligence.** Diligence is the practicing of careful and unceasing attention and being conscientious in everything we do.

43. **Trustworthiness.** Trustworthiness is truthfulness and faithfulness combined.

44. **Gentleness.** Gentleness is the ability to be patient and kind, and expressed by a continual compassionate leniency towards all people.

45. **Discernment.** Discernment is the ability to distinguish between right and wrong, between what is more expedient or not, and what is best.

46. **Truthfulness.** Truthfulness is the ability to speak and act in an honest, open, just and righteous way.

47. **Generosity.** Generosity is the ability to be unselfish with a readiness to give freely.

48. **Kindness.** Kindness is that generally warm-hearted, friendly and well-meaning interaction with others. Kindness is seen in the thoughtfulness and consideration with which we deal with people.

49. **Watchfulness.** It is the action and activity of paying close attention to one's own, and other's lives, especially as it impacts others positively for Christ's sake.

50. **Perseverance.** Perseverance is the inbred ability to endure through difficult and hard times.

51. **Honouring.** To value honoring is to be respectful in gesture, words and behaviour.

52. **Submissive.** Submission is the self-determined subjection to the will of another. For us it is our submission to the Will and Word of God.

Spiritual Disciplines

1. Prayer.
2. Fasting.
3. Stewardship.
4. Reading, meditating and practicing the Word of God.
5. Worship.
6. Simplicity.
7. Servanthood.
8. Obedience and submission.

Phase Three in Discipleship – Developing Gifts and Purpose Driven Skills.

1. Gift Discovery Course. DISC. Weekend.
2. Walk through the Bible Course. Weekend.
3. Faith sharing Course. Weekend.
4. Overcoming Course. Weekend.
5. Group Leader Training Course. Weekend.

Phase Four in Discipleship– Discipling Fruit-producers.

Phase Five in Discipleship – Multiplying the Body.

Chapter Nine - Phase Three in Church Planting – Congregating the Discipleship groups.

COMMENTS FROM WORLD LEADERS

Dr. **Larry Stockstill** – Emeritus Senior Pastor of Bethany World Prayer Center, and president of the Surge project. (*Planted 26'000 churches in 114 nations.*)

"Dr. Vorster's work is truly amazing. I predict a church planting explosion in the earth through these thorough and simple yet advanced teachings to world church planters. Coupled with his own experience and success, there is no nation that will not benefit from this entire program being implemented. Congratulations to you as the reader for finding a jewel for your life!"

Dr. Ranjit Abraham – Secretary General of the New Delhi Church of God in India. (4500 churches in India.)

"A Detailed and thorough account of the concept, the book beautifully evaluates every aspect of the pioneer's journey of church planting. I specifically connected with the section about discipleship, which is critical in ensuring that the pioneer's fruit is multiplied and his vision is fulfilled beyond his own lifetime. This is something that all ministries must focus on to see the Kingdom built continuously and diligently.

All in all, it is a great guidebook for evangelists and ministers, irrespec-

*tive of the stage of life and ministry they are at, **to understand the heart, calling and fervour that goes behind church planting across the world.** I congratulate Dr Hendrik Vorster for being able to consolidate his experiences with church planters globally and bring us his unique perspective on the concept. I pray this book may reach and bless many on their pioneering journey for the Lord!*

Dr. Bob Rodgers – Senior Pastor, Evangel World Prayer Center, Louisville, KY.

"***Dr. Hendrik Vorster** is one of the **leading church planters in the world**. His years of **successful experience** in what is necessary to start a church are recorded **in this powerful book**. If one follows these steps, **your church will multiply**, then multiply again just as the churches grew in the New Testament. **I highly recommend this book** to any Pastor and prospective Church Planter.*"

Dr. Ed Delph – President of Nation Strategy.

"*I like where Dr. Hendrik is going in his new book, **Church Planting**. **It's a kingdom approach to church planting**. He connects contrasting kingdom keys that every church planter should be aware of for planting a God-breathed church.*

***He connects Truth and Spirit**, and not just the usual Truth or Spirit approach to church planting. **He connects** evangelism and discipleship; fruit of the Spirit and the gifts of the Spirit; favor with God and favor with man; the art of being led by God and the ability to plan and set goals; prayer as well as hard work. You don't often see the ability to integrate these crucial keys to successful church planting and maturing.*

*In one sense, **it's not just church planting that matters; it's the kind of church that's planted** that matters. **Hendrik captures this perfectly**. Let there be light!*"

. . .

Rev Dr. Margaret Court AO, MBE – President and Senior Minister of Victory Life International (Network of churches in over 22 nations.)

"I believe the church is poised for an outpouring from God – an awakening! It is our responsibly to arise and be prepared for this powerful season. Hendrik J. Vorster's book, Church Planting, comes to do just that. This word base, spirit led book ***is packed with insight, wisdom and practical principles to enable the church to thrive.*** *With over 30 years experience in planting and overseeing thousands of churches,* ***I believe this book will practically equip and prepare the body of Christ to "go and make disciples of all nations."***

Dr. John Bond – Chairman of Compassion Australia & World zone Leader of DCPI for Southeast Asia & Pacific Islands.

"Drawing from his diverse experiences across the world over many years Dr. Vorster provides us with ***a comprehensive step by step*** *outline* ***of the why, the how to's, the possibilities, the spiritual foundations, the essentials, the practicalities*** *and the joys and thrills of church planting.*

You can go to a relevant section and read it as a guide because ***this book of books is a comprehensive thesaurus on Church Planting***. *Hendrik has lived this, breathed this, practiced this and based this book on his years of doing this!* ***This is not a book of theory***, *but one, which has been* ***born in the International kiln of church planting***. *This a priority read if you want to plant a church!*

Pastor Renier Pelser – Secretary General of the Full Gospel Church of God in Southern Africa.

"I believe one of the most significant challenges in today's church is that of the know-how of planting churches is missing and people quickly get stuck in their comfort zones of existing within "safe environments." ***Here is a blueprint of the how, the why, and practical advice*** *from all angles that makes this "nearly" impossible to fail. It is God's command, and therefore He uses tools like my friend of Bible school days,* ***Dr. Hendrik Vorster, who gives exceptional tips and counsel***, *from* ***a well-prepared, success-***

proven book, *that will guide any disciple of Christ thoroughly to the cause of God's heart to plant Churches."*

Apostle Robert Kasaro – Founder and Senior Minister of Jesus Calls Worship Center in the Kingdom of Swaziland.

*"**This is a must-read** for every Believer who understands God's heartbeat for the end time agenda. Dr. Hendrik Vorster offers deep insights and precise instructions through **a much needed and well-researched resource** for Church Planting. **This book is practical and relevant,** and will provoke you to also take action."*

Pastor Tony Cameneti – Senior Pastor of Rhema Family Church in Brisbane, Australia

*"Wow! As church planters and pioneers we immediately recognized the content of this book as being extremely valuable. Simply put, the pioneer church planter will know what to do before a church plant and after the launch be prepared to organize and grow the church. This is one of the few complete books on these important elements of planting and pastoring. **We highly recommend this book** to not only the new church planter, but also to those who have been in ministry for years."*

FOREWORD

I've had the privilege of having many godly, apostolic friends. These men and women know how to hear from God, by faith believe God for the impossible, and are full of vision and dreams to advance the kingdom of God. They are some of my most precious gifts.

One of those people is Dr. Hendrik Vorster. For many years Hendrik has been a member of the Church Growth International board. He has helped me, given me wise advice, and has been a deeply loyal brother and friend in the faith. I can't thank him enough for his kindness to me.

God gave Hendrik Vorster a dream that most would think impossible. The dream was to plant hundreds of churches in Australia, Vietnam, Thailand, India, the Philippines, and other nations. That dream is being fulfilled today and his impact as a leader has influenced church planters in over 70 nations on 5 continents. His ministry, Cornerstone Ministry International is truly fulfilling a dream given by God for such a time as this. Dr. Vorster tells me that I have been a mentor to him. As a son in the faith, I pray for him that his dedication and faith will increase his supernatural vision to reach masses of lost people.

In his latest book, Dr. Vorster writes about key factors for church planting, for growing a church, and for ensuring that a church remains healthy. He has given an amazing amount of information that covers numerous essential details for the church planter. I highly recommend his book: **Church Planting: How to Plant a Dynamic Church**. It is one of the finest treatments of this subject that is available. You too can be a church planter. This book will give you a spiritual "**blueprint**" to help in your success.

Like Dr. Vorster, I too have had a vision to plant churches and raise up godly leaders with vision. The church that I planted in Seoul, Korea had very humble beginnings. We began in a small tent in a destitute part of a devastated city. I had a burning desire to bring hope to the hopeless. God miraculously moved, healed, delivered people, and brought hope for a tremendous future. Our Lord has continued to give us grace as we have planted or assisted others to plant many thousands of churches.

Someone has said that "church planting" is the greatest way to grow God's kingdom. The new church begins with new converts who receive reconciliation in Christ. They are baptized in water and baptized in the Holy Spirit. They frequently desire to share their newfound faith with their families, friends, and neighbours. I have no doubt that church planting is a primary tool that our Lord uses to advance the Church globally. Please find help in your church planting endeavours from this book.

Yonggi Cho

INTRODUCTION TO CHURCH PLANTING

M atthew 16:18-19 (NIV)

"18 *And I tell you that you are Peter, and on this rock* **I will build my church**, *and the gates of Hades will not overcome it. 19* **I will give you the keys** *of the kingdom of heaven; whatever you bind on earth will be bound in heaven, and whatever you loose on earth will be loosed in heaven.*"

I will build My Church

Jesus gave us two incredible promises: 1. That He would build His Church, and 2. That the gates of hell would not be able to stand against her. He also promised to give us the keys to advance His kingdom work. The extent, to which we keep these truths in the forefront of our minds, and work as Partners alongside Jesus, is the extent to which we will see dynamic Churches planted around the world.

Our journey will explore what we can learn from the Word of God and how Jesus build His Church and taught His Disciples to build the Church. After equipping thousands of Church Leaders, over the past 32 years, in over 70 nations, spanning 5 Continents, from Evangelicals to Charismatics, I have learnt that there are definite keys to successful Church Planting.

Keys are principles from God's Word, which, when applied, used and adhered to, almost have a supra cultural, determined outcome. Godly Principles apply in every culture and socio-economic sub structure. Wherever the Lord determined His Kingdom to advance is where the principles of the Word of God will apply. Through my experience in extensively working both within developed and developing nations, I've observed these principles effectively applied.

I trust that this book will be of assistance to you in understanding the way to building and growing a more successful and fruitful ministry in Church Planting. Church Planting is both exciting and challenging at the same time. It is an expression of one of the most biblical ways of evangelising and expanding the Kingdom of God.

May the Lord give us a spirit of understanding and knowledge as we take this journey together. I will attempt to prime our hearts with an awareness of the huge challenge before us, an appreciation for the call of God to ministry, an understanding for the power of prayer, the importance of developing sound spiritual values and disciplines, developing leadership qualities, both within ourselves and within those whom we will disciple, and attending to administrative systems.

May your heart, for seeing the lost suitably reached, be enlarged and your vision for planting churches be expanded. My prayer is that you will be encouraged by the possibilities and that you will find yourself taking heart at the task before us.

Dr. Hendrik J. Vorster

THE CHALLENGE TO PLANT NEW CHURCHES

Never in history has the task before us been so enormous and compelling. The challenge, to preach and reach every tongue, tribe and nation with the Good News of Jesus Christ is increasing at disproportionate rates. If we consider the net world population growth, compared with the conversion rate within the Church, if we consider the moral depravity and falling away, if we consider the real financial economic position of nations, not to speak of the average person in the street, if we consider the health and welfare of people, if we consider the true educational level within the world compared to the tempo at which knowledge is increasing, we have to conclude that the task is huge. Never has the opportunity to make a tangible and sound difference been at such a premium as what it is now.

We have an opportunity to make a difference, and I think it is time for those who can, who have, and are able, to dig down deep and go, or help those who can, to reach our generation with the Gospel of Jesus Christ.

We are challenged, not only by the enormity of the statistics which are available, but also from an eschatological perspective, and it is from this challenging dimension that I wish to take my departure to present to us the challenge before us.

The Biblical challenge

Three Scriptures compel us to rethink the task before us. They are not
the only Scriptures, which harness our attention, however for the
purpose of this chapter they will suffice. Though many of us have, in a
sense, become immune to the compelling message within these Scriptures, we nevertheless need to allow the Holy Spirit to quicken them in
our hearts again.

The first, of many, present to us the scope of the task at hand.
Jesus' mission was clear and that mission was that the message of the
Kingdom of God would be *'preached in all the world, unto all nations.'*

> Matthew 24:14 (KJV) "[14] And ***this gospel of the kingdom
> shall be preached in all the world*** for a witness unto all
> nations; and then shall the end come."

The extent to which the Gospel will be preached is declared, and
expressed, in this message from the Lord Jesus. Through this declaration He confirmed many prophetic utterances that this 'message,' will
be preached *'to the ends of the earth.'* In His final commission to His
Followers, He gave them instruction to 'go, and teach all nations.' I
believe the zeal of the Lord will accomplish this desire to bring the
good news of Jesus to all *'ethnos'* nations.

In my travels around the world I have never seen such a bursting
forth of the Call of God upon young people like I have seen during the
last few years. The Lord is calling a new generation into His service
who would cross the unchartered waters, and go where no other generation have gone before. I believe this generation, of Called Servants of
God, will be the generation who will finish the task of taking the
whole gospel to the whole world.

This challenge is further defined through our second Scriptural
challenge in Revelation 5 verse 9, where the Apostle John shares a
vision he had. He saw the twenty-four elders worshipping before the
Lord and then they started to sing a song of praise to the Lamb for
purchasing unto himself a kingdom and priests ***'from every tribe and
language and people and nation.'*** This vision encapsulates for us the

extent to which the gospel would reach the ends of the earth. If the vision is anything to go by, and I believe it does, then we are challenged with the more than 6000 (2016 - Joshua Project Statistics) tribes, which have never, not even once, had the gospel preached to them.

> Revelation 5:8-10 (NIV) [8] And when he had taken it, the four
> living creatures* and the twenty-four elders* fell down
> before the Lamb. Each one had a harp* and ***they were
> holding golden bowls full of incense, which are the
> prayers* of the saints*** [9] And they sang a new song: "You
> are worthy* to take the scroll and to open its seals, because
> you were slain, ***and with your blood* you purchased* men
> for God from every tribe and language and people and
> nation.*** [10] ***You have made them to be a kingdom and
> priests* to serve our God,*** and they will reign on the
> earth."

We are challenged to take the whole Gospel to the whole world, and that includes taking it to every tribe and language and people and nation.

Another Scripture, already mentioned in part, which calls for our considered attention is the well known 'Great Commission' or 'Finishing Task' in Matthew 28 verses 18-20 which presents to us a packaged instruction, which, beyond the emphasis which most of us grew up with, of it being an instruction to primarily "go", in essence challenges us to take this gospel, not only to simply share it, but to ensure that those who hear the gospel be discipled into obedient followers of Christ.

For some, this means just sharing their faith, and by sharing their faith they've fulfilled their obligation to the Great Commission. I believe the Great Commission is truly a commissioning Scripture for effective Discipling and culminating into Church Planting. The part of the Great Commission, which we more often emphasize, is the ***'go, and make disciples'*** part, however, the Great Commission ends with a full stop, only after including '***baptism*'** and '***teaching the disciples to obey everything*.**' The message of the Kingdom of God will only grow and expand to the extent to which each one of us become earnest in presenting and fulfilling the whole commission. This could only be executed within the confines of a body of believers.

I grew up in Africa, and we have a saying: "It takes a mother to give birth to a child, but a community to raise a child." This, I believe to be true about the process of discipleship, or as we commonly know it, fulfilling the Great Commission. It takes a Church to help a child of God grow up in their faith, and that comes through the collaborated efforts of a body of believers.

What is that commission to us as Believers?

> Matthew 28:19-20 (KJV) "[19] Go ye therefore, and teach all nations, baptizing them in the name of the Father, and of the Son, and of the Holy Ghost: [20] Teaching them to observe all things whatsoever I have commanded you: and, lo, I am with you always, even unto the end of the world. Amen."

The challenge this Great Commission poses to us today is to responsibly execute all of it, and that is only possible within the confines of a Church Body, albeit that be where 'two or three gather together' in His Name. Like Jesus modelled and taught His disciples in a gathered group, so too should we, not just share our faith, but gather those who accept Christ as their Lord and Savior, baptize them, and teach them to obey everything the Lord Jesus taught us through His Word and through His Holy Spirit.

Barna Research

The Barna research group started a research project among professing Christians in 1993, which they published in December 2013, to determine the extent to which believers share their faith. Their research showed an alarming, and increasing, low level of participation of believers actually sharing their faith.

The challenge exists not only to spread the Word to the ends of the earth, but the researchers found, also to mobilize those within the Church to actually take up their responsibility to go, and share. The challenge is therefor twofold, both in getting believers to share, as well as mobilizing them to share.

Why don't people share their faith anymore?

John Daniel posted this research document in christianpost.com on July 12, 2013, sighting his findings as to why people don't share their Faith as freely as they possibly should. The top 12 reasons were, and please indulge my paraphrasing of his excellent research:

"Fear, of being ridiculed, disapproved and persecuted by the world, especially those who have authority over us parents, spouses and bosses,"

"Not feeling they are qualified."

"Just wanting to keep their jobs."

"Complacency, lack of compassion, passion and laziness."

"Too many worry about being politically correct."

"Influenced by a worldly culture."

"A lack of training and don't know How to share."

"A feeling of not being strong Christians with strong faith."

"Few people believed what they said they believed in."

"They embrace false beliefs."

"They don't know the Gospel clearly and rightly."

"They don't see the example from Church leaders."

Jesus challenged His disciples in Acts 1 verse 8 to be His Witnesses in Jerusalem, Judea, Samaria, and unto the ends of the earth.

We are challenged!

We are challenged! We are Biblically challenged to take this Gospel, this Faith, and share it with everyone, that by all means, all people will hear, and make every effort to bring those who believe into an obedient relationship with Jesus Christ. This challenge is huge. It only takes this generation to not share their faith, and then we will find the challenge before us insurmountable. Let us pray and pay so that those who want to and sense the urgency of this Call of God on their lives can go and preach this Gospel of Jesus Christ, and plant Churches where no man has ever gone before.

The Moral Challenge

From a worldly perspective, the world is crying out for help. Never have we experienced such turmoil in the world, with all the wars, human displacements, and migrations, and human trafficking. There is the challenge between of this war between Islamic extremists, and those not upholding their belief system. There is such an assault on the hearts and minds of people. The depravity of mankind is at an all time high. It is truly like in the days of Noah where every inclination of man is wrought with perverseness.

Reports tell us that some 30 million children and woman might be caught in the sex trafficking industry. Their souls cry out to be delivered. Their souls cry out to receive the hope only Christ can bring. We have never before seen such an onslaught on the morality of the people. The over exposure to violence, wars, verbal and physical abuse is seen all around us on a daily basis. The extent to which people, especially children are exposed to this kind of moral abuses through television, computer games, and even children programs, pose us with an even greater challenge to bring the light of the Gospel of Jesus to the Darkness around us. The open and free access to pornography through the increasing amount of mobile and media devices have brought much depravity in the hearts and minds of nations. The innocence of nations has been raped in a sense. The moral onslaught is rife.

> Matthew 24:37-39 (NIV) [37] As it was in the days of Noah, so
> it will be at the coming of the Son of Man. [38] For in the
> days before the flood, people were eating and drinking,
> marrying and giving in marriage, up to the day Noah

entered the ark; [39] and they knew nothing about what would happen until the flood came and took them all away. That is how it will be at the coming of the Son of Man.

To understand the context of Jesus' warning here in Matthew 24, we have to take a look back in Genesis when Noah was called upon to build an ark. He built an ark and he preached a message for people to make right with God.

Genesis 6:5 (AMP) "[5] The Lord saw that the wickedness of man was great in the earth, and that every imagination and intention of all human thinking was only evil continually."

Genesis 6:11-12 (AMP) "[11] The earth was depraved and putrid in God's sight, and the land was filled with violence (desecration, infringement, outrage, assault, and lust for power). [12] And God looked upon the world and saw how degenerate, debased, and vicious it was, for all humanity had corrupted their way upon the earth and lost their true direction."

These few verses give us a quick insight into what Jesus meant when He referred to the days of Noah. There existed an unhealthy environment of lust, greed, violence, desecration, viciousness, where every inclination and intention of all human thinking was only evil all the time. You can't, but draw the same direct parallel between then and the way things are now, as with the days of Noah. The moral depravity is everywhere. In the midst of this compelling situation in the days of Noah God found Noah to be just, righteous and walking in habitual fellowship with Him, and therefor he found Favour with the Lord.

Genesis 6:8-9 (AMP) "[8] But Noah found grace (favor) in the eyes of the Lord. [9] This is the history of the generations of Noah. Noah was a just and righteous man, blameless in his [evil] generation; Noah walked [in habitual fellowship] with God."

We, the Church of Jesus Christ, the Believers, are challenged to walk in the same uprightness and righteousness of Noah. We are called upon to keep our flavour. It is only through the Church that the light of the Gospel can continue to shine in the midst of the darkness that exists in the heart of society. Maybe a Word of encouragement to those of you who read this book with faith-filled hearts, we have the hope given us through the Lord Jesus, that "the gates of hell will not prevail." I pray that the reality of the state of affairs in the world would encourage us to embrace the challenge rather than push us into a position of despair and despondency. Let's pray that God would use us to bring Light into Darkness.

The Population Growth Challenge.

Since the turn of the century, the world population grew with almost 75 million people per year. Earlier this year (2016) we topped 7.4 Billion people. Last year the net world population growth was around 78 million people. That means that the net population growth was an average of 113000 people every day. These people need to be reached. They need to hear the gospel of Jesus. They need to know. They need to be gathered.

If the average church size is 85 people per congregation then we need more than a million new churches per year, just to gather the yearly increased harvest. If the average Cell group or Home group is 15 people, then we need just over 5'600'000 new Cell group leaders to accommodate and reach the annual net world population growth. If this stands to be true of the present challenge before us, how much more do we need to reach out and plant new Churches to reach the present harvest?

Matthew 9:37-38 [NIV] "The harvest is plentiful but the workers are few! Ask the Lord of the Harvest, therefor, to send out workers into his harvest field."

We urgently need to pray to the Lord of the harvest for more workers. If you are one of those who answered to the Call of God, take a moment to pray that God would give you workers to bring the harvest in alongside you. We need millions of harvesters just to meet the current population growth challenge, and we are not even presenting the overall world population. May God stir our hearts to respond to His Call.

The Unreached People Groups Challenge.

We remain challenged by the great Commission and the desire of the Lord, that all people from every tribe, nation and language would hear the Gospel, at least once. The Joshua Project research shows that we still have an unfinished task. According to their published research results as at June 2016, there still remained an enormous task before us. Someone has to go.

May the Lord of the harvest put a vision for reaching some of these people groups in your heart. According to this research findings there still is a total of 6671 wholly Unreached People groups. We still have 3803 Partially Reached People groups. We still have 1106 Minimally Reached People groups, and 1679 Formerly or Falsely Reached people groups.

The fact remains that there are whole Tribes, language groups, and ethnic groups who have never, not even once, heard the Gospel of Jesus Christ. 60% of the, to be reached, harvest is in Asia. 28% of this, to be reached, harvest remains in Africa and the Middle Eastern Countries.

It might just be that God is calling you to go and reach them! As you read this book, allow the Lord of the Harvest to find a man and a woman, in you, whom He can send, whom He could use to reach these people. God is calling and challenging men and woman to go and plant a Church among these people. The enormity of this challenge, especially within the 10/40 window, cannot be overlooked. We are challenged.

All People Groups
by Reachedness Status

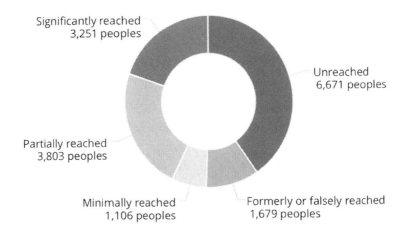

Significantly reached
3,251 peoples

Unreached
6,671 peoples

Partially reached
3,803 peoples

Minimally reached
1,106 peoples

Formerly or falsely reached
1,679 peoples

A good resource to look at is that published by the Joshua Project on their website at the end of June 2016.

But this challenge is not only to go into rural and remote areas, this harvest of unreached people groups might be closer to us than what we think.

The Urbanization Challenge.

The ever-increasing amount of people flocking to urban areas calls for our urgent attention. We need a rethink on the way to reach urban people. The complexities around confined spaces, time restraints, work environments and cultures compete with our historical approaches of Church Planting. Learning from those who have been able to effectively reach their city dwellers should be at the forefront of our pursuits.

UN Research

A report by the United Nations, Department of Economic and Social Affairs, Population Division (2014) reports as follows:

"World Urbanisation Prospects: The 2014 Revision

• Globally, more people live in urban areas than in rural areas, with 54 per cent of the world's population residing in urban areas in 2014. In 1950, 30 per cent of the world's population was urban, and by 2050, 66 per cent of the world's population is projected to be urban.

• Today, the most urbanised regions include Northern America (82 per cent living in urban areas in 2014), Latin America and the Caribbean (80 per cent), and Europe (73 per cent). In contrast, Africa and Asia remain mostly rural, with 40 and 48 per cent of their respective populations living in urban areas. All regions are expected to urbanise further over the coming decades. Africa and Asia are urbanising faster than the other regions and are projected to become 56 and 64 per cent urban, respectively, by 2050.

• The rural population of the world has grown slowly since 1950 and is expected to reach its peak in a few years. The global rural population is now close to 3.4 billion and is expected to decline to 3.2 billion by 2050. Africa and Asia are home to nearly 90 per cent of the world's rural population. India has the largest rural population (857 million), followed by China (635 million).

• The urban population of the world has grown rapidly since 1950, from 746 million to 3.9 billion in 2014. Asia, despite its lower level of urbanisation, is home to 53 per cent of the world's urban population, followed by Europe (14 per cent) and Latin America and the Caribbean (13 per cent).

•Continuing population growth and urbanisation are projected to add 2.5 billion people to the world's urban population by 2050, with nearly 90 per cent of the increase concentrated in Asia and Africa.

• Just three countries—India, China and Nigeria— together are expected to account for 37 per cent of the projected growth of the world's urban population between 2014 and 2050. India is projected to add 404 million urban dwellers, China 292 million and Nigeria 212 million.

• Close to half of the world's urban dwellers reside in relatively small settlements of less than 500,000 inhabitants, while only around one in eight live in the 28 mega-cities with more than 10 million inhabitants.

• Tokyo is the world's largest city with an agglomeration of 38 million inhabitants, followed by Delhi with 25 million, Shanghai with 23 million, and Mexico City, Mumbai and São Paulo, each with around 21 million inhabitants. By 2030, the world is projected to have 41 mega-cities with more than 10 million inhabitants. Tokyo is projected to remain the world's largest city in 2030 with 37 million inhabitants, followed closely by Delhi where the population is projected to rise swiftly to 36 million. Several decades ago most of the world's largest urban agglomerations were found in the more developed regions, but today's large cities are concentrated in the global south. The fastest growing urban agglomerations are medium-sized cities and cities with less than 1 million inhabitants located in Asia and Africa.

• Some cities have experienced population decline in recent years. Most of these are located in the low-fertility countries of Asia and Europe where the overall population is stagnant or declining. Economic contraction and natural disasters have contributed to population losses in some cities as well.

As the world continues to urbanise, sustainable development challenges will be increasingly concentrated in cities, particularly in the lower-middle income countries where the pace of urbanisation is fastest. Integrated policies to improve the lives of both urban and rural dwellers are needed."

Understanding and reaching those living in urban areas should be at the forefront of those seeking to following the Call of God to ministering to those who will become urban dwellers. The research highlight the fact that the greatest urbanisation will take place in India, China and Nigeria where there will be an estimated 404 million new urban dwellers over coming years. We need to train and equip our people to go and prepare for this harvest of souls.

Even though this draws our urgent attention and effort, we still need to consider the remaining 40% of unreached people groups who will still live in populations smaller than 500'000 people.

I was reading the story of Jonah the other day and it struck me again that this whole message and sending of Jonah was because there was a hundred and twenty-thousand people living in that city. God expressed concern for the multitude of people living there.

Jonah 4:11 (NIV)

[11] But Nineveh has more than a hundred and twenty-thousand people who cannot tell their right hand from their left, and many cattle as well. Should I not be concerned about that great city?"

If the hundred and twenty-thousand people living in Nineveh caught the attention of God, how much more should it not arrest our attention into action when we look at the ever-increasing growing population of our cities.

The Age demographical Challenge.

For a decade or more we focused our attention to reaching the increasing amount of young people, however, that focus on the young should again shift to include people of all ages. It remains true that the most responsive people to receive Jesus as their Lord and Saviour come from the age group of under 15, and at present we have around 26% of young people in that age bracket. The shift, which needs our focused attention, is the harvest we failed to reach in their teens who now is part of the increasing group of 15-65 year olds.

With the life expectancy increasing from 58 in 1970 to a life expectancy of 71 in 2013, we are granted a few extra years to reach those whom have lived their lives without Christ. The population growth is expected to increase but not to the proportions we've seen in previous generations. From a fertility rate of 4.7 children per woman in the 1970's it has dropped significantly to 2.5 children per woman in 2013. This means that we will have a proportionate age demographic in the future.

God is calling men and woman of all ages into His service. God needs you! Don't say you're too young, or you're too old. God need you to go and reach the lost and plant new Churches that will reach every age.

The Migration Challenge.

The past decade or more, more than ever before, we've seen major people migrations take place around the world. Over centuries there's been major people migrations and displacements around the world. My forefathers came to Southern Africa in the 1600's. At that time their was a major exploration of continents and many desired the adventure of going on exploration expeditions to discover the unknown world.

Sadly not all migrations and people movements was the result of choice. Wars and political unrest, genocide, racial and religious wars caused many mass migrations throughout the ages. The result of these people displacements brought new opportunities and challenges. Many revivals came about as a result of these migrations.

The Book of Acts tells us that Jesus' original intention was that His disciples would be His witnesses both in Jerusalem, Judea, Samaria and the ends of the earth, however, we find them confined to Jerusalem until a persecution broke out, and as a result of this mass people migration or displacement, the gospel eventually spread, but this came by default and not by intention.

> Acts 1:8 (NIV) [8] But you will receive power when the Holy Spirit comes on you; and you will be my witnesses in Jerusalem, and in all Judea and Samaria, and to the ends of the earth."

> Acts 8:1 (NIV) [8:1] And Saul was there, giving approval to his death. On that day a great persecution broke out against the church at Jerusalem, and all except the apostles were scattered throughout Judea and Samaria.

> Acts 8:4 (NIV) [4] Those who had been scattered preached the word wherever they went.

Acts 11:19-21 (NIV) [19] Now those who had been scattered by
the persecution in connection with Stephen traveled as far
as Phoenicia, Cyprus and Antioch, telling the message only
to Jews. [20] Some of them, however, men from Cyprus and
Cyrene, went to Antioch and began to speak to Greeks also,
telling them the good news about the Lord Jesus. [21] The
Lord's hand was with them, and a great number of people
believed and turned to the Lord.

As sad as what it was that these people had to flee as a result of
persecution, it most certainly became a torch-bearing exercise for the
advancement of the Kingdom of God.

Global people migrations

Today we have the Syrian migration. Millions have been displaced
through war. We hear many testimonies of these displaced Syrians who
have now given their lives to Christ. The opportunity to reach these
displaced people is a wonderful and rare opportunity.

We have the Ethiopian and Southern African migration resulting in
major Xenophobian attacks whereby thousands of people are loosing
their lives. Just think of the hostilities between Muslim extremist and
the Christians in Northern African countries like Nigeria. We have the
Mexican migration into North America. Within Asia we have the
constant migration of people attempting to flee their own to find a
better life elsewhere.

Regardless of the cause or reason for these migrations, these
people, at their most vulnerable, need Jesus. They need us. May we
cease the moment and hear if the Father is not calling us to go and
plant a Church among these displaced or migrated people.

We have so many testimonies coming through of migrants coming
to faith in Jesus Christ, both through supernatural and outreach
means. We praise God for every soul that is reached.

God might be calling you to go and reach those who have been
displaced. May the Lord of the Harvest find you today! This is equally

as huge a challenge as much as what it presents to us an enormous opportunity to share the Gospel and plant new Churches.

Church Planting is the most effective form of evangelism.

Dr. C. Peter Wagner, in his Book "Church Planting for a greater harvest" says: "*the most effective methodology for evangelism is church planting.*" He goes on to say that his research shown that an average of 46 people come to the Lord through each and every new church that is planted. His research shows that the most effective methodology of evangelism is through Church Planting. May the Lord of the Harvest help us to work smarter and not just harder.

Conclusion

May we never cease to ask the Father for workers to bring in the harvest. The safest and most secure place to bring the harvest into, is the local church. That local church might start as, or operate as a small group, but that is where the harvest needs to be brought into. I believe God is calling more men and woman, to face the challenge for world evangelization, than what many seem to think.

There might be people in your family, group, congregation, or even if you are a pastor reading this book, who actually sense the call of God on their lives. You might be the one whom God is challenging to take the challenge. Let's face the challenge before us and go and plant churches to reach our generation for Christ.

2

PHASES OF CHURCH PLANTING

There are basically five phases to planting a dynamic Church, three of which happens prior to the Church being constituted, and one after her going public.

Phase One - The Calling, Vision and Preparation Phase

Phase One describes the Calling, Vision and Preparation Phase, where we ensure that we depart on this exciting journey with a clear Call of God upon our lives, a Holy Spirit Inspired Vision, the Empowerment of the Holy Spirit, well established Spiritual Disciplines, and under the Discipleship of a Godly Discipler.

Phase Two - The Discipleship Phase

Phase Two describes the Discipleship Phase. The Discipleship Phase marks the first steps in planting a Fruit-producing, multipliable Church by finding our Disciples, our worthy men and woman, and this is a key landmark during this phase. The Discipleship Phase is also the phase where we develop and establish our God-ordained DNA through the process of discipleship. If you do this right, it most certainly guarantees success.

During this phase we also mobilize our disciples from learners to practitioners. Another landmark during this phase is that we put things we've learnt into practice, and one of the key steps towards a fruit-producing life is leading someone to the Lord, baptizing them, as well as having a consistent, life share-able relationship in Christ. This phase is also landmarked by our disciples gathering their disciples into groups for effective ministry, teaching and discipleship them.

Phase Three - The congregating and formulization of the Discipleship groups phase

Phase Three describes the congregating, and the formalizing of the Discipleship groups. Some of the key landmarks during this phase are the formulation of the Church constitution, refining the Church structure, and appointing office bearers. During this phase we organize the Discipleship Group Leaders, by appointing some Elders, some as Deacons, and some into key administrative and organizational roles. Establishing a sound Administrative system and appointing Key staff is essential during this phase.

Attention is given to formulizing the liturgy for the congregational services. Until this point most, if not all, of the growth came through personal evangelism, however, during this phase corporate harvesting events are planned and developed to not just reach our Jerusalem, but also our Judea, Samaria and the ends of the earth. We organize our disciples into body ministry areas. During this phase look for the right place to bring everyone together. It is essential to effective Church Planting that we have each of these in place to truly have a New Testament Church foundation to build upon. This phase is also defined by the development and implementation of systems to maintain the health and welfare, and continued growth of the Church. (Systems are defined in the Chapter on systems.)

Phase Four - The Church-launching Phase

Phase Four describes the Church-launching Phase. This phase is landmarked by the Discipleship Groups congregating for Weekly Worship, observing the Sacraments and Celebration. During this phase we start seeing this body of Believers going public as a unified Body where each one does its part to build the Church up. During this phase the Church mobilizes herself into a corporate harvesting machine. By maintaining the DNA of Discipleship and keeping its focus on seeking and saving the lost, the church will traject herself on a pathway of continued growth. You will find Timothy's raised, Paul's released, and the Kingdom of God expanding in various and wonderful ways.

Phase Five - The Maturing and Daughtering Phase

Phase Five describes the Maturing and Daughtering Phase. Healthy churches reproduce, and this is mostly observed by their ability to continue to plant new churches. Instead of being alarmed by some seemingly wanting to break away to start their own ministries, rather embrace the cycle of seeing our spiritual sons and daughters mature and coming ministers and leaders in their own right. Some will stay with you and some will want to go. If you observe their destiny before they do, you could actually make the whole process of multiplication a pleasant one, and release them in a God-honoring way. Churches need to multiply to continue to grow.

3

PHASE ONE OF CHURCH PLANTING - THE CALLING, VISION AND PREPARATION PHASE

I n Church Planting it is true that a Holy Spirit inspired Vision, combined with a Called Servant of God, Empowered by the Holy Spirit, living a disciplined, Spiritual, relational life in Christ, under the Discipleship of a Mature Follower of Jesus Christ, will most certainly advance the prospects for successful and efficient Discipleship and ultimately dynamic Church Planting. Having the right man in the right location, at the right time, will most certainly provide for Kingdom advancing successes.

 "a Holy Spirit inspired Vision, combined with a Called Servant of God, Empowered by the Holy Spirit, living a disciplined, Spiritual, relational life in Christ, under the Discipleship of a Mature Follower of Jesus Christ, will most certainly advance the prospects for successful and efficient Discipleship and ultimately dynamic Church Planting."

— DR. HENDRIK J. VORSTER

During this initial phase of Church Planting we lay a deep and solid foundation upon which we could truly build a ministry that will greatly advance the Kingdom of God, as well as endure the test of time. The diligence we apply in making thorough preparations will ensure that the Vision God gave us will be accomplished.

I have outlined what I see as the essential foundations to be laid in order that the following phases will be build on the right foundations. They follow. These are not necessarily in a sequential order, but they are definitely all critically important for establishing a rock solid ministry.

a. Affirm the Call of God.

Step One is to make your Calling sure and Fast. We need to make sure that we are called to lead the planting of a Church. Everyone is called to be part of Church Planting, but not all carry that anointing to lead the planting of a new church. The Apostle Peter said in his second Epistle that the brothers should "***make their calling and election sure***."

> **2 Peter 1:10 KJV** "*10 Wherefore the rather, brethren,* **give diligence to make your calling and election sure**: *for if ye do these things, ye shall never fall.*"

The Apostle Paul in his various Pastoral letters encourage leaders to "***know the hope of their calling.***" In other words to know "***why***" God called them, and for "***what purpose***" He called them. This should be the same for us. We need to affirm that we have been called by God to fulfil a divinely inspired vision and mission.

> **Ephesians 1:18 KJV** "*18 The eyes of your understanding being enlightened;* **that ye may know what is the hope of his calling**, *and what the riches of the glory of his inheritance in the saints,*"

The Apostle Paul, in his instruction and equipping of Timothy, taught him about the *"High Calling"* of God. Being called by God to lead His people and to advance His Kingdom is most certainly a special privilege. This high Calling should be treasured and upheld with the honour it deserves.

> **2 Timothy 1:9 KJV** "9 *Who hath saved us, and called us with an holy calling, not according to our works, but according to his own purpose and grace, which was given us in Christ Jesus before the world began,"*

The writer to the Hebrews speaks of this *"High Calling"* in Hebrews 3 verses 1-2 (NIV) and Hebrews 5 verses 4-5.

> *Hebrews 3:1-2 (NIV)* "*[1] Therefore, holy brothers and sisters, who share in the* **heavenly calling***, fix your thoughts on Jesus, whom we acknowledge as* **our apostle and high priest***. [2]* **He was faithful to the one who appointed him***, just as Moses was faithful in all God's house."*

> Hebrews 5:4-5 (KJV) *[4] And* **no man taketh this honour unto himself***, but* **he that is called of God, as was Aaron***. [5] So also Christ glorified not himself to be made an high priest; but he that said unto him, Thou art my Son, to day have I begotten thee.*

It is clear, from Scripture, and from our experience in the field, that God definitely calls certain people to lead the oversight and advancement of the expansion of His Kingdom. No one takes this honour upon himself, but, just as God chose and appointed Aaron to be the High Priest, so He chooses men to be His Servants to serve in the ministry of leading and advancing His Kingdom through Church Planting.

The Apostle Paul, in his letter to the Romans, says that we are *"Called for a purpose."* Things work out for those who live according to the Call and Purpose of God on their lives.

Romans 8:28 KJV *"28 And we know that all things work together for good to them that love God, **to them who are the called according to his purpose**."*

Although this Scripture is a Word of encouragement to every Believer, it does emphasize that there is a Divinely Inspired Purpose for the Call of God upon our lives.

To prepare oneself for a lifetime of ministry, one has to affirm that you are Called of God to pioneer a New Church.

b. Vision.

Step two is to make sure that you pursue God's Vision and not our own. The Power of Vision and having a Vision from God is incredibly important for successful Church Planting.

 Every new season starts with a vision.

Every new season starts with a vision. The word of God teaches us that: *"**Without a Vision people perish**"* We will explore this in detail in the chapter on the Call of God. It is important that we keep the example and teaching of our Lord Jesus in the forefront of our hearts and minds when He repeatedly emphasized the fact that He was only doing what His Father commissioned and assigned for Him to do. We should take earnest heed to this advice and example if we want to see dynamic Churches planted and multiplied through our lives and ministries.

John 5:30 KJV *"30 I can of mine own self do nothing: as I hear, I judge: and my judgment is just; **because I seek not mine own will, but the will of the Father which hath sent me**."*

John 5:19-20 AMP *"19 So Jesus answered them by saying, I assure you, most solemnly I tell you, **the Son is able to do nothing of Himself (of His own accord); but He is able to do only what He sees the Father doing, for whatever the Father***

*does is what the Son does in the same way [in His turn].
20 The Father dearly loves the Son and discloses to (shows)
Him everything that He Himself does. And He will disclose
to Him (let Him see) greater things yet than these, so that you may
marvel and be full of wonder and astonishment."*

Having a Vision from God, and constantly doing what the Lord shows you to do will ensure a lifetime of fulfilled ministry. The Apostle Paul found the truth of this in his ministry when he made many attempts to preach the Word of God in regions outside of the specific assignment and instruction of God.

Acts 16:6-10 AMP *"6 And **Paul and Silas passed through
the territory of Phrygia and Galatia, having been
forbidden by the Holy Spirit to proclaim the Word** in
[the province of] Asia. 7 And when they had come opposite Mysia,
**they tried to go into Bithynia, but the Spirit of Jesus
did not permit them.** 8 So passing by Mysia, they went down to
Troas. 9 [There] **a vision appeared to Paul in the night: a
man from Macedonia stood pleading with him and
saying, Come over to Macedonia and help us! 10 And
when he had seen the vision, we [including Luke] at
once endeavoured to go on into Macedonia, confidently
inferring that God had called us to proclaim the glad
tidings (Gospel) to them.**"*

This portion clearly outlines to us the paramount importance of pursuing God's Vision for dynamic Church Planting. It was there, in one of the towns of Macedonia, in Philippi, where he straight away met Lydia, the dealer in purple dyed clothing, stayed in her house, and from there the Gospel spread throughout the entire region.

 God has a plan, and He wants to reveal His plan to us!

Having a clear vision from God before you venture into planting a new church is essential. The Church is His and **He has a plan** of how He desires to reach every man and woman on this planet. **He reveals this plan to us** through visions and dreams. I pray that you too will receive your Divine Mandate and Assignment from God. Having a Vision from God allows you to build your ministry on a solid foundation, one with which you can face the enemy. The Apostle Paul encouraged his young disciple, whom he calls his "son," to fight this battle by constantly reminding himself of the prophecies once made about him.

I encourage you to go and fast and pray, go on a prayer retreat, and seek God for His specific assignment and vision for what He wants to do through you. Ephesians 2 verse 10 tells us that He already prepared things for us to do before the foundation of the earth, so it is essential that we step into that vision he has for us right from the beginning.

Step two is therefor a step to ensure that you pursue God's Vision.

c. Wait for Empowerment.

Step Three is waiting to be endued with Power from on High before you start. Jesus, after His Baptism in water and the Baptism with the Holy Spirit, went into the desert for a 40 day Fasting and Prayer time. This period was by all measures an empowering time for Him since we see that from that combined period of Fasting and Prayer, and receiving the empowerment of the Holy Spirit, He came forth with Power, and Signs and Wonders followed Him.

> **Mark 1:13-28 KJV** "*13 And he was there in the wilderness forty days*, *tempted of Satan; and was with the wild beasts; and the angels ministered unto him. 14 Now after that John was put in prison,* ***Jesus came into Galilee, preaching the gospel of the kingdom of God,*** *15 And saying, The time is fulfilled,* ***and the kingdom of God is at hand: repent ye, and believe the gospel***.

One of the remarkable things we see, when Jesus started His earthly ministry, was the miracles that followed His preaching. He

healed many and delivered them from evil spirits because God was
with Him.

> **Mark 1: 21-23 KJV** "*27 And they were all amazed, in so much
> that they questioned among themselves, saying, What thing is
> this? What new doctrine is this? For with authority
> commanded he even the unclean spirits, and they do
> obey him. 28 And immediately his fame spread abroad
> throughout all the region round about Galilee.*"

Jesus demonstrated and gave us an example to follow. **First, be
equipped, and empowered by the Holy Spirit, before you start
your ministry.** This is the same message that He not only modelled,
but also commanded His Disciples to follow. He clearly instructed
them not to leave Jerusalem until they received the empowerment
from on High.

> **Acts 1:4-5 KJV** "*4 And, being assembled together with them,
> commanded them that they should not depart from
> Jerusalem, but wait for the promise of the Father, which,
> saith he, ye have heard of me. 5 For John truly baptized with water;
> but ye shall be baptized with the Holy Ghost not many
> days hence.*"

The Apostolic Church Leaders modelled this kind of waiting before
they went out. In the Church in Antioch, even after the Holy Spirit
spoke and commissioned Barnabas and Saul, they first fasted and prayed,
and only afterwards they laid their hands on them and sent them out.
You will recall of Paul's conversion and that Jesus appeared to him, in
person, and called him for the work that he did, however, even though he
carried such a tremendous Calling upon his life, he never went out until
the Holy Spirit spoke and they completed a period of Fasting and Prayer.

> **Acts 13:2-4 AMP** "*2 While they were worshiping the Lord
> and fasting, the Holy Spirit said, Separate now for Me*

Barnabas and Saul for the work to which I have called
them. 3 Then after fasting and praying, they put their hands
on them and sent them away. 4 So then, being sent out by the
Holy Spirit, they went down to Seleucia, and from [that port]
they sailed away to Cyprus."

So, here we see how the Apostles' Barnabas and Paul was only sent out and commissioned after a time of Fasting and Prayer. The result of following this process and instruction of the Lord resulted in tremendous successful and dynamic Church Planting. Later in that same chapter we read how the Word of God spread throughout the entire region.

When we are willing to wait before we go, we will experience the same kind of results and success. The entire Old Testament teaches us the importance of not running ahead of God, but to seek Him in everything prior to doing things. The times where the people of God simply assumed that He would be with them and went on their own accord into things, they encountered defeat after defeat, however, the times when they sought the Lord, He gave them success over their enemies, even in the more impossible situations.

Acts 13:49 AMP "*49 And so the Word of the Lord [concerning*
eternal salvation through Christ] scattered and spread
throughout the whole region."

Dynamic Church Planting takes place when we do things God's way and when we patiently wait for His empowerment before we go. The very thing that defines us as men and woman of God is the Anointing we carry upon our lives. Be sure to not go until you've received that empowerment.

d. Spiritual Disciplines.

Step Four is to ensure that you have well-developed Spiritual Disciplines. Spiritual Disciplines are both important and necessary for our spiritual growth as well as keeping us empowered for a lifetime of ministry.

There are a number of Spiritual Disciplines. All of these Spiritual Disciplines will be discussed in my book *"The Values and Disciplines of the Kingdom of God,"* but suffice to mention in this Chapter that the disciplines of **Fasting and Prayer, Reading and meditating upon the Word of God, Worship, Witnessing, Contentment, Simplicity, Submission and Obedience**, are some of the most important disciplines to develop.

If some, or all, of these mentioned disciplines are not already well established in your life, may I recommend that you start today, to put into place a priority and schedule of 1-2 hours per day, every day of the week, where you intentionally encounter with the Father, His Son and the Holy Spirit. My recommendation, if you are new to this, is that you start reading at least **5 Psalms, 1 Chapter in Proverbs**, and **1 Book in the New Testament**. Church Planters are predominantly early adopters, and therefor need to be at the forefront of High Capacity Learning and adoption.

You will never be able to reproduce what you don't already have well established in your own life first. These, among many form the solid spiritual foundation to ensure that you maintain the anointing of God upon your life as well as keep you in step and in touch with what God is saying and wanting to do, in and through you. It is by building these Spiritual disciplines into your life that you will keep yourself in and out of season bearing good and lasting fruit.

e. Discipler.

Step 5 is to ask God for a Discipler, unless you've already been approached to be Discipled. The fifth most important step to take in preparing to plant dynamic Churches is having a Discipler who will help and guide you to accomplish the vision God has given you.

"A Discipler is someone who has been where you want to go, has the qualities, and character, you desire to have established in your life, and is willing

to help you to reach your full potential, and fulfil your God-given goal."

Biblically, I see that, in most cases, if not all, **it is the Discipler who approaches the Disciple** and then the Disciple has an option whether to follow or not. Elijah approached Elisha. Jesus called His Disciples to disciple them. The Apostle Paul was such a Discipler to many and he serves as a great example of one who was found, discipled, and then went on to fulfill His God-given purpose and did the same with many other disciples.

1 Kings 19 tells us the story of when Elijah, led by the Holy Spirit, went and called Elisha to follow him. This portion both help us see that the Discipler called the Disciple and that the Disciple was developed as he or she faithfully followed in the footsteps of the Discipler.

> **1 Kings 19:19-20 NIV** *"19 So **Elijah went from there and found Elisha** son of Shaphat. He was plowing with twelve yoke of oxen, and he himself was driving the twelfth pair. **Elijah went up to him and threw his cloak around him. 20 Elisha then left his oxen and ran after Elijah.** "*

Another example come from the Lord Jesus Himself when He called His Disciples to follow Him.

> **Matthew 4:18-20 NIV** *"18 As Jesus was walking beside the Sea of Galilee, **he saw two brothers**, Simon called Peter and his brother Andrew. They were casting a net into the lake, for they were fishermen. 19 **"Come, follow me," Jesus said, "and I will send you out to fish for people." 20 At once they left their nets and followed him.** "*

This example of the Lord Jesus became the practice throughout the New Testament as well as in the New Testament Church. Barnabas went to Tarsus where he called Saul (Paul) to follow him. They went to the Church in Antioch from where they were commissioned to go out.

Initially we read about Barnabas and Saul, in that order, and then later on we see Saul taking the lead.

> **Acts 11:25-26 NIV** *"25 Then **Barnabas went to Tarsus to look for Saul, 26 and when he found him, he brought him to Antioch**. So for a whole year Barnabas and Saul met with the church and taught great numbers of people. **The disciples were called Christians first at Antioch**."*

When the Apostle Paul went on his way he went to Lystra and called Timothy to be his disciple. Timothy followed Paul and we see that the Word of God spread throughout the whole region.

> **Acts 16:1-5 NIV** *"1 **Paul came to Derbe and then to Lystra, where a disciple named Timothy lived**, whose mother was Jewish and a believer but whose father was a Greek. 2 **The believers at Lystra and Iconium spoke well of him. 3 Paul wanted to take him along on the journey**, so he circumcised him because of the Jews who lived in that area, for they all knew that his father was a Greek. 4 **As they travelled from town to town, they delivered the decisions reached by the apostles and elders in Jerusalem for the people to obey**. 5 So the churches were strengthened in the faith and grew daily in numbers."*

Jesus called us to "Go" and to make "Disciples" of all nations. We see this pattern modelled throughout the Pastoral Epistles with frequent phrases like "follow me as I follow Christ" or "follow my example" or "you became models to the church." Every single Pastoral Epistles is built on the model Christ set before them. They obeyed God's Call to make Disciples and so, through their example, led and discipled many. It was this foundational pattern that allowed the New Testament Church to grow and in relatively a short space of time they won their entire world for Christ, and even infiltrated and reached the entire Roman Empire.

This all came as a result of disciples being discipled well. We will never be able to develop the DNA of Discipleship in our churches unless and until we ourselves submit ourselves to be developed and discipled by a Godly Discipler.

 "Serve your way up."

— Dr. Hendrik J. Vorster

In this regard, I learned a wonderful lesson from the Word when I was still a young man, and it came from the Words of Jesus to His Disciples in Matthew 20 verses 26-28:

Matthew 20:26-28 (NIV) *"26 Not so with you. Instead, **whoever wants to become great among you must be your servant**, 27 and **whoever wants to be first must be your slave**— 28 just as the Son of Man did not come to be served, but to serve, and to give his life as a ransom for many."*

This Scripture taught me to "Serve my way up." I sought opportunities to serve great men and woman of God, and whilst sitting at their feet to learn from them and follow in their footsteps, God grew and developed me into what I am today. By being a servant to men and woman of God it brought me close enough that I could learn and observe the values of the Kingdom of God in operation. This step will put you ahead of any peer. Submission to a Godly Discipler will bring you to a place of making authentic disciples yourself.

4

THE CALL TO CHURCH PLANTING

A fter years of research and study, I concluded, that the first, and most important step in the journey of planting a Church, is that you need to be called by God. The Bible is a compilation of men and woman who answered the call of God on their lives. All of them had to fulfill a Divine Purpose in the Salvatory Acts of God. He equipped each and every one of them with His Holy Spirit, whom enabled them to carry out the calling with which He called them. Their obedience, submission and fulfillment of the Call is clearly applauded throughout Scripture. Each one's calling was different and unique, and even though there might be many similarities, or things that might, on the surface, seem to be common, their Calling and Purpose was uniquely different.

 There is a wave of People responding to the Call of God.

I have not seen so many people respond to the call of God to full time ministry as I've seen it these last few years. In every nation I go and minister I bring a message on the Call of God, and might I say I have never seen such an overwhelming response to the Call of God upon people, of all ages. Many young people respond to the Call of

God to give their whole lives unto the service of the Lord, but more surprising is the amount of people, from all ages, even elderly people, who respond by saying:

 "Here am I, send me!"

In one sense, we are all called. 1 Peter 2 verse 10 tells us that **we have been called "out of darkness into the light**." Galatians 1 verse 6 speaks about being **called "into the grace of Jesus Christ**" which in essence means to be **called unto salvation**.

2 Thessalonians 2 verses 13-14 tells us that, we have been chosen by God, to be saved, and that God called us. These references, among many, highlight the fact that all of us carry in one way, or another, the call of God upon our lives, however, what we're exploring today is the specific, and high calling of God and specifically the Apostolic Calling.

> 2 Thessalonians 2:13-14 (KJV) "*[13] But we are bound to give thanks always to God for you, brethren beloved of the Lord, because God hath from the beginning **chosen you to salvation** through sanctification of the Spirit and belief of the truth:*
> *[14] **Whereunto he called you by our gospel**, to the obtaining of the glory of our Lord Jesus Christ.*"

Church Planting is quite a specified field. We will endeavour to explore the Calling of the person, the purpose for which God Calls, the Place to where He Calls, the Responsibilities of the Called, and the Enabling required for the Call to Church Planting.

The High Calling of God.

The writer to the Hebrews speaks of this High Calling in Hebrews 3:1-2 (NIV) and Hebrews 5:4-5.

> *Hebrews 3:1-2 (NIV.) "[1] Therefore, holy brothers and sisters, who share in the **heavenly calling**, fix your thoughts on Jesus, whom we acknowledge as **our apostle and high priest**. [2] **He was***

faithful to the one who appointed him, just as Moses was faithful in all God's house."

Hebrews 5:4-5 (KJV) *[4] And **no man taketh this honour unto himself**, but **he that is called of God, as was Aaron**. [5] So also Christ glorified not himself to be made an high priest; but he that said unto him, Thou art my Son, to day have I begotten thee.*

A Call from Heaven

A few things stand out for me in these two verses. In the **first** place, he speaks of a "**Heavenly calling**." This call seems to be a higher calling, yet He includes the brothers and sisters in his address, **who share** in the Heavenly Calling. The **second** thing that stands out for me is **The Purpose** for which Jesus was called and appointed. We see that he was called to be "**our Apostle and High Priest**." In the **third** place, I see that God **appointed** Jesus to that office or ministry, to which He was called. In the **fourth** place I see that **Jesus was faithful** to the One who called and appointed Him. The message I take from this is that God Calls people, for a Specific Purpose, and upon answering the call, He appoints them in that ministry or office. Those who are Called, have the responsibility to remain faithful to the One who Appointment them.

I am not speaking about accepting a call to a position in some Church or Missions organisation, which might be a necessary step as you walk into your destiny, but a Heavenly Call should always precede such pursuits into Church Planting. I believe that you need to have a Call from Heaven to be effective in ministry, and for the Purpose of this book, I will go on to say that, due to the high risk involved in Church Planting, it is absolutely essential that you receive a Call from God before you venture into Church Planting. There clearly exist, at least in my mind, a Calling from God, for a Specific Purpose and Function, and upon proving yourself faithful and obedient, the ultimate Appointment into the office or ministry to which God called you.

Affirm the Call of God.

It is absolutely essential that you affirm the Call of God upon your life. The Apostle Peter, in his second Epistle, exhorts us to affirm the Call of God, and I would say, the Purpose of God, in our lives.

> 2 Peter 1:10 (AMP) he says: "10 *Because of this, brethren, be all the more solicitous and eager* **to make sure (to ratify, to strengthen, to make steadfast) your calling and election;** *for if you do this, you will never stumble or fall."*

Make your calling sure and fast.

Those who have affirmed the Call of God upon their lives should only pursue Church Planting. Only those who firmly decided to do whatever the Lord wants them to do, and to go wherever His Call would take them, should venture in. You can't try it out, or see how it goes, the stakes are to high for those who work on the rock face of where the Kingdom of God advances against the forces of darkness. It's not a regular job, it's a Call, an assignment, and the eternal destiny of people depends on it for someone to press through the obstacles and provide a safe haven where they could be saved, delivered, nurtured and matured in their relationship with the Lord Jesus. You need to be sure that this is what God wants you to do.

Show yourself approved for the Call.

The Apostle Paul gave this advice to the young disciple Timothy that he should study to show himself approved by God. Preparing ourselves for the task before us is an essential part of being greatly used by the Lord.

> 2 Timothy 2:15 (KJV) "[15] **Study to show thyself approved unto God,** *a workman that needeth not to be ashamed, rightly dividing the word of truth."*

2 Timothy 2:15 (AMP) "[15] **Study and be eager and do your utmost to present yourself to God approved (tested by trial)**, *a workman who has no cause to be ashamed, correctly analyzing and accurately dividing [***rightly handling and skillfully teaching]*** *the Word of Truth."*

The young man Timothy knew the Scriptures. He grew up in a Household of Faith. His Grandmother and mother were both believers and taught him the Word of God.

2 Timothy 1:5 (NIV) "[5] I have been reminded of your **sincere faith, which first lived in your grandmother Lois** *and in your mother Eunice and, I am persuaded,* **now lives in you also.**"

Having a faith that's been passed down from your parents is one thing, but making it your own for others to see it in you is another. The proofing of one's Faith comes through persevering trials and proving that one's faith is firmly established on the Word and obedience to the teachings of Jesus, regardless of what might be popular or commonly accepted in society.

The process of proving to God that you are faithful, obedient and trustworthy is both exciting and challenging. Exciting since you live the adventure of pleasing the Lord through living out His Will and Purpose and obediently following His instructions. Challenging since on that path of learning to be obedient we learn a whole lot about ourselves and of persevering through many trials.

I pray that you will allow the Showing yourself to be an Approved Servant of God process to be successful in your life and ministry.

Called for a Purpose.

God has a specific purpose for each person in the Body of Christ. Each one of us has an assigned purpose and place in the Body. Not all are called to be Church Planters. No one should ever feel that they are less fortunate because they are not specifically called to Church Planting.

We learn from Romans 8:28 and Ephesians 1:11 that God calls for a purpose. There is always purpose in God's call upon our lives.

> Romans 8:28 (KJV) "*[28] And we know that all things work together for good to them that love God, to them who are the called according to his purpose.*"

> Ephesians 1:11 (KJV) "*[11] In whom also we have obtained an inheritance, being predestinated according to the purpose of him who worketh all things after the counsel of his own will.*"

Called for a Purpose

We, who are called by God, who accept His calling, and who are then appointed to the Body of Christ, in a variety of offices, some of which is seen in Ephesians 4:11, we have this weight of responsibility to fulfil the specific Call of God upon our lives. May I emphasise again that of course there exist upon each and every believer a call from God, however, what I am exploring here is the Apostolic Call of God.

You might recall that when God called Jeremiah, He told Him that He placed this Call, to be a Prophet, upon his life before he was born. For Church Planters, God's calling of men and woman, is to serve primarily in the Apostolic or Evangelistic Office, or as the Message Bible says; "as missionaries."

> Jeremiah 1:5 (NIV) "*[5] "Before I formed you in the womb I knew you, before you were born I set you apart;* **I appointed you as a prophet to the nations.***"*

I sense that we are in the middle of a new move of God, whereby He is calling a new generation into His service. You might be one of them. I pray that the Father will inspire you to make your calling sure and fast, as you read the pages of this book.

Empowerment for the Call.

Those whom God calls, He also anoints with special gifts to enable them to be determined blessings to the Church, but also, to endure the hardship and persecutions that accompany this ministry. The call to Apostleship is one of the most spectacular but also one of the most challenging. May those whom He calls to lead the planting of Churches around the world rise in this hour to the call and designation of our Lord's service. Be a called out people to declare His Mighty deeds among the nations.

At the beginning of Jesus' earthly ministry He received the empowerment of the Holy Spirit.

> *Matthew 3:16 (NIV) [16] As soon as Jesus was baptized, he went up out of the water. At that moment heaven was opened, and he **saw the Spirit of God descending like a dove and lighting on him**.*

The Gospel of Luke goes on to say that Jesus was full of the spirit when He was led into the wilderness to be tempted by the devil.

> *Luke 4:1 (NIV) "[4:1] Jesus, **full of the Holy Spirit**, returned from the Jordan and was led by the Spirit in the desert,"*

Jesus affirmed this Anointing from on High when He went into the Synagogue on the Sabbath day.

> *Luke 4:18 (NIV) "[18] **The Spirit of the Lord is on me, because he has anointed me to preach good news to the poor**. He has sent me to proclaim freedom for the prisoners and recovery of sight for the blind, to release the oppressed,"*

> *Acts 10:38 (NIV) "[38] how **God anointed Jesus of Nazareth with the Holy Spirit and power**, and how he went around doing good and healing all who were under the power of the devil, because God was with him."*

After giving His disciples the Great Commission, He gave them the instruction to wait, before they go out, for the promise of the Father. We now know it is the empowerment of the Holy Spirit. We need the empowerment of the Holy Spirit if we want to be effective in the planting of new churches.

> Acts 1:4-5 (NIV) "*[4] On one occasion, while he was eating with them, he gave them this command:* **"Do not leave Jerusalem, but wait for the gift my Father promised,** *which you have heard me speak about. [5] For John baptized with water,* **but in a few days you will be baptized with the Holy Spirit."**

> Acts 1:8 (NIV) "*[8] But* **you will receive power when the Holy Spirit comes on you;** *and* **you will be my witnesses** *in Jerusalem, and in all Judea and Samaria, and to the ends of the earth."*

The empowerment the Apostles received brought great enablement to their lives. We see a Peter boldly preaching and declaring the Gospel of Jesus Christ on the day of Pentecost. We see him, and others, performing Mighty miracles and healings with the empowerment of the Holy Spirit. This empowerment of the Holy Spirit gave Stephen the strength to endure the stoning until his body gave way unto death.

To be effective in Church Planting, or any ministry for that matter, you need the empowerment of the Holy Spirit upon your life. The Holy Spirit will guide you, direct you, empower you, strengthen you and constantly comfort you.

Not that my life is anything in comparison to these mighty Apostles, but I've found that the Holy Spirit's empowerment on my life brought tremendous endurance and strength. I am constantly aware of His Mighty Power effectively working in my body as I travel extensively around the globe to equip those called to Church Planting.

We've spoken about being called for a purpose and being empowered by the Holy Spirit for that Call. Now I want us to look at the Apostolic Call and the places and people to whom God Calls.

The Apostolic Calling.

I see that Jesus first called a number of people to be His followers, and then subsequent to their faithful following, He appointed some as Apostles. I see an order in which the Heavenly Call of God works. **First**, He calls people, and then upon their yielding, obedience and faithfulness, he appoints them to one of the Offices, such as those named in Ephesians 4:11.

> *Ephesians 4:11 (NIV) "So Christ himself gave some to be apostles, some to be prophets, some to be evangelists, and some to be pastors and teachers,"*

Jesus first called unto Himself Disciples to follow Him in Matthew 4 verses 19-22

> Matthew 4:19-22 (NIV) *"Come, follow me," Jesus said, "and I will send you out to fish for people."* **At once they left their nets and followed him.** *Going on from there, he saw two other brothers, James son of Zebedee and his brother John. They were in a boat with their father Zebedee, preparing their nets. Jesus called them,* and **immediately they left the boat and their father and followed him.**"

Jesus called His Disciples and we see that they "**at once**" left their nets and followed Him. His teachings seemed hard to understand for those who were minimally minded and engaged, yet to His disciples, whom He later would appoint as Apostles, proofed Faithful.

In Matthew chapter 10, Mark chapter 3, and Luke chapter 6, we read of a subsequent designation and appointment, from among all the Disciples who followed Jesus, to be Apostles. So, Jesus first called, it seems, a number of disciples to follow Him, and then after a period of time He went up on the Mountainside, prayed through the night, and then called 12 of them up onto the Mountain where he appointed them as Apostles, to send them out to preach, and then He came down the mountain with His Apostles by His side and joined the rest of the

Disciples and a great multitude of people who came to hear Him speak and heal them. It is such an honour to be given such a designation, or any for that matter.

> Mark 3:13-18 (NIV) The Appointing of the Twelve Apostles "
> [13] Jesus went up on a mountainside and called to him
> those he wanted, and they came to him. [14] He appointed
> twelve—**designating them apostles—that they might**
> **be with him and that he might send them out to**
> **preach** [15] and to have authority to drive out demons.
> [16] These are the twelve he appointed: Simon (to whom he
> gave the name Peter); [17] James son of Zebedee and his
> brother John (to them he gave the name Boanerges, which
> means Sons of Thunder); [18] Andrew, Philip, Bartholomew,
> Matthew, Thomas, James son of Alphaeus, Thaddaeus,
> Simon the Zealot ."

> Luke 6:12-13 (KJV) "[12] And it came to pass in those days, that
> he went out into a mountain to pray, and continued all night
> in prayer to God. [13] And when it was day, **he called unto**
> **him his disciples: and of them he chose twelve, whom**
> **also he named apostles**;"

> Luke 6:17 (KJV) "[17] And **he came down with them**, and
> stood in the plain, **and the company of his disciples**, and
> a great multitude of people out of all Judaea and Jerusalem,
> and from the sea coast of Tyre and Sidon, which came to
> hear him, and to be healed of their diseases;"

It seems clear from these Scriptures that there was a Secondary choosing or designation by the Lord, from among all His disciples, to the Apostolic Calling, an essential calling and designation for those who dream of working on the forefront of where the Gospel will be preached and established.

The Apostle Paul tells us that it is God, in His Divine Wisdom and Grace, who choose and give certain called people as gifts to the

Church, in the form of "Specially Anointed and Appointed People." Ephesians 4:8 and 11 tells us that God gave special grace to some and gave them as gifts to the Church.

Ephesians 4:8 says: "8 this is why it says: '*When He ascended on high, He took many captives and **gave gifts to his people**.*" The Greek word used for "**gifts**" is the word "χαριτοω" - "charitoo;" from the root word "charis"; to grace, or to indue with special honor: — to be highly favoured. These, highly favoured people, have been given as gifts to the Body of Christ, to equip them. Ephesians 4:11-13 concludes the statement in verse 8, and says:

> Ephesians 4:11-13 (NIV) "*11 **So Christ himself gave the apostles, the prophets, the evangelists, the pastors and teachers,** 12 to equip his people for works of service, so that the body of Christ may be built up, 13 until we all reach unity in the faith and in the knowledge of the Son of God and become mature, attaining to the whole measure of the fullness of Christ.*"

The gifting, calling and anointing as an Apostle, is a primary determination for successful Church Planting. You are highly favoured if you strongly sense this calling and anointing upon your life.

God calls specific people for specific purposes, and for the purpose of successful Church Planting, He calls people to be Apostles. This empowering and affirmation come from the Holy Spirit. It is He who gives you the Grace to function in the Apostolic. The Greek Word is "αποστολοσ" - "apostolos;" meaning; a delegate; specially, an ambassador of the Gospel; officially commissioned by Christ ("apostle") (with miraculous powers): — ***apostle, messenger, he that is sent***.

If you are called to Church Planting, then you would have sensed the Call of God upon your life, followed it in obedience, and now you've been given an increased responsibility by being called into the Apostolic ministry as a Missionary. When you sense this Call and Anointing upon your life, you'll become aware of the specific purpose of the Call of God upon your life.

Macedonian Call.

Jesus said, in the Great Commission to *"go and make disciples of all nations"* however, what we see unfold in Scripture is that it meant that they could only go wherever the Lord purposes them to go. They had to go where the Lord wanted them to go.

We find in Acts 13 that the Lord finally releases the Apostles Paul and Barnabas to go out from the local Church in Antioch to fulfil the Call of God upon their lives, however we see that they quickly learned a powerful principle and that is to only go where the Spirit leads, for only there you will find open doors and success. Let's take a few moments and explore one of the Apostle Paul's experiences in the regions of Phrygia and Galatia.

> *Acts 16:6-10 (NIV) Paul's Vision of the Man of Macedonia "[6] Paul and his companions traveled throughout the region of Phrygia and Galatia, having been kept by the Holy Spirit from preaching the word in the province of Asia. [7] When they came to the border of Mysia, they tried to enter Bithynia, but the Spirit of Jesus would not allow them to. [8] So they passed by Mysia and went down to Troas. [9] During the night Paul had a vision of a man of Macedonia standing and begging him, "Come over to Macedonia and help us." [10] After Paul had seen the vision, we got ready at once to leave for Macedonia, concluding that God had called us to preach the gospel to them."*

I'm sure you could see clearly what transpired here. Even though the Lord Jesus commanded them to go and preach the gospel into the whole world, the specific place where they should have gone needed to be under the directive of the Holy Spirit. Later on, in fact, most of the tremendous successes he enjoyed in ministry came from the region of Asia, however, I believe it was as and when the Lord directed him in that way. The same is true for us, we need to be preaching the Gospel where He directs and by His assignment.

Over the years I have watched so many pastors take appointments to new congregations and see them fail, time and time again. As daunting as what it sounds, I still propose that prior to taking your next faith leap that you will go into a time of fasting and prayer and first find the perfect will of God as to where He wants you to go. My advice would be that you don't concern yourself with what you think of the assignment but rather to walking in obedience to the will of the Father. Obedience is better that the years you will spend being frustrated and exhausted.

The leading of the Lord is so important and this is one of the pet topics of the Apostle Paul in his various addresses to the Churches, but more importantly, it is what Jesus taught and modelled to us. Over and over again Jesus shared and taught us this powerful principle of only doing and going where the Holy Spirit would have us go.

> *John 4:34 (NIV) [34] "My food," said Jesus, "is to do the will of him who sent me and to finish his work.*

> *John 6:38 (NIV) [38] For I have come down from heaven not to do my will but to do the will of him who sent me.*

> *John 5:19 (NIV) [19] Jesus gave them this answer: "I tell you the truth, the Son can do nothing by himself; he can do only what he sees his Father doing, because whatever the Father does the Son also does.*

> *John 5:30 (NIV) [30] By myself I can do nothing; I judge only as I hear, and my judgment is just, for I seek not to please myself but him who sent me.*

Through the words of the Lord Jesus we learn the importance, as servants of God, to do and go where the Lord leads us by His Spirit. It is true what Jesus taught in John 15 that *"we can do nothing without Him."*

The one thing we all desire, is to bear lasting fruit. The fruit of our labours come on the back of obediently following Him to where He leads us to do the Will of the Father as expressed to us by the leading of His Spirit.

Romans 8:14 (KJV) "[14] For as many as are led by the Spirit of God, they are the sons of God."

Living a Spirit directed life affirms us as His sons!

Galatians 5:25 (NIV) "[25] Since we live by the Spirit, let us keep in step with the Spirit."

The Jewish and Gentile Call.

May I briefly draw our attention to the specifics of the assignment of God to us as His servants. The Lord wants to save people from every language, tribe and nation, and therefor, it is not uncommon for Him to give specific people a specific call for a specific people group. Rarely does He assign Apostles to many people groups.

Jesus came and declared His assigned people group. On one occasion, as we read in Matthew 15:24, a Canaanite woman begged Him to heal and restore her daughter, He declared that He was "*only sent to the Lost sheep of Israel.*"

Matthew 15:24 (NIV) "[24] He answered, 'I was sent only to the lost sheep of Israel.'"

Matthew 10:5-6 (NIV) "[5] These twelve Jesus sent out with the following instructions: 'Do not go among the Gentiles or enter any town of the Samaritans. [6] Go rather to the lost sheep of Israel.'"

Jesus' primary people group to whom He ministered was the people of Israel. He only went to those to whom He was assigned to go.

We have two defining examples in the Book of Acts who help us understand the specifics of the Call of God upon our lives. We have the Apostle Peter called to preach the Gospel to the Jews and we have the Apostle Paul called to primarily preach the Gospel to the Gentiles.

The Apostles Peter and Paul carried upon their lives different purposes. Galatians highlight for us the specific purpose of this heavenly Call of God upon their lives.

> Galatians 2:7-9 (NIV) "*[7] On the contrary, they saw that **I had been entrusted with the task of preaching the gospel to the Gentiles, just as Peter had been to the Jews**. [8] For God, who was at work in the ministry of **Peter as an apostle to the Jews**, was also at work in **my ministry as an apostle to the Gentiles**. [9] James, Peter and John, those reputed to be pillars, gave me and Barnabas the right hand of fellowship when **they recognized the grace given to me**. They agreed that we should go to the Gentiles, and they to the Jews.*"

Both concluded, as their ministry profile developed, that God assigned and called them specifically to preach the Gospel to an assigned group of people. So, even though the instruction is to '*go into all the world and preach the Gospel to all nations*,' we can and should only go where He leads, for that is where you will experience the grace to succeed.

Afterword

I pray you too will be one of this new generation of Church Planters who will courageously follow the call of the Lord to wherever He might lead you, to do whatever He desires you to do, to the people group or nations to whom He calls you to, to fulfill His Call.

We are so privileged to be called and to participate in this High Calling of God. Make every day count. Use every opportunity to learn, experiment and to obediently follow the voice of the Holy Spirit.

5

TWELVE CHARACTERISTICS OF CHURCH PLANTING LEADERS

As I studied the characteristics of dynamic Church Planting Leaders around the world, I came across a few shared characteristics. These are not conclusive, however for the purpose of our study they will be very helpful in affirming how God has prepared you to be a next generational Church Planting Leader. Also, these are not in any specific order, but definitely all common among the greatest leaders, both in New Testament days as well as in our day.

Obedience

The primary attitude for every dynamic Church planter is that of obedience. The same heart attitude that allowed Joshua and Caleb to enter into the Promised Land is also the same heart attitude that allowed New Testament Believers to possess their Promised Lands. The Believers had the same Faith to obey God's Call.

Jesus taught His Disciples both the importance of hearing God's Word and obedience to do it.

Luke 11:28 (NIV) "28 He replied, "Blessed rather are those who hear the word of God and obey it.""

The Apostles walked in this same obedience to the Word of the Lord to them.

> Acts 5:29 (NIV) "29 Peter and the other apostles replied: "We must obey God rather than human beings!"

The best place you could ever be is where God desires you to be. Every new assignment we ever took on was only based on obedience to a "Rhema" Word of the Lord. When God called my wife and I out of South Africa to go to Australia, we went. We knew that the best place for us to be is where His Grace leads us.

Prayer and Fasting

Spiritual disciplines greatly advance our Church Planting efforts. Jesus started His ministry after a period of Fasting and Prayer. We see that He prayed often and at times even spent whole nights in prayer.

The Disciples were men of prayer. One of the hallmarks of the New Testament Believers was that of meeting regularly for prayer.

> Acts 1:14 (NIV) "14 **They all joined together constantly in prayer**, along with the women and Mary the mother of Jesus, and with his brothers."

> Acts 2:42 (NIV) "42 **They devoted themselves** to the apostles' teaching and to fellowship, to the breaking of bread and **to prayer**."

Every decision was bathed in prayer prior to them pursuing anything. It was after a night of prayer that Jesus chose His Disciples. It was during a time of Fasting and Prayer in the Church in Antioch that the Holy Spirit spoke and gave Barnabas and Saul their "Great Commission."

> Acts 13:2-3 (NIV) 2 While **they were worshiping the Lord and fasting, the Holy Spirit said**, "Set apart for me Barnabas

and Saul for the work to which I have called them." 3 So
after they had fasted and prayed, they placed their hands
on them and sent them off.

One of the hallmarks of most, if not all, dynamic Church Planting
Leaders is their practice of Fasting and Disciplined Prayer lives. As I
studied the lives of the great Revivalists I found that almost without
fail that all of them practiced fasting. Some practiced fasting at least
one day a week and others undertook periods of dedicated fasting,
some for three days, seven days, fourteen days, twenty-one days and
forty days.

I listened to the late Doctor Jerry Falwell as he shared the incredible testimonies as a result of his periods of extended fasting and
prayer. I saw it in the lives of Doctor David Yonggi Cho, Doctor
Enoch Adeboye, Doctor Fred Roberts, Ed Roebert, Cesar Castellanos,
Mario Vega, Haroldt Weitzs, Jentezen Franklin, Oral Roberts, Nicky
Van der Westhuizen, and Katherine Kuhlman. I have seen that these
leaders led their ministries to be the largest and most powerful
ministries in their nations after and through consistent periods of
fasting and prayer.

For years now we've encouraged our movement around the world
to undertake 21 days of fasting and prayer at the beginning of the year.
I believe that it is this time of dedicated focus on fasting and prayer
that has allowed us to see churches planted in over 70 nations. We've
seen many miracles of healing and provision.

Biblical Preaching and the Teaching of the Apostles.

The Apostles made a deep commitment to preach and teach sound
biblical doctrine, as inspired by the Holy Spirit.

> Acts 2:42 (NIV) "42 They devoted themselves to ***the apostles'
> teaching*** and to fellowship, to the breaking of bread and to
> prayer."

The Apostles impressed their disciples to preach sound doctrine.

They encouraged their disciples to preach the Word in season and out of season and to be unrelenting in preaching the Word. The Word of God is powerful, active and useful, and we would be wise to use the latent power in it to minister to people.

> Titus 2:1 (NIV) "1 You, however, **must teach** what is appropriate to **sound doctrine**."

> 2 Timothy 4:2 (NIV) "2 **Preach the word**; be prepared in season and out of season; correct, rebuke and encourage— with great patience and careful instruction."

One of the stark differences I've seen between many popular preachers and those who really impact and advance the Kingdom of God, is their ability to preach a sound Gospel message based on the Word and from the Word. Those who truly advance the Kingdom of God are those who preach the Word of God.

Holy Spirit

The primary person and partner for successful Church Planting is the Holy Spirit. No journey in Church Planting is possible without the powerful work and ministration of the Holy Spirit.

This was true in the live of Jesus, and throughout His earthly ministry. Jesus received the Holy Spirit as He came out of the waters of baptism. The Holy Spirit immediately led him into the Wilderness where He was tempted for forty days. We frequently read about Him referring to the Holy Spirit's guidance and direction. In fact He stated that He was fulfilling the prophesy, penned down by Isaiah.

> Luke 4:18-19 (NIV) 18 "**The Spirit of the Lord is on me**, because **he has anointed me** to proclaim good news to the poor. He has sent me to proclaim freedom for the prisoners and recovery of sight for the blind, to set the oppressed free, 19 to proclaim the year of the Lord's favor."

Acts 10:38 (NIV) "38 how ***God anointed Jesus of Nazareth with the Holy Spirit and power***, and how he went around ***doing good*** and ***healing all*** who were under the power of the devil, because God was with him."

The Gospel of John ascribe many and great things to the Holy Spirit. Jesus promised that the Father would send the Holy Spirit to those obey Him and keep His commandments.

John 14:26 (NIV) "26 But the Advocate, ***the Holy Spirit***, whom the Father will send in my name, ***will teach you all things*** and ***will remind you of everything I have said to you***."

The One Promise Jesus insisted that His Disciples wait for was that of the Baptism of the Holy Spirit. The impact of the Baptism of the Holy Spirit on the Apostles was profound. Immediately after the Baptism of the Holy Spirit, Peter unashamedly stood up and delivered a powerful message and then started an awe-inspiring ministry that transformed the world.

The one constant reference, throughout the Book of Acts, is the reference to the Holy Spirit. He spoke, He led, He kept, He healed and He built and grew the Believers. On a number of occasions we see how the Apostles ministered "in the Power of the Holy Spirit," and being "Full of the Holy Spirit," and being "led by the Holy Spirit." They were full of the Holy Spirit and were most certainly led by the Holy Spirit and definitely ministered in the power of the Holy Spirit. There are literally tens of Scriptures throughout the Book of Acts referencing the Holy Spirit and His participation in the work of God in saving people, delivering and healing them, encouraging and growing them.

Acts 8:29 (NIV) "29 The Spirit told Philip, 'Go to that chariot and stay near it.'"

The result of this one act of obedience of Philip was that an Ethiopian Eunuch was saved, baptised and he saw Philip translated.

Whilst the Church in Antioch was fasting and praying the Holy Spirit spoke and gave Barnabas and Saul their "Great Commission" which ultimately resulted in many churches being planted in Asia through the lives of these obedient Apostles.

Acts 13:2, 4. (NIV) "*2 While they were worshiping the Lord and fasting,* **the Holy Spirit said**, '**Set apart for me Barnabas and Saul for the work to which I have called them.**' *4 The two of them,* **sent on their way by the Holy Spirit**, *went down to Seleucia and sailed from there to Cyprus.*"

There is no doubt that the Holy Spirit is an active Agent of God in the salvation of men, in their growth and development, and in their empowerment and commissioning to fulfill their part in building and expanding the Kingdom of God.

Every revival is a work and demonstration of the Holy Spirit in and through His Servants. Every great ministry has the Holy Spirit as a Directing and Empowering Force behind them.

I've seen the work of the Holy Spirit in the lives and ministries of truly great men and woman of God around the world. Doctor Yonggi Cho refers to the Holy Spirit as his senior Partner in growing the world's largest Church in Seoul, South Korea. His emphasis on the work and presence of the Holy Spirit is heard in every message he delivers. The Evangelist Benny Hinn, refers to the Holy Spirit as his Senior Partner. During his ministry he saw thousands of people receive their healing by the powerful working of the Holy Spirit.

I witnessed Enoch Adeboye in Nigeria as He operated under the Power and direction of the Holy Spirit. Thousands received Christ as their Lord and Savior. Thousands received healing and miracles. The Redeemed Christian Church of God houses over 1 million people during their monthly Holy Spirit Weekends. This church planting movement now boasts churches on every continent, and that just in the past 30 plus years.

The great Evangelist Reinhard Bonnke ascribes the success of his ministry to the work of the Holy Spirit. He is possibly the greatest evangelist Africa has ever seen. Every crusade sees hundreds of thousands of people saved, healed and delivered. This is only possible with the powerful working of the Holy Spirit.

Our ministries would experience the same demonstration of the Power of God as we yield to the instructions of the Holy Spirit, and allow His Power to flow through us as His vessels.

Signs and Wonders.

Our openness to the Person of the Holy Spirit, and our willingness to acknowledge His Presence and operation in our lives will unlock the supernatural power and manifestation of the Spirit in and through our ministries. As we acknowledge His work and Presence we witness the unlocking of His Power.

The early church grew as they witnessed the powerful working of the Holy Spirit in the lives of the Apostles and Believers. Jesus promised, *"These signs shall follow those who believe."* As Believers discover and avail themselves to the Holy Spirit Gifts inside of them, they become witnesses of this Mighty Working Power of God.

Acts 2:43 (NIV) "43 Everyone was filled with awe at the *many wonders and signs performed by the apostles."*

Acts 5 verses 12 and 16, among many, tells us that, *"The apostles performed many signs and wonders among the people,"* and that, *"many people were healed."*

The Apostles were not the only people to whom the Gift of the Holy Spirit was promised. In fact the Apostle Peter, in his great message on the Day of Pentecost, declared that, *"This promise is for all who put their faith in Christ as Lord."* That promise still stands. Even though for many centuries the Church did not operate in the Gifts of the Holy Spirit, or widely recognized the Baptism of the Holy Spirit, as an integral part of the growth and development as a Believer, He nevertheless existed and worked. As with the reformation, the Church rediscovered the true tenants of the faith. When the Church rediscovered the importance and value of the Baptism of Believers the Church found herself renewed again. With every new or renewed discovery of that which made the early Church significant, the Church grew and developed.

In the 1800's there was a renewed awareness of the Person and work of the Holy Spirit, and as Believers pursued a deeper relationship with Him, they testified that they experienced the "Baptism of the Holy Spirit." Andrew Murray, a Dutch Reformed Minister in South Africa wrote extensively about his and their encounter with this Outpouring of the Holy Spirit. The Azusa Street Revival, the Welsh Revival, the ministries of John G. Lake, George Whitfield and others around the world at turn of the 20th century brought an awakening to the Person and Power of the Holy Spirit. The Pentecostal and later the Charismatic Movement was birthed during the 20th century.

As I observed the advancement of the Kingdom of God in recent years in China, India, Pakistan, Africa, South East Asia, Latin America, the Pacific Islands Region and most of the European Nations, it is through this latter movement that most of the Kingdom Advancement takes place. The Pentecostal Movement has grown to over 500 million adherents in 2011, according to one Global research exercise.

As more and more people across the Church and Denominational spectrum open up to the work of the Holy Spirit, we see that the Church prospers greatly. If you desire to have a Kingdom advancing ministry in Church Planting then you most certainly will be wise to embrace the Person of the Holy Spirit as an integral part of your ministry. You too will witness, *"these signs following"* in your life and ministry.

Apostolic

The early Church embraced the apostolic and being an apostolic people. Jesus first introduced the idea of the Apostolic when He chose, from among His Disciples, twelve Apostles.

Luke 6:13 (NIV) "13 When morning came, **he called his disciples**

to him and **chose twelve of them, whom he** *also*
designated apostles."

These Apostles held their designation with pride and ultimately took the Message of Christ to the ends of the earth.

The Apostolic ministry continued throughout the New Testament Church era. We see that Paul enforces the notion in his letters to the Romans, Ephesians and Corinthians. He refers to himself and Timothy as Apostles

> *Ephesians 4:11 (NIV) "11 So Christ himself gave the apostles, the prophets, the evangelists, the pastors and teachers,"*

> *1 Thessalonians 1:1 (NIV) "1 Paul, Silas and Timothy, To the church of the Thessalonians in God the Father and the Lord Jesus Christ: Grace and peace to you."*

Prophetic

The Prophetic Word is present in every successful Church plant. One of the Hallmarks of dynamic Church Planting Leaders is their ability to move in the prophetic. Their positive attitude towards the future and what it holds is infectious. In one sense we bring a prophetic message of hope every time we minister a Rhema Word of the Lord. I can't but think that every one of those messages that get delivered in services are prophetic in nature. They bring hope to the listener and when yielded to accomplish exactly what was delivered. May we heed with caution as we weekly deliver messages that bring hope.

Pastoral

Caring for the harvest is as important as reaching them. One of the things we have learnt from the Apostle Paul is his unrelenting care for the churches he planted. He constantly share his care and concern for the church's wellbeing. Every great dynamic church planting Leader share this pastoral care for those entrusted to their care.

Evangelistic

The lifeblood of every ministry is her successful reaching and assimilating lost people. Without new people coming into the Kingdom of God, no expansion of the Kingdom of God can take place. At the core of every church planter's heart is the desire to see souls saved. I've watched one dynamic leader after the next, and almost without exception, they all use every opportunity to share the message of salvation. We use every opportunity to reach out to the lost and to lead them to Christ.

Discipleship

Discipleship stands central to bringing people to maturity and fruitfulness. One of the consistent desires shared by almost every church leader I speak to is their desire to mobilize their body of Believers to be Disciples and to make Disciples. The example of the Lord Jesus eternally stands before us as one to follow. The Apostles were effective in reaching their world by being intentional about making disciples. On at least two occasions we read how the Apostles were intentional about ministry to the Disciples. In fact the believers were called disciples throughout the Acts of the Apostles. It was clearly all about making disciples.

> Acts 14:21-22 (NIV) "21 **They preached the gospel** in that city and **won a large number of disciples**. Then **they returned to Lystra, Iconium and Antioch, 22 strengthening the disciples and encouraging them** to remain true to the faith. "We must go through many hardships to enter the kingdom of God," they said."

> Acts 19:9 (NIV) "9 But some of them became obstinate; they refused to believe and publicly maligned the Way. So Paul left them. **He took the disciples with him and had discussions daily in the lecture hall of Tyrannus.**"

I believe, and see, that those who earnestly desire to make an impact in their community will be intentional about making Disciples.

Servanthood

Serving the poor, orphans, elderly and widows will validate our faith. The Apostle James was very clear in his pastoral message to the church in James 1 verse 27. He exhorted them, and us, to look after the poor, the orphans and widows.

> James 1:27 (NIV) "27 Religion that God our Father accepts as pure and faultless is this: to look after orphans and widows in their distress and to keep oneself from being polluted by the world."

Looking after the poor, and caring for the elderly, the widows and orphans form an essential part the ministry of every great ministry.

Biblical Structures

Organizational structures provide stability to growing church movements, not for lording it over but for smooth fulfillment of the purpose of God. Every constituted church should have at minimum an organizational chart, mapping out the different hierarchical orders and presenting all the various ministries in an easy to understand flowchart.

Afterword

These characteristics are seen and observed in most of those who I see accomplish great and amazing things in advancing the Kingdom of God. I pray that these be developed and bestowed upon your life and ministry.

6

CHURCH PLANTING TERMINOLOGY

 Why do we speak about Church Planting?

Terminology

We often hear the terminology '***Church Planting***' being used, referring to the activity of advancing and multiplying Churches in more places around the world. In searching for a suitable terminology, let us look at some terms and attempt to find resonance in the Bible.

Church

What is the Church? Who is the Church? What defines the Church to being the Church?

Definition

- The Church is the **collective body of believers**, known as the Church, both when we congregate or when we meet separately in two's or three's.

- The Church is defined as those who, by faith, responded to the Call of God to Salvation. Jesus first introduced us to this concept, the Church.
- The Church refers to those who responded to the Call of God to come out of darkness into the light. The Greek word for Church is "**Ekklesia**" which means "**called out people.**"
- The Church refers to the Body of Believers in one place together as well as to all those gathered in different countries, nations and places, **collectively.**
- The Church is Church when at least two or three gather together, for **Spiritual worship** of the Triune God, sharing in the **sacraments**, and intentionally encouraging and building each other up as each one administers their **spiritual gifts**, and witness to those outside of the faith, and disciple those who accept Christ as Lord in their lives.

The Church we refer to when we talk about Church Planting is not a reference to the place where the believers meet together, but a reference to those believers who gather together for the purpose of **Scriptural worship, preaching, prayer** and **administering the sacraments of Baptism** and **the Lord Table (Communion.)** We refer to those believers in Christ who meet under His Lordship, to worship Him, to Learn from Him, and receive their encouragement and assignments from Him.

The Church is not the Place but the people who gather together. However, the Church neither simply describes all those who gather together in a meeting place. The Church specifically refers to those who responded to the call, out of darkness. The Church might meet together with unbelievers, or unbelievers might come together with the believers such as we read about in 1 Corinthians 14, but that does not make them the Church. The Church consist of those who confess Jesus as the Lord over their lives. When Jesus returns to fetch His Church, it will only be those who confessed Him as their Lord and Saviour, who will be saved in that day.

Matthew 16:18 (KJV): "*[18] And I say also unto thee, That thou art Peter, and upon this rock **I will build my church**; and the gates of hell shall not prevail against it.*"

Ephesians 1:22 (KJV) "*[22] And hath put all things under his feet, and gave him to be the head over all things to the church,*"

Ephesians 5:23-24 (KJV) "*[23] For the husband is the head of the wife, even **as Christ is the head of the church**: and **he is the saviour of the body.** [24] Therefore **as the church is subject unto Christ**, so let the wives be to their own husbands in everything.*"

1 Corinthians 1:2 (KJV) "[2] Unto the church of God which is at Corinth, to them that are sanctified in Christ Jesus, called to be saints, with all that in every place call upon the name of Jesus Christ our Lord, both theirs and ours:"

Church Building.

The first instance where we hear about the Church in the New Testament came from the words of the Lord Jesus Himself when He spoke about 'building His Church.' An appropriate term would have been 'Church Building,' since we have significant reference to validate such a terminology.

Matthew 16:18 (KJV) "[18] And I say also unto thee, That thou art Peter, and upon this rock **I will build my church**; and the gates of hell shall not prevail against it."

Romans 15:18-20 (NIV) "[18] I will not venture to speak of anything except what Christ has accomplished through me **in leading the Gentiles to obey God** by what I have said and done— [19] by the power of signs and miracles, through the power of the Spirit. So from Jerusalem all the way around to Illyricum, **I have fully proclaimed the gospel**

of Christ. [20] It has always been my ambition **to preach the gospel where Christ was not known,** so that **I would not be building on someone else's foundation.**"

In this portion of Scripture we find the confluent terms of the Great Commission, namely '**Preaching,**' and **Building**'

What is known to us today, is that the Apostle Paul was in fact '***Building Churches***' in these regions. Giving credence to use '**Church Building**' as a terminology is further endorsed by his use of '*not building on someone else's foundation.*'

> 1 Corinthians 14:12 (NIV) "[12] So it is with you. Since you are eager to have spiritual gifts, **try to excel in gifts that build up the church.**"

> Ephesians 2:19-22 (NIV) "[19] Consequently, you are no longer foreigners and aliens, but fellow citizens with **God's people** and **members of God's household,** [20] **built on the foundation** of the apostles and prophets, with **Christ Jesus himself as the chief cornerstone.** [21] In him **the whole building is joined together** and **rises to become a holy temple** in the Lord. [22] And **in him you too are being built together** to **become a dwelling** in which God lives by his Spirit."

> 1 Corinthians 3:10 (NIV) "[10] By the grace God has given me, **I laid a foundation as an expert builder,** and someone else is building on it. But each one should be careful how he builds."

> 1 Peter 2:5 (NIV) "[5] you also, like living stones, **are being built into a spiritual house** to be a holy priesthood, offering spiritual sacrifices acceptable to God through Jesus Christ.

Church Multiplication.

If we take the 'Church Building' pathway, then multiplication would be the desired outcome. Multiplying Churches should be the aspiration of every Church Leader. When God made man, He blessed them and commanded them "to be Fruitful and to multiply."

> Genesis 1:26-28 (KJV) "[26] And God said, Let us make man in our image, after our likeness: [27] So God created man in his own image, in the image of God created he him; male and female created he them. [28] And God blessed them, and God said unto them, ***Be fruitful, and multiply***, and replenish the earth, and subdue it:..."

> Genesis 9:1 (AMP) "[9:1] AND GOD pronounced a blessing upon Noah and his sons and said to them, Be fruitful and multiply and fill the earth.

> Genesis 35:11 (AMP) "[11] And God said to him, I am God Almighty. Be fruitful and multiply; a nation and a company of nations shall come from you and kings shall be born of your stock;

> Jeremiah 23:3-4 (AMP) "[3] And I will gather the remnant of My flock out of all the countries to which I have driven them and will bring them again to their folds and pastures; and they will be fruitful and multiply. [4] And I will set up shepherds over them who will feed them. And they will fear no more nor be dismayed, neither will any be missing or lost, says the Lord.

Church Planting.

Finally, "**Church Planting**" has become the popular terminology describing the organic nature of founding new Churches. There are a few concepts to embrace, for us to understand the popularised term –

*"**Church Planting**."* This action and activity of how and where the Church is multiplied could be called many things, but in the absence of the Lord calling it *"**Church Planting**,"* we have to draw on a number of Scriptures to validate or authenticate this terminology.

Let us therefor explore the relevant use of *"**Church Planting**,"* as an appropriate term to use in describing the action and activity of establishing new congregations. **Firstly**, it draws on the concept that the righteous is metaphorically compared to, or described as *"**Trees planted**,"* in Scripture.

> *Isaiah 60:21 (NIV) "[21] Then will all your people be righteous and they will possess the land forever. **They are the shoot I have planted, the work of my hands**, for the display of my splendor.*

> *Isaiah 61:3 (NIV) "[3] ...They will be **called oaks of righteousness, a planting of the LORD** for the **display of his splendor**."*

These two references combine the Messianic purpose of Christ for the Church with His redemptive purpose for us by **"planting"** the **"righteous"** and calling them **"Oaks of righteousness."** This notion is further expanded by His expressed desire to see this **"Oak of right- eousness"** become a showpiece **"for the display of His splendour."**

> *Psalms 1:3 (NIV) "[3] **He is like a tree planted by streams of water, which yields its fruit in season and whose leaf does not wither. Whatever he does prospers**."*

Again we see, those in right standing with God, referred to as **"trees planted,"** with the added concept of **"bearing fruit."**

So, in the **second place**, we have the **"fruit-bearing"** concept connected to the **"tree"** concept. This fruit-bearing connection brings us to Jesus speaking about us, as Believers, bearing fruit in John 15. As branches of the "Vine," we need to grow and bear lasting fruit.

> John 15:5 (NIV) "[5] "**I am the vine; you are the branches**. If
> a man remains in me and I in him, he will bear much fruit;
> apart from me you can do nothing."

Another example is found in Psalms 92:12-14. Here we have an
expansion of the "**Tree**" concept, by firstly describing how the righteous "**flourish like a palm tree,**" and "**grow like a cedar**."

> Psalms 92:12-14 (NIV) "12 **The righteous will flourish like a
> palm tree, they will grow like a cedar** of Lebanon;13
> **planted in the house of the Lord**, they will flourish in
> the courts of our God.14 **They will still bear fruit in old
> age**, they will stay fresh and green,"

In the **Third place**, we connect the "**tree,**" "**fruit-bearing**" and
"**growth**" to the "**House of the Lord.**" The health of these "trees"
are described by the longevity of their fruitfulness, "**they will still
bear fruit in old age, they will stay fresh and green.**" This Scripture also brings together the concept of being "**planted**" in the
"**House of the Lord.**"

> Jeremiah 12:2 (NIV) "[2] **You have planted them, and they
> have taken root; they grow and bear fruit**. You are
> always on their lips but far from their hearts.

The "**House of the Lord**" is growing and bearing fruit as the
righteous continue to be planted, or we could rightly say that as the
righteous continue to grow and bear lasting fruit, the "**House of the
Lord**" will be firmly planted and multiply.

It is this later concept of "**multiplication**" that we find in Acts 9
verse 31, where "**the church throughout the whole Judea and
Galilee and Samaria**" was "**edified**", and continued to "**increase
and was multiplied.**"

Acts 9:31 (AMP) "[31] **So the church throughout the whole of Judea and Galilee and Samaria** had peace and **was edified [growing in wisdom, virtue, and piety]** and walking in the respect and reverential fear of the Lord and in the consolation and exhortation of the Holy Spirit, continued to increase and was multiplied.

Acts 9:31 (NLTSE) "[31] **The church** then had peace throughout Judea, Galilee, and Samaria, and it became stronger as the believers lived in the fear of the Lord. And with the encouragement of the Holy Spirit, **it also grew in numbers**.

Healthy churches will grow and multiply.

Acts 2:47 (KJV) "[47] Praising God, and having favour with all the people. And **the Lord added to the church daily such as should be saved**.

Colossians 2:6-7 (NIV) "[6] So then, **just as you received Christ Jesus as Lord**, continue to live in him, [7] **rooted and built up in him**, strengthened in the faith as you were taught, and overflowing with thankfulness.

Afterword

We have to conclude therefor that, since the Church is organic in nature, growing and maturing, the more appropriate term to use would be one reflective of that organic nature, hence "**Church Planting**."

Isaiah 61:3 (KJV) "[3] To appoint unto them that mourn in Zion, to give unto them beauty for ashes, the oil of joy for mourning, the garment of praise for the spirit of heaviness; **that they might be called trees of righteousness, the planting of the LORD,** that he might be glorified.

7

PHASE TWO OF CHURCH PLANTING - DISCIPLESHIP

L et us take a moment and briefly look at the steps we need to take in Phase Two to establish a fruit-producing, disciple-making multiplying movement. I say briefly since this represents only a synoptic overview of the phase, whilst the heart of this phase lies in the Process of Discipleship, which is expanded in a separate chapter.

As I travelled throughout the nations, one question repeats itself in private conversation with almost every aspiring church leader:

"Can we talk about the most effective way of making disciples?
What have you found to be effective?"

Well, this is my brief and humble submission through studying the Scriptures and observing the activities and actions of nation-changing leaders and churches around the world.

For the purpose of this book, and this discussion on phases, it is important that we will pursue the most expedient way of planting dynamic churches. Let us heed to the example of the Lord Jesus when He started His ministry on earth, and the pattern He set for us to follow.

Step One - Evangelizing and preaching the Word of God.

Step 1 is to start evangelising and preaching the Word of God where God called you to go and plant a church. When both John and Jesus started their ministries, they both started by preaching **the Message of Repentance.**

John, the Baptist, after receiving His Call, went throughout the countryside around the Jordan and preached this message of Repentance. Jesus on the other hand preached both in the Synagogues, the Marketplaces and in some countryside places. In other words He preached in the established places of worship as well as in the streets where the mass of the people were. Jesus also ministered on a one-to-one basis to people like Zacchaeus as well as the Samaritan Woman, with tremendous effects.

> Luke 3:2-3 (NIV) "2 ...the word of God came to John ... 3 He went into all the country around the Jordan, preaching a baptism of repentance for the forgiveness of sins."

> Matthew 4:17 (NIV) 17 From that time on Jesus began to preach, "Repent, for the kingdom of heaven has come near."

Phase Two of planting Dynamic churches start when we evangelise and preach the message God gave us, in the place where He assigned to us to go.

 Where do we evangelize and preach?

We use every opportunity the Lord gives us, to connect with people and intentionally share the Message He put in our heart. Engaging in sharing our faith is essential. Many times this "*using every opportunity*" brings you to opportunities to go into people's houses, into hospitals and even into businesses, to pray and share.

Jesus started His ministry by preaching everywhere and in the Synagogues. Everywhere meant in the markets, in the countryside, next to the Sea of Galilee, and in the homes of many. When you go with the specific purpose of evangelising and preaching, you will find yourself at the right place at the right time most of the time. I pray that you will have sensitive awareness for the opportunities God open before you to share your faith with people. God will always send you to a place where He already prepared the hearts of the people for the message He placed in your heart.

Paul and Lydia

This is what the Apostle Paul did after receiving his "**Macedonian Call**." He went and looked for a place to pray, and that is where he started sharing the Word. This is also the place where He found a "Worthy" woman in whose house they lodged for a while whilst preaching the Word.

> Acts 16:13-15 (NIV) 13 On the Sabbath we went outside the city
> gate to the river, where we expected to find a place of
> prayer. *We sat down and began to speak to the women
> who had gathered there.* 14 One of those listening was a
> woman from the city of Thyatira named *Lydia, a dealer in
> purple cloth*. She was a worshiper of God. *The Lord
> opened her heart to respond to Paul's message.* 15 When
> she and the members of her household were baptized, she
> invited us to her home. "If you consider me a believer in the
> Lord," she said, "*come and stay at my house*." And she
> persuaded us.

This is one of many beautiful examples of dynamic church planting. A Called man of God, sent out by the Will of God from a local Church, by the Holy Spirit, and Full of the Holy Spirit, with a Heavenly Assignment, and the result is a new church is planted.

Wherever God called you to go, go with the message that God placed in your heart, seek a place where you can sit down and share that message. If it is a Message from God, and you are where He sent you, then you will find open hearts with those who will receive the message.

Jesus and the Samaritan Woman

One day Jesus stopped at a well where some woman drew some water. It was here that Jesus met the Samaritan woman. Her life was forever changed by this encounter with Jesus.

Philip and the Ethiopian Eunuch

When Philip was commissioned to go to a certain road, he went, and that is where he found the Eunuch reading the Word of God. Being prompted by the Holy Spirit He went and opened the Word of God to the Eunuch. The Eunuch's life was forever changed because of that encounter and sharing the Word of God.

We read in many places how Jesus preached the Word to the throngs of people who came to Him for healing and deliverance. There are many examples in the Bible. For us it is important to go, under the direction of the Holy Spirit and share the Word God places in our hearts. The Discipleship journey starts with us leading people to accept Jesus as Lord over their lives.

How to evangelise?

There are many, and effective, ways to share your faith. We know of the Evangelism Explosion Strategy, the Four Spiritual Laws, The John 3 verse 16 gospel presentation, Service Evangelism, Prayer Evangelism and many more. Your circumstance will determine which one is the most effective to be a witness for Jesus.

Bishop Dr. Dag Heward-Mills

One of my friends, Bishop Dr. Dag Heward-Mills, shared his testimony of how God asked him to start with tent crusades all over Ghana. He was reluctant at first, since he didn't think that it would work in Ghana, and he felt that it was something that was done previously and served its purpose, but would not work any longer. Well, after a period of time he became convinced that this was indeed the strategy that God wanted him to use to share the Gospel. Well, when he shared his testimony, he reported that they have received over 1 million decision cards for salvation and he then had over 1000 churches around the world, in just over 10 years. God's strategy is the best strategy!

The Best Strategy

The best strategy has to be one engulfed in sharing the message of Jesus Christ. I've had many people come to me and tell me that they are going to do church planting and their strategy is to incite people to play bingo, or other board games, and hopefully after some time they will find an opportunity to share their faith. My advice is that you should rather trust God for divine opportunities to share your faith, and be an example.

We are all called and anointed to be witnesses. The best and by far the most effective witness and testimony we can carry in our lives is a changed life.

Step 2 – Finding "Worthy men."

Step 2 is to find "Worthy men" to disciple. John Maxwell says: "Everything rises and falls on Leadership," well, I humbly submit ***"Church planting rises and falls on Discipleship."*** The quality of Disciples we make will determine the impact their lives will have on others around them.

The extent to which you will be able to make Disciples is the extent to which your church will grow in a healthy way. **Disciples are those men and woman where your Peace will find rest in their hearts.** You know that you have found a Disciple if they, out of their own free will, express a desire that you help them grow in their faith, however, even then, be wise in who you Disciple. ***Build the strongest team*** that you are able to lead for the Lord Jesus.

The Lord Jesus set the example.

The Lord Jesus set a pattern and model when He started His ministry on earth with **worthy** men. Even though Jesus declared in Luke 4 that the "***Spirit of the Lord is upon me to preach the Good News to the Poor***" He never started His ministry with poor people. He started His ministry with "***Worthy men***."

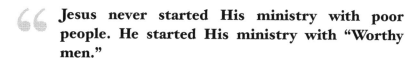

> **Jesus never started His ministry with poor people. He started His ministry with "Worthy men."**

We see that Jesus one day was walking by the sea of Galilee and He got into a boat "***belonging***" to Simon Peter. Peter was not just a Fisherman, no, he was the owner of a fishing boat, and if we read the whole portion we see that he had a crew, and so did his partners, James and John. Just think about it: "How many people do you know who own their own boat?" Not many I guess. Why? The answer is simple: "boats are too expensive." Can you imagine owning a boat 2000 years ago. I think that you will agree, they were "Worthy men." These four Fishermen were "Worthy Men" whom Jesus called to be His disciples. The Bible also tells us that they had a crew (companions.)

> **Luke 5:3 (NIV) "3 He got into one of the boats, the one belonging to Simon,** and asked him to put out a little from shore. Then he sat down and taught the people from the boat."

> **Luke 5:9-11 (NIV) "9 For he and all his companions were astonished** at the catch of fish they had taken, 10 and **so were James and John, the sons of Zebedee, Simon's partners.** Then Jesus said to Simon, **"Don't be afraid; from now on you will fish for people."** 11 So they pulled their boats up on shore, left everything and followed him."

Luke also tells us that He then went past the Tax booth of Levi and called him to follow Him.

> **Luke 5:27-28 (NIV)** "*27 After this, Jesus went out and saw a tax collector by the name of Levi sitting at his tax booth. "Follow me," Jesus said to him, 28 and Levi got up, left everything and followed him.*"

Levi was a "**Worthy man.**" In those days the Tax Collectors were like the wealthiest people around. They were like Bankers who rolled in the money.

We know from Colossians 4 verse 14 that Luke was a doctor. A doctor is regarded as a "worthy" person in our day. How much more would he have been regarded as a "Worthy" man 2000 years ago? We can see that these disciples were worthy men since they were **Fishermen, a Tax Collector and a Doctor**. We also know that **Judas** handled the money, hence we could assume that he was a worthy man as well who could be trusted with the Lord's finances.

The principle of starting with "Worthy" men and woman.

When Jesus sent out His Disciples to go and preach the Gospel, He gave them this same wonderful strategy. I believe this strategy will serve you well in planting dynamic Churches.

> **Matthew 10:11-13 (NIV)** "11 Whatever town or village you enter, *search there for some worthy person* and stay at their house until you leave. 12 As you enter the home, **give it your greeting. 13 If the home is deserving, let your peace rest on it;** if it is not, let your peace return to you."

Finding a **Worthy man**, a House of Peace or a Man of Peace in the town, suburb or place where God calls you to go and plant a Church, is essential. These are the "worthy" people through whom the Gospel message will be advanced. Always look for people who could and would take the message you bring to them, further.

A "Worthy Man" defined.

A **Worthy man** is defined by being a man of **worth**. Worthy people are **visionary.** They are the people who love to be involved with people who have a vision. The only vision poor people have, is what you have on offer for them, whereas worthy people **will help you fulfill the vision** God gave you. If you share a vision with worthy people they will frequently ask and offer their help to see that vision fulfilled. Worthy people are people who **take action** and **take responsibility**. You would be wise to ask God for "Worthy" men and woman to start your new ministry with.

A "***worthy man***" could be **a man or a woman** or a couple. A worthy man is someone who runs his or her **own business**, small or large, or **manages or leads a business, organization or industry**. A worthy man **could be the principle** or department head of a **School, College or Educational institution**. The worthy man **is distinguished by their stand, reputation and stature** in the community.

The Apostle Paul practiced it in his Church Planting ministry.

The Apostle Paul, when he planted the church in Philippi, found this principle in operation. You will recall that he had this "Macedonian Call" and straightaway went to the region of Macedonia to preach the Word of God there. Acts 16 verses 12-15 tell us this amazing affirmative story of this principle being applied. It was there that he immediately met a "**Worthy Woman**" called **Lydia**. She invited them to her house, where they stayed until the church was established.

Another example came from when Paul planted the church in Corinth. He met a "Worthy Man and Woman." Aquila was a tentmaker like him. Once he found this "Worthy Man" he stayed with them and from there the Church grew.

Acts 18:1-3 (NIV) "*[18:1] After this, Paul left Athens and went to* **Corinth**. *[2]* ***There he met a Jew named Aquila***, *a native of Pontus, who had recently come from Italy with **his wife***

> *Priscilla*, *because Claudius had ordered all the Jews to leave*
> *Rome. Paul went to see them, [3] and because* ***he was a***
> ***tentmaker*** *as they were,* ***he stayed and worked with them***."

The Principle passed on from Paul to Timothy.

Interestingly, and most noteworthy for us is the fact that the Apostle
Paul gave this same advice to his disciple, and spiritual son, Timothy.
In 2 Timothy 2 verse 2 we read that he advised Timothy to "***entrust to***
reliable people" the things he learnt and observed from Paul. He
advised him to entrust these truths to people "***who will also be quali-***
fied to teach others."

One of the essentials to planting dynamic churches is starting with
the right people. ***Worthy and reliable people*** need to be ***your first***
disciples. If you truly follow the example that the Lord gave us, you
too will establish a work that will last long after you're gone to be with
the Lord. Starting your ministry with the right people will ensure fruitfulness and multiplication.

Most Pastors I speak to have this dream of having a ministry that
would see spiritual sons and daughters multiply their work, however,
few see their dreams realised as they are surrounded with the wrong
calibre of people.

Where do we find these "Worthy Men" to be our Disciples?

We could find these "worthy men" in two primary areas:

1. Home church. They could be those whom God gives you right
from the start from within your current Church, such as was the situation with the Apostles Paul and Barnabas in the Church in Antioch
when the Holy Spirit called them to go out on their first Missionary
journey. We read this amazing story in Acts 13 verses 1-5.

2. Mission field. These disciples could be found by sharing the
Gospel among those who come to the Lord through the preaching of
the Word such as what we find in Acts 19 verses 1-12.

Fast and pray before you call "worthy men" as your Disciples.

This process of finding and choosing disciples always starts with a season of Fasting and Prayer. Jesus spent a night praying before He chose His Disciples. God chose Paul and Barnabas during a time of Fasting and Prayer in the church in Antioch.

The process of finding your disciples to disciple might take you three to nine months. It will require some serious focus, diligence and efficiency. It is far better to start a new ministry with people whom you led to the Lord, and show a strong commitment to be discipled by you. New believers are more easily led and discipled.

I remember, before I met my wife, I always wondered how I will know, and then when it happens, you know. Well, for those of you who have been blessed to be married to a wonderful man or woman of God will know what I talk about. Well, the reason for my brief divergence is this: Ask God for His choice of Disciples for you. Rather focus your attention on finding your twelve than running after every "**Tom, Dick or a Harry**," who does not want to follow, learn or put the Word of God into practice. The Church of Jesus Christ would be so much stronger and larger if we spent our energies on prayer and earnest pursuit of those who God chose for us to Disciple. May we always carry the Great Commission close to our hearts, and with wisdom choose and make the best Disciples we are able to lead.

Matthew 28:19 (NIV) "*[19] Therefore go and make disciples of all nations, baptizing them in the name of the Father and of the Son and of the Holy Spirit,*"

As you go, seek and save the Lost, and teach them to observe everything the Lord taught you.

Step 3 is to Disciple the "worthy men."

Finding Disciples is one thing, but "*teaching them to observe*" is another. Jesus called us to teach our Disciples the very things He taught His Disciples. Remember, the early Church never had the New Testament like we have it today. They had the Apostles teaching them and their teachings became known as the "*Apostles Teachings*." The

"Apostles Teachings" was really just Jesus' Teachings, which they conveyed and taught the New Believers.

 Discipleship is the intentionally process of teaching someone the teachings of Jesus.

Discipleship is the intentionally process of teaching someone the teachings of Jesus. Developing a clearly defined process of Discipleship is essential to fulfilling the Great Commission of Jesus.

> **Matthew 28:20 NIV** *"20 and **teaching them to obey everything I have commanded you**. And surely I am with you always, to the very end of the age."*

Through the parable of the Sower in Matthew 13 verses 3-9, we learn that the condition of the disciple's heart is of great importance to have the desired outcome of making a *'fruit-producing'* disciple.

Where do we start?

It is essential to determine the Outcome of your discipleship program before you start making disciples.

Simply said:

- *What would the Disciple look like when you've discipled him or her?*
- *What qualities and characteristics would they have and exhibit when you're done with them?*
- *How will you take what Jesus taught His Disciples and teach your Disciples?*

Here are some good guidelines to consider in determining your God-directed process of Discipleship:

1. **Determine the qualities and characteristics** you wish to see formed and characterized in the Disciples you are making.
2. **Determine a pathway** of accomplishing and developing each one of those goals, qualities and characteristics in their lives.
3. **Prioritise these steps** to ensure that you reach the determined outcome.

Start with "saved" people.

It is only fitting to start any Discipleship Journey with a module on getting people "**Born again**." Not that this is the work of man, but for man being instrumental in praying that God would open the hearts of men; bring them to a place of remorse of their sins, and ultimately repentance of their sins. Our prayers of petition are encouraged throughout Scripture.

When people respond to the Grace of God, they are "Born again," their lives changed, renewed, and regenerated. Let us take a few moments and look at what such a Process of Discipleship looks like. This process have been tested and tried in many countries with great success.

Discipleship Process Overview

Let's quickly look at the whole process and then revisit each step later on.

There are basically Five Steps in the Process of Discipleship:

1. Salvation.

The first stage is the stage of leading someone to an enduring encounter with Jesus Christ. It is the phase of leading them to make a firm decision to make Jesus the Lord of their lives, solidify that decision through Baptism and laying a strong foundation for their faith.

2. Establishing Roots, Values and Spiritual Disciplines.

During this stage we teach our Disciples to observe the Values of the Kingdom, while establishing spiritual Disciplines. These Values and Spiritual Disciplines become the Spiritual Roots of their Faith.

3. Developing Gifts and Skills.

During this Phase we help our Disciples to discover the Gifts of God upon their lives. We help them develop their Gifts and Skills to fulfil the purpose of God upon their lives. This is an equipping phase.

4. Being Fruitful.

The key to a process of Discipleship is putting Gifts and Skills into practice. Being Fruitful also deals with us living a life worth following. Winning Souls is bearing fruit. Being Fruitful is helping your Disciples to effectively equip their Disciples through the Process of Discipleship.

5. Multiplication.

This phase its marked by our Disciples making disciples, and launching their Disciples into their own God-given purpose.

Diagram 1. Discipleship Foundation Cycle

Step One – Salvation.

The first step in the Process of Discipleship is therefor to make sure that people are "**Born again**." The Discipleship journey will only bear fruit if it is built on the Foundation of Salvation. Faith is about being adopted into a family, the Family of God.

Phase One explores the essentials to allow the incorruptible Seed of God's Word to take root in our lives so that we can believe and be saved. The writer to the Hebrews outlines the **six foundational principles** in following Christ.

> Hebrews 6:1-2 (NKJV) "*1 Therefore, leaving the discussion of **the elementary principles of Christ**, let us go on to perfection, not laying again **the foundation** of **repentance from dead works** and of **faith toward God**, 2 of **the doctrine of baptisms**, of **laying on of hands**, of **resurrection of the dead**, and of **eternal judgment**.*"

Within these two verses we find the **elementary principles** of life in Christ, the only foundation upon which a living relationship with Jesus Christ is possible. They are **1. Repentance from dead works, 2. Faith towards God, 3. Baptisms, 4. Laying on of Hands, 5. Resurrection of the dead, and 6. Eternal judgment.** If we build our relationship upon these elementary principles and add to them spiritual disciplines and the development of good and sound spiritual roots, it will set us up for tremendous growth and we will see the Seed of God produce in us fruitfulness.

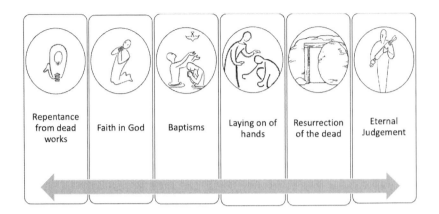

| Repentance from dead works | Faith in God | Baptisms | Laying on of hands | Resurrection of the dead | Eternal Judgement |

| Elementary Principles of Salvation

These six foundations were installed and taught to every New Believer. Laying a solid and sound foundation to build one's faith on is essential to build a spiritual house that will withstand the storms of life.

The expanded content description is in the Chapter on "The Process of Discipleship," however, the full content of this Foundational Series on Discipleship is contained in my Book; "**Discipleship Journeys – Step One – Salvation**."

Step 2 – Establish Spiritual Roots, Values and disciplines.

Once you have a "***Born Again***" Believer then you can start the investment process of instilling the Values of the Kingdom of God in the Believer. If you build spiritual values and disciplines into people who have never bowed their knees to the Lordship of Christ, you are building on sand. As I mentioned earlier, if you are going to build people up then make sure that you build in those lives that has Christ as their Rock and Foundation.

Values.

I always wondered where to start once people committed their lives to Christ. When I look at how Jesus did it, remembering that He started His Discipleship journey with people who left everything to follow Him, **I find that Jesus started by teaching His Disciples the Values of the Kingdom of God.** One of the biggest challenges we face in ministries is sitting with people who are "churched" but never adopted and applied the values of the Kingdom of God in their lives.

There are over 80 discern-able Values that Jesus taught in the Gospels. I will draw our attention to the first 8 Values, which Jesus taught in His Sermon on the Mount. Let us briefly consider:

1. **Humility.** Humility is the quality of having a modest or subjected view of one's own importance.
2. **Penitence.** Penitence is the value of mournful, reflective living.
3. **Meekness.** Meekness is the consistent characteristic of submissiveness.
4. **Spiritual Passion**. Spiritual passion is the value of giving, and expressing oneself fully in one's faith.
5. **Merciful**. To be Merciful is to be filled with grace towards all people, being constantly mindful of how much we've been forgiven of.
6. **Purity**. Purity is characterized by freedom from immorality, adultery and sinful contamination, and is a value of the Kingdom of God.
7. **Peacemakers**. A peacemaker is someone who actively steps up in every adversarial situation to work towards a peaceful outcome.
8. **Patient endurance under suffering.** It is the ability to endure through unjust treatment because of your faith, and even go beyond the expected response to such attacks by acting in a non-retaliatory way.

In fact I have determined and narrowed the values down to **52 Kingdom Values**. In my Book: **"The Values of the Kingdom of God"** I have outlined and explored these in my book for adoption and application in our lives.

Assimilating the Values of the Kingdom of God is one thing, however, maintaining them in our lives is another, and **it is** therefor **equally important to establish spiritual disciplines**, which will ensure that these Values are kept and maintained.

The second area of development in the young Believer's life is Spiritual Disciplines.

Spiritual Disciplines.

Spiritual disciplines are habits, practices, and experiences that are designed to develop, grow, and strengthen our inner man. Spiritual disciplines build the capacity of our character and keep the values, we aspire to assimilate into our lives, intact. Spiritual disciplines form the structure within which we train our soul to obey.

1. Prayer.
2. Fasting.
3. Stewardship.
4. Reading, meditating and practicing the Word of God.
5. Worship.
6. Simplicity.
7. Servanthood.
8. Obedience and submission.

There are many spiritual disciplines to explore and assimilate into our daily lives. *The Spiritual Disciplines of Fasting and Prayer, Stewardship, Simplicity, Servanthood, studying and meditating on the Word of God,* are some of the most valued disciplines to uphold. You can read more on these in my Book on "*Spiritual Disciplines of the Kingdom of God.*" Spiritual disciplines will keep the fire of God burning ablaze inside of you.

Step 3 – Discovering and developing our Spiritual Gifts, and developing ministry skills to fulfil God's Purpose on our lives.

The third phase of Discipleship deals with us discovering and developing our spiritual gifts, where we develop ministry skills to fulfill our calling in service of the Lord and we continue to grow strong and healthy roots to ensure that we, both bring forth healthy fruit, as well as, withstand the evil temptation of the enemy.

Character Building happens when we apply the Values of the Word of God on a consistent basis. This is the phase where we become overcomers by the Confession of our mouths and the application of the Word of God. This stage is also marked by our skill and gift development. This is a continuation of the "Young men" phase.

1. Gift Discovery Course. Weekend.
2. Survey of the Bible Course. Weekend.
3. How to share your Faith Course. Weekend.
4. Overcoming Course. Weekend.
5. Shepherd, Group Leader Training Course. Weekend.

These five weekend encounters are designed to help the Disciples develop skills and abilities that would assist them in fulfilling the purpose of God in their lives. The details of each are explored further in the dedicated chapter on "The Process of Discipleship."

Step 4 – Discipling Fruit-producers.

The fourth phase of Discipleship deals with us bearing Fruit through consistently putting into practice what we've learnt, and by living a life of love, worth following, and shepherding those entrusted to our care.

This Step is all about producing fruit through application of learnt experiences and Gift discovery and use. I am always excited about this phase since it is always great to disciple obedient practitioners. At this stage of the journey they are mature and diligent followers of the Lord Jesus. They are accountable.

1. Walking with purpose.
2. Build purposeful relationships. Finding Worthy Men/Woman.
3. Priesthood. Praying effectively for those entrusted to you.
4. Caring compassionately.
5. Walking worthily.
6. Walking in the Spirit.
7. Practicing hospitality.

Step 5 – Multiplying the Body.

The fifth step of Discipleship deals with our Disciples multiplying themselves through their Disciples, by helping and guiding them to consistently put into practice what they've learnt through their union with Christ. We model it to them, and they model it to their Disciples, by living a life of love worth following, and shepherding them into their purpose.

Fruitfulness and Multiplication.

The fifth step in the process of developing as a disciple is to develop in the gifts and graces upon our lives until we become fruitful and through us the Kingdom of God starts multiplying, disciples.

Fruitfulness refers to the ability of a disciple to win souls for Christ.

Multiplication refers to the disciples to make fruit-producing disciples.

Reproducing through others.

The key elements of this step in the process of Discipleship is to reproduce and multiply the Body of Christ through strengthening and encouraging your Disciples to be models and worthy examples to their Disciples, as well as help your disciples to being fruitful and to multiply. Through this step we equip our Disciples to go higher and deeper in their own walk with God.

The art of being a Discipler.

It requires you to be a Facilitator, who knows the Voice of the Holy Spirit, and one who has the heart of a Shepherd. We therefor encourage that you teach the Disciples to:

1. **The Discipler's Characteristics. Living a life worthy to be reproduced in others.**
2. **The Discipler's meetings.**
3. **The Discipler's prayers.**
4. **The Discipler's advice.**
5. **The Discipler's encouragement.**
6. **The Discipler's focus.**

In Conclusion on the Disciple making process, this is not conclusive, as we constantly have new emphasis highlighted to us by the Holy Spirit.

Step 4 - Gather the "worthy men" into groups.

Discipleship happens best in groups. One of the strategies we learnt from Jesus through the way He discipled His Disciples was that He discipled them in a group. Rarely do we see Him doing one on one discipling. Jesus sometimes discipled His Disciples in two's or three's, however, most of the time, He discipled the together in a group.

We read in Matthew 5 when Jesus started discipling His Disciples. He started by *calling them together* and then He taught them in a group. One of the successes I've seen around the world of effective discipleship is that it happens in groups.

Time-wise.

In a time where we need to be wise with our time, it maximises our time to equip our disciples by doing it in a group. If you are disciplined and focused, the teaching and equipping part can be concluded in a 2 hour gathering once a week.

Accountability.

Learning in groups provide for an opportunity to be accountable, not just to the Leader, but also to one another. It is amazing to see how people grow and develop in a group. One of the models for effective learning is of course our schools. Nowadays even more so with the adjustments in how they work in interactive groups in classes. The world is picking up on something Jesus actually taught. When you shift the responsibility to learn and grow on to the individual, the pressure to counter perform and live up to the trust given creates an atmosphere where people can truly grow and develop. The peers consciously and unconsciously become an accountability group.

Collaboration.

In a group, the Disciples learn from one another, and learn to work together as a team. When Jesus sent His disciples out to put into practice what He taught them, He sent them out two by two. It is this "two by two" that we need to put into practice with our Disciples. When they start bringing people to Salvation, one of the strategies is to appoint the stronger "worthy" men to lead a group of these new believers alongside one of the less confident "worthy" men from your Discipleship group. Teach your Disciples to work together.

Afterword

Remember, Jesus encouraged this team approach when reaching out, and the Holy Spirit did it when He called Barnabas and Saul from the Church in Antioch. The Apostle Paul, through what we've learnt from his pastoral letters, frequently travelled together with his disciples.

THE PROCESS OF DISCIPLESHIP

After years of research and observing successful models around the world, I want to humbly submit a process of Discipleship that I've seen work effectively.

 The early Church was highly effective.

We have to agree that the early church was quite effective in Discipleship. In relatively a short space of time they were able to impact almost the entire known world, even the mighty Roman Empire. **How did they do that?** Well, my research showed that for at least the first few hundred years after Christ, there was a foundational approach with every new believer. It developed into *"The Didache"* or otherwise known as "The teaching of the Twelve Apostles." In their book on the research of Professor Liddle, on the existence of "The Teaching" Alexander Roberts and James Donaldson argue the existence and use even as late as 1886.

The Teaching

*"**The Teaching**,"* as it was often referred to consisted of: (indulge my paraphrasing.)

1. The two ways and the First Commandment.

2. The Second Commandment and the forbidden sins. (*10 Commandments summarised.*)

3. Other forbidden sins. (*Values of the Kingdom of God as taught by the Lord.*)

4. The Precepts. (*Spiritual disciplines.*)

5. The way of death. (*Avoid all evil at all cost.*)

6. Against false teachers, and food offered to idols.

7. Baptism.

8. Fasting and Prayer, and the Lord's Prayer.

9. Thanksgiving (*the Eucharist.*)

10. Prayer after Communion.

11. Apostles, Prophets and Teachers.

12. Receiving Christians. (*Practicing hospitality.*)

13. Support of Prophets.

14. Christian Assembly on the Lord's Day.

15. Bishops and Deacons. Christian proofing.

16. Watchfulness and the Coming of the Lord.

As these traditional manuscripts were largely based on the various Teachings of the Apostles, we see that a strong emphasis came from Hebrews chapter six. Six of the Foundational Teachings of Christ, and of the various Gospels and Pastoral Letters to the Churches, was encapsulated in "the teaching."

When I researched contemporary models such as the *G12 model* of Pastor Cesar Castellanos (***Win, Consolidate, Disciple, and Send,***) I saw that the emphasis was very strong on getting someone saved, properly and then consolidating that decision before taking them through a discipling process.

One of the churches that I researched grew to over 25'000 people in attendance in just over 17 years. They continue to lay a strong emphasis on getting people saved and baptised prior to taking them through their discipleship process.

Start with "Born Again" people.

It is therefor fitting to start any Discipleship Journey with a module on getting people "**Born again**." Not that this is the work of man, but for man being instrumental in praying that God would open the hearts of men; bring them to a place of remorse of their sins, and ultimately repentance of their sins. Our prayers of petition are encouraged throughout Scripture.

When people respond to the Grace of God, they are "Born again," their lives changed, renewed, and regenerated.

Let's quickly look at the whole process and then revisit each step on.

There are basically Five Steps in the Process of Discipleship;

1. Salvation.

The first stage is the stage of leading someone to an enduring encounter with Jesus Christ. It is the phase of leading them **to make a firm decision to make Jesus the Lord** of their lives, solidify that decision through Baptism and laying a strong foundation for their faith.

2. Establishing Roots, Values and Spiritual Disciplines.

During this stage we teach our Disciples to observe the Values of the Kingdom, while establishing spiritual Disciplines. These Values and Spiritual Disciplines become the Spiritual Roots of our Faith.

3. Developing Gifts and Skills.

During this Phase we help our Disciples to discover the Gifts of God upon their lives. We help them develop their Gifts and Skills to fulfill the purpose of God upon their lives. This is an equipping phase.

Diagram 1. Discipleship Foundations Cycle.

4. Being Fruitful.

The key to a process of Discipleship is putting Gifts and Skills into practice. Being Fruitful also deals with us living a life worth following. Winning Souls is bearing fruit. Being Fruitful is helping your Disciples to effectively equip their Disciples through the Process of Discipleship.

5. Multiplication.

Our Disciples making and launching their Disciples into their purpose mark this phase.

Step One – Salvation.

The first step in the Process of Discipleship is to make sure that people are "**Born again**." The Discipleship journey will only bear fruit if it is built on the Foundation of Salvation. Faith is about being adopted into a family, the Family of God.

Phase One explores the essentials to allow the incorruptible Seed of God's Word to take root in our lives so that we can believe and be saved. The writer to the Hebrews outlines the **six foundational principles** in following Christ.

> Hebrews 6:1-2 (NKJV) "*1 Therefore, leaving the discussion of **the elementary principles of Christ**, let us go on to perfection, not laying again **the foundation** of **repentance from dead works** and of **faith toward God**, 2 of **the doctrine of baptisms**, of **laying on of hands**, of **resurrection of the dead**, and of **eternal judgment**.*"

Within these two verses we find the elementary principles of life in Christ, the only foundation upon which a living relationship with Jesus Christ is possible. They are **1. Repentance from dead works, 2. Faith towards God, 3. Baptisms, 4. Laying on of Hands, 5. Resurrection of the dead, and 6. Eternal judgment.** If we build our relationship upon these elementary principles and add to them spiritual disciplines and the development of good and sound spiritual roots, it will set us up for tremendous growth and we will see the Seed of God produce in us fruitfulness.

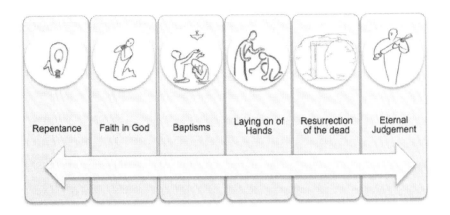

| Repentance | Faith in God | Baptisms | Laying on of Hands | Resurrection of the dead | Eternal Judgement |

Departure Point.

The departure point in following Christ is to understand sin and its impact on our wellbeing. We need an understanding of our need for a Saviour. Christ provided Redemption by dying on the cross of Calvary for our sins. We can be saved and redeemed from our sins, by acknowledging our sinfulness, and by confession and repent of our sins, and receiving His forgiveness. The goal of this process is that we might be restored in our relationship with our Heavenly Father, His Son and with the Holy Spirit.

How can we be "Saved?"

- To be "*SAVED*" requires two worlds to meet: **the Divine** and **Human worlds**.
- To be "*SAVED*" requires mankind to respond affirmatively to the divine work of God; through the Redemptive work of Christ on the Cross, by paying for our sins, and through the Holy Spirit's conviction inside of us.
- To be "*SAVED*" is also the process of being "*Born Again*" to become a "*Child of God.*"
- To be "**Saved**" is to be "*Converted.*"

From a human perspective, this process of becoming a Child of God is called: "*Conversion,*" and is the voluntary change in the mind of a sinner, on one the one hand, *from sin*, and on the other hand, *to Christ*. This human perspective is not the result of human initiation, but a mere response to the work of the Holy Spirit inside of us. The *turning from our sin is called Repentance*, and the *turning to Christ is called Faith*.

- **To be "Saved" is to be "Regenerated."**

From a Godly perspective, this process is called "*Regeneration,*" and is the act of God whereby God makes us new creations, creates in us a new heart and puts a new spirit within us. God removing our sin, the wall of separation between Him and us, and Him making us holy and pure as He is, and declaring us righteous further extends this act of God. This is when we are "**born again**."

Let's take our first step into this exciting Discipleship journey by looking at Part 1, of 6 in our Discipleship Journey.

Step One – Repentance of dead works.

The departure point, in following Christ, should be "*repentance*" from dead works. Many think that they can come closer to God by doing good works, but there is only one way to come close to God and that is through Faith in Jesus Christ.

The Fall of Adam and Eve had devastating effects for mankind.

Adam and Eve sinned. They made a choice to disobey God in the Garden of Eden and through their actions of disobedience **sin came** and **death came**, and through their disobedience **separation from the Presence of God** came.

> 1 Corinthians 15:21-22 (NKJV) "*21 For since **by man came death**, by Man also came the resurrection of the dead. 22 For as in Adam all die, even so in Christ all shall be made alive.*"

Sin separates us from God.

The Bible says that: "*All have sinned and fall short of the Glory of God.*"

> Isaiah 59:2 (NKJV) "2 But *your iniquities have separated you from your God*; And *your sins have hidden His face from you, So that He will not hear.* "

What will redeem us from sin?

The only redeeming price for sin is the blood of Jesus. Jesus Christ came and paid the price for our sins so that we, through putting our faith in Him, will receive forgiveness of our sins.

> 1 Peter 1:18-19 (NKJV) "*18 knowing that you were not redeemed with corruptible things*, like silver or gold, from your aimless conduct received by tradition from your fathers, 19 **but with the precious blood of Christ, as of a lamb without blemish and without spot.**"

We need a Saviour!

Christ is our Saviour.

Christ is our Saviour. Only He can take our sins away. Only He made a way to take away our sins and to bring us into a restored relationship with the Father.

> Matthew 1:21 (NKJV) "*21 And she will bring forth a Son, and you shall call His name Jesus, for **He will save His people from their sins.**"

Christ died for our sins.

Christ showed His love towards us *by dying on our behalf, to pay for the penalty of our sin* and *to deliver us from the power and stronghold of sin.* He became the Lamb that was slain for the redemption of our souls. He gave His live that we, who deserved to die for our sins, might live.

Unless we make a heartfelt decision to turn away from our sins with true repentance, no enduring change is possible. There are a number of essential, non-negotiable landmarks for this discipleship journey to be successful, and this is most certainly one of them. Only start this discipleship journey if you want to turn from your sins and follow Christ.

On the day of Pentecost, Peter stood up and boldly preached a message, calling everyone to **"repent, be baptised and to wait for the gift of the Holy Spirit."**

> Acts 2:37-38 (NKJV) *"37 Now when they heard this, they were cut to the heart, and said to Peter and the rest of the apostles, "**Men and brethren, what shall we do?**" 38 Then Peter said to them, "**Repent, and let every one of you be baptized** in the name of Jesus Christ for the remission of sins; **and you shall receive the gift of the Holy Spirit.**"*

What does it mean to "Repent?"

Repentance means that you make a roundabout turn in your **thoughts** and **actions**. Repentance is to change your mind and actions to conformity to the Will and purpose of God.

> **"Repentance is a place we come to in our lives where we look at our lives with sorrow, reflect over our actions with remorse, and then turn away from our sins, change our course, our views and accept the Will of God, over ours."**
>
> — DR. HENDRIK J. VORSTER

Repentance is seen in the remorse we express.

The way we give expression to this "change of heart and mind" is that we express true sorrow for our actions, behaviour and sins, and then confess our sins.

> 2 Corinthians 7:9-11 (NKJV) "*9 Now I rejoice, not that you were made sorry, but that **your sorrow led to repentance.** For you were made sorry in a godly manner, that you might suffer loss from us in nothing. 10 **For godly sorrow produces repentance leading to salvation,** not to be regretted; but the sorrow of the world produces death. 11 **For observe this very thing, that you sorrowed in a godly manner:** What **diligence** it produced in you, what **clearing** of yourselves, what **indignation,** what **fear,** what **vehement desire,** what **zeal,** what **vindication!** In all things you proved yourselves to be clear in this matter.*"

Hence we could say that repentance means more than being sorry for what has been done, although ***sorrow always accompanies true repentance. Repentance also means that we stop sinning,*** deliberately. ***True sorrow will lead to repentance and that will lead you to salvation.***

How do we "Repent"?

- **We Repent when we accept the Holy Spirit's conviction of our sins inside of us.**

The Bible says that the Holy Spirit is now that active agent working inside of us to help us come to a place of repentance. **The Holy Spirit convicts us of sin.**

> John 16:8-11 (NKJV) "*8 And when He (Holy Spirit) has come, **He will convict the world of sin,** and of righteousness, and of judgment: 9 **of sin, because they do not believe in Me;** 10 of*

righteousness, because I go to My Father and you see Me no more; 11 of judgment, because the ruler of this world is judged."

- **We come to repentance when we make confession of our sins.**

We have this assurance that when we confess our sins that He will forgive us our sins and cleanse us.

1 John 1:9 (NKJV) "***9 If we confess our sins, He is faithful and just to forgive us our sins and to cleanse us from all unrighteousness.***"

The thoroughness with which this repentance is done, will produce tremendous changes. The relief will be tangible. Sin weighs us down.

The next part is extremely important! The next part runs **concurrently** with the first and that is to put your faith in Jesus as your Saviour.

Step Two – Faith in God.

The second part of being born again is to "***put your faith in God***." Jesus, spoke to Nicodemus and explained to him that he needed to be '***Born again***' to enter into the Kingdom of God. Unless a person ***repents***, places their ***faith in God***, and ***accepts Christ as their Lord*** and Saviour, no conversion or regeneration can take place. Christ describes this conversion experience as being "***born again.***" Being "***Born Again***" marks the beginning of our discipleship journey. This is not possible until we've accepted Christ's redemptive work on the cross, and bowed to His Lordship in our lives.

John 3:3-5 (NKJV) "3 Jesus answered and said to him, "Most assuredly, I say to you, **unless one is born again, he cannot see the kingdom of God.**" 4 Nicodemus said to Him, "How can a man be born when he is old? Can he enter a second time into his mother's womb and be born?" 5 Jesus answered, "Most assuredly, I say to you, **unless one is born of water and the Spirit, he cannot enter the kingdom of God**."

To be '**Born again**" requires of us to "**repent**" of our sins, **yield** to the conviction of the Holy Spirit inside of us, AND, *put our faith in Jesus Christ*.

People place their faith in many things. They place their faith in themselves (**humanism,**) in things like possessions (**materialism,**) traditions - especially those of their forefathers (**traditionalism,**) religion (**pharisaism,**) and many other things or people, except in God.

For true conversion and regeneration to take place in our lives we need to also bow our knees to His Lordship, Jesus Christ, and make Him the Lord of our lives. **We need to put our faith in Him.**

How do I put my faith in Jesus Christ?

The English language has two words to describe the same principle: a noun, FAITH; and a verb, TO BELIEVE.

- **We believe that Jesus is the Son of God.**

The first place we need to look at, in putting our faith in God, is **who** we put our faith in. Jesus is at the centre of this journey.

Jesus is a man who lived 2000 years ago.

The Apostle Matthew records an appearance of an Angel to Joseph, when he learnt that his fiancé was pregnant and explored options to privately leave her, where the Angel made it abundantly clear that she became pregnant by the Holy Spirit, something too wonderful for us to comprehend, and confirmed to him that she was bearing "**Immanuel**" - meaning: "*God with us.*"

Matthew 1:23 (NKJV) "23 "Behold, *the virgin shall be with*

child, and bear a Son, and they shall call His name ***Immanuel***," which is translated, "***God with us***.""

The Apostle Matthew gives us a few accounts where they heard a voice from Heaven saying that Jesus was God's Son. The first was when He was baptized, and the second was when He was on the Mountain of Transfiguration.

Matthew 3:17 (NKJV) "17 And suddenly a voice came from heaven, saying, "**This is My beloved Son**, in whom I am well pleased.""

Jesus once asked His Disciples who people say that He was. The Apostle Peter stated, and it is recorded in Matthew, that He is "the Christ, the Son of the Living God."

Matthew 16:15-16 (NKJV) "15 He said to them, "But who do you say that I am?" 16 Simon Peter answered and said, "You are the Christ, **the Son** of the living God.""

We believe Jesus is the Son of God.

- **We believe that He died on the Cross of Calvary for our sins.**

What did Jesus do on earth?

Throughout the New Testament, especially the first few that are called the Gospels, we learn that Jesus came to "***take away the sins of mankind***." His earthly assignment was declared from the beginning.

Matthew 1:21 (NKJV) "21 And she will bring forth a Son, and you shall ***call His name Jesus***, for ***He will save His people from their sins***.""

- **We believe that He rose from the dead and is alive and seated on the right hand of God the Father.**

Before Jesus died on the cross He declared to His Disciples that He would rise from the dead. This was an amazing message, and one profoundly confronting to a society that lived as if this life is all that there is. He spoke on the resurrection, and eternal life. Faith in Jesus is about believing in eternal life, but that life is only secure because Jesus rose from the dead.

> Romans 14:9 (NKJV) "9 For to this end ***Christ died and rose and lived again***, that He might be Lord of both the dead and the living."

- **We believe that forgiveness for our sins is found from the Lord Jesus Christ.**

The ability and continued willingness to forgive is one of the most valuable attributes to embrace in any person's life, yet who brings forgiveness to our lives when we have sinned, to such an extend that we experience true release of the guilt and condemnation? Only in Jesus Christ do we find such forgiveness from sins. Putting our faith in Jesus, is believing that He forgives us of all our sins, and redeems us through His blood.

> Ephesians 1:7 (NIV)
> [7] ***In him we have redemption through his blood, the forgiveness of sins***, in accordance with the riches of God's grace."

We believe that if we confess our sins then He will forgive us and remove our sins. This is such an amazing promise: that upon confession of our sins, that God will forgive us. Confession of sins requires us to be honest both with ourselves and with God.

- **We come to believe, when we place our trust in Christ, to be our Lord and Savior.**

Believing is essential, but the essential I am talking about is trusting Him to be our Master.

We have the beautiful example in Acts 16 when Paul and Silas was in prison. The Lord sent an earthquake and all the prisoners chains came off and all the prison doors were opened. The jailer got such a fright that he wanted to kill himself. The Apostles Paul and Silas stopped the Jailer from killing himself, and shared the Good News of Jesus with him. He and his household accepted Jesus into their lives. They believed and got baptized.

Acts 16:30-31, 33b, 34c (NKJV)
"30 And he brought them out and said, "Sirs, **what must I do to be saved?**" 31 So they said, "**Believe on the Lord Jesus Christ, and you will be saved**, you and your household.""
"33 ... And **immediately he and all his family were baptized**. 34...; and he rejoiced, **having believed in God** with all his household."

The Jailer asked the question that we are exploring right now: "***What must I do to be saved?***" The answer came immediately: **"Believe on the Lord Jesus Christ, and you will be saved."**

That message is still the same today: **"Believe on the Lord Jesus Christ, and you will be saved."**

When we believe in Jesus, we put our faith in Him. We believe it from our hearts and therefor confess it with our mouths. Putting our faith in God requires both the believing of the heart and the confession with the mouth. This is also what the Word of God teaches us in Romans 10 verse 9:

Romans 10:9 (NKJV)
"***9 that if you confess with your mouth the Lord Jesus and***

believe in your heart that God has raised Him from the
dead, you will be saved."

I have often seen people come under deep conviction of the Holy
Spirit for their sins, repent of them, but they never put their faith in
Jesus to be the Lord over their lives. For true transformation to take
place in our lives we need to transition our faith from ourselves to
having faith in God for our entire lives.

 "For true transformation to take place in our lives we need to
transition our faith from ourselves to having faith in Jesus for
our entire lives."

— Dr. Hendrik Vorster

Step Three – Baptisms.

Step 3, as outlined in the Scripture below, speaks of "**Baptisms**" in the
plural. We have the Baptism into the Body of Christ, the Baptism of
Believers, and the Baptism of the Holy Spirit. We have a number of
Biblical examples to emphasise this progression from Regeneration
(Baptism into the Body of Christ,) to Baptism in water, to receiving
the Baptism of the Holy Spirit.

> Hebrews 6:1-2 (NKJV)
> "*1 Therefore, leaving the discussion of the elementary principles of*
> *Christ, let us go on to perfection, not laying again the foundation of*
> *repentance from dead works and of faith toward God, 2 of **the***
> ***doctrine of baptisms**, of laying on of hands, of resurrection of*
> *the dead, and of eternal judgment.*"

Baptism into the Body of Christ.

In one sense we already discussed the first Baptism into the Body of
Christ in our previous sessions, when we discussed about being "Born
again." This is a work of God through the Holy Spirit at regeneration.

1 Corinthians 12:13 (NIV 1984)

13 For ***we were all baptized by one Spirit into one body—*** whether Jews or Greeks, slave or free—and ***we were all given the one Spirit to drink***."

In this session we explore the next step, of baptism, as one of the ordinances instituted by Christ for His followers to obey. Baptism marks the next necessary step for those who turned their backs on their past sins and turned towards Christ as Lord and who desire to live their lives in union with Christ. Baptism is that step of obedience signifying one's unification with the death and resurrection of Jesus Christ.

The Baptism of Believers.

The Baptism of Believers is a ceremonial action we take to submerse ourselves in water, signifying our death to sin and the world, and burying our old selves, but then also, to signify, as we come out of the water, rising up to a new life with Christ through our reliance on His resurrection Power.

In Biblical order we find, firstly, that when we accept Christ as Lord, through conversion, we are baptised into the Body of Christ. That regeneration process marks our immersion into the Body of Christ, however, Baptism marks our installation into the Body of Christ. It could be explained by comparing the election of a president of a country. They might be elected, but only take office once they are installed or sworn in. Baptism is that "swearing in" ceremony. It is an outward affirmation of change of mind and direction and of an inner regeneration.

Jesus emphasized that **believers** should be baptised, as a necessary step after believing.

Mark 16:16 (NIV)

[16] Whoever believes and is baptized will be saved, but whoever does not believe will be condemned.

Baptism of the Holy Spirit.

Towards the end of Jesus' ministry He emphasized to His Disciples the importance of water baptism and the subsequent Baptism with the Holy Spirit.

> Acts 1:5 (NIV)
> [5] For John baptized with water, but in a few days you will be baptized with the Holy Spirit."

The Apostles preached the Gospel, and then immediately after people responded to the message, emphasized that these new believers should be baptised, and they received the Holy Spirit. The Apostle Peter presented this later Baptism as a promise from the Father.

> Acts 2:37-38 (NKJV)
> "37 Now when they heard this, they were cut to the heart, and said to Peter and the rest of the apostles, "Men and brethren, **what shall we do?**" 38 Then Peter said to them, **"Repent, and let every one of you be baptized** in the name of Jesus Christ for the remission of sins; **and you shall receive the gift of the Holy Spirit.**"

When Philip finished sharing the Gospel with people, he immediately baptized those who believed his message and placed their faith in Jesus Christ.

> Acts 8:12 (NIV)
> [12] But **when they believed** Philip **as he preached the good news** of the kingdom of God and the name of Jesus Christ, **they were baptized**, both men and women.

The Apostles were quite intentional in their pursuit of new believers. Once people accepted the Word of God, they immediately taught them about baptism as a means of sealing their new found faith with a public demonstration of solidarity with Christ, and then as an immediate follow up of their obedience to go through the waters of baptism, laid their hands on them to receive the Holy Spirit.

Acts 8:14-17 (NIV)

'[14] **When the apostles** in Jerusalem **heard that** Samaria **had accepted the word of God**, they sent Peter and John to them. [15] When they arrived, **they prayed for them that they might receive the Holy Spirit**, [16] because the Holy Spirit had not yet come upon any of them; **they had simply been baptized** into the name of the Lord Jesus. [17] **Then Peter and John placed their hands on them, and they received the Holy Spirit**."

Acts 19:4-7 (NIV)

[4] Paul said, "John's baptism was a baptism of repentance. **He told the people to believe in the one coming after him, that is, in Jesus**." [5] On hearing this, **they were baptized into the name of the Lord Jesus**. [6] When **Paul placed his hands on them, the Holy Spirit came on them**, and they spoke in tongues and prophesied. [7] There were about twelve men in all.

In these few verses, among many New Testament examples, we find examples of an order of how the Apostles discipled. *We clearly see the progression from conversion/regeneration, to baptism in water, to baptism in the Holy Spirit.* These three basic initial elements of the Discipleship journey are essential starting blocks. We see that the disciples were intentional, to preach the Gospel, and then ensure that these new believers were Baptised, and then let them receive the Holy Spirit.

Step Four – Laying on of hands.

The Laying on of Hands is an extremely important foundation to establish in the life of a Believer. God is Mighty and His Power and Authority is Supreme, yet one of the amazing things of this Mighty

God is, that He chooses to use people through whom He speaks and ministers.

The Laying on of hands is that ministry that takes places where God touches others, through His commissioned servants, to commission certain people for specific divine purposes, to make conciliation, to bring healing to the sick, and to bestow gifts, especially the Gift of the Holy Spirit.

Throughout the Old Testament we see that ***the laying on of hands was practiced in the commissioning of people for divine service and purposes***. On all occasions ***the laying on of hands came from a direct instruction from the Lord***, and it should therefor always be upheld and honoured as such as we practice this in the Church.

Moses commissioning Joshua.

In Numbers 27 we read the account of when God said to Moses to commission Joshua as his successor.

Numbers 27:18-20 (NKJV)
"18 And ***the Lord said to Moses***: "Take Joshua the son of Nun with you, a man in whom is the Spirit, ***and lay your hand on him***; 19 ***set him before Eleazar the priest and before all the congregation, and inaugurate him in their sight.*** 20 ***And you shall give some of your authority to him,*** that all the congregation of the children of Israel may be obedient."

Numbers 27:23 (NKJV)
"23 ***And he laid his hands on him and inaugurated him, just as the Lord commanded by the hand of Moses.***"

Deuteronomy 34:9 (NKJV)
"9 ***Now Joshua*** the son of Nun ***was full of the spirit of wisdom, for Moses had laid his hands on him***; ***so the***

children of Israel heeded him, and did as the Lord had commanded Moses."

We learn from this "Laying on of hands," that Joshua was inaugurated, and received authority and the "spirit of wisdom."

Appointment of Deacons.

When the early Church elected Spirit-filled Deacons to help with the ministry of serving, the Apostles laid their hands on them and commissioned them for that purpose in the presence of the whole church.

Acts 6:3-6 (NKJV)

"3 Therefore, brethren, seek out from among you seven men of good reputation, full of the Holy Spirit and wisdom, ***whom we may appoint over this business***; 4 but we will give ourselves continually to prayer and to the ministry of the word."

5 And the saying pleased the whole multitude. And ***they chose Stephen***, a man full of faith and the Holy Spirit, and ***Philip, Prochorus, Nicanor, Timon, Parmenas, and Nicolas***, a proselyte from Antioch, 6 ***whom they set before the apostles; and when they had prayed, they laid hands on them.***"

Commissioning of Barnabas and Saul.

In the church in Antioch, when the Holy Spirit commissioned Barnabas and Saul (the Apostle Paul) for a specific mission, the church leaders who were present, under the instruction of the Holy Spirit, commissioning them by the laying on of hands.

Acts 13:3 (NKJV)

"1 Now in the church that was at Antioch there were ***certain prophets and teachers***: Barnabas, Simeon who was called

Niger, Lucius of Cyrene, Manaen who had been brought up
with Herod the tetrarch, and Saul. 2 *As they ministered to
the Lord and fasted, the Holy Spirit said*, "Now *separate
to Me Barnabas and Saul for the work to which I have
called them.*" 3 **Then**, *having fasted and prayed, and
laid hands on them, they sent them away.*"

It is this "*laying on of hands*" that was honoured and regarded in
the early church, both by the people who were "commissioned" and
"anointed" for their "higher calling" and service, and by those who
observed the 'Laying on of Hands." These men and woman were held
in high regard, since the Lord set them apart by the "laying on of
hands" for their service.

The foundation of the "laying on of hands," and upholding it in our
lives is therefor in one sense an honouring of the Lord's choosing of
men and woman to lead in the affairs of the church, and an honouring
of the "anointing" that comes as a result of this "laying on of hands."
We show that we value this foundation in our lives when we honour
those whom the Lord set aside for specific purposes and upon whom
hands were laid in the presence of God and the congregation.

Without valuing this foundation, we wont value the setting aside of
some for spiritual purpose, and neither will we value their appointment
over us. With valuing the Foundation of "laying on of hands" come
both a respect for those on whom hands have been laid as well as for
the position in which God placed them.

Healing came through the laying on of hands.

In the New Testament we find that Christ laid His hands on the
sick and they got well.

Luke 4:40 (NIV 1984)
"40 When the sun was setting, the people brought to Jesus all
who had various kinds of sickness, and *laying his hands on
each one, he healed them*."

Jesus encouraged and instructed Believers to lay their hands on the sick so that they will recover.

> Mark 16:18 (NKJV)
> "18 they will take up serpents; and if they drink anything deadly, it will by no means hurt them; *they will lay hands on the sick, and they will recover.*""

Spiritual gifts are imparted through the laying on Hands.

The early Church placed a high value on the Apostles laying hands on them. It was regarded and received as if it was the Lord Himself laying His Hand on them. The Laying on of Hands was and is a powerful tool in the Hands of God to bring healing, impart Spiritual Gifts, and to set people apart for service unto the Lord.

> Acts 8:17-19 (NIV 1984)
> 17 Then *Peter and John placed their hands on them, and they received the Holy Spirit.* 18 When Simon saw that the Spirit was given at the laying on of the apostles' hands, he offered them money 19 and said, "Give me also this ability so that everyone on whom I lay my hands may receive the Holy Spirit."

> 2 Timothy 1:6 (NIV 1984)
> "6 For this reason I remind you to *fan into flame the gift of God, which is in you through the laying on of my hands.*"

The use of the 'Laying on of Hands" is therefor something to be treated with the utmost respect and reverence. We, on God's behalf, and under His instruction, lay our hands on people to impart blessing, pardon, healing or some Spiritual Gift or empowerment. These should be practiced with care and consideration. On the other hand, we show the value we place on God's choosing of servants, by honouring and obeying those who administer such "laying on of Hands," on His behalf.

Step Five – Resurrection of the dead.

The Resurrection of the dead is an essential constituent of our faith in Christ. Through embracing this truth, about the resurrection, we embrace the fact that 1. Christ rose from the dead, as He said He would, and 2. We too will rise again, either for eternal life, or unto eternal damnation.

Since Christ rose from the dead, we embrace the Resurrection of the dead.

One of the essentials teachings we as Believers embrace is the teaching on the "**Resurrection of the Dead**." Our entire Gospel hinges on the fact that **Jesus rose from the dead**. He is Alive, and through Him we can truly embrace eternal life!

1 Corinthians 15:20-21 (NIV 1984)
"*20 But Christ has indeed been raised from the dead, the firstfruits of those who have fallen asleep. 21 For **since death came through a man, the resurrection of the dead comes also through a man.***"

Since Christ rose from the dead, we too shall rise from the dead to eternal life.

Every Believer should live daily with this eternal hope in his or her heart, since Christ rose from the dead, we too shall rise from the dead to eternal life. When Jesus comes back, He is coming to fetch us, His children, to be with Him for eternity. We should live with this eternal hope in our hearts.

1 Thessalonians 4:16 (NIV 1984)
"16 For the Lord himself will come down from heaven, with a loud command, with the voice of the archangel and with the trumpet call of God, and **the dead in Christ will rise first**."

By embracing the Resurrection of the dead we embrace the second coming of Christ.

Jesus is coming back again, and we as believers should live as those who expect to stand before Him one day and give account of our life on earth. We will be without excuse on that day since Christ paid a high price to pave the way for us to have eternal life.

Matthew 25:31-32 (NKJV)

"31 *"**When the Son of Man comes in His glory**, and all the holy angels with Him, then **He will sit on the throne of His glory. 32 All the nations will be gathered before Him, and He will separate them one from another**, as a shepherd divides his sheep from the goats."*

Matthew 25:34 (NKJV)

"34 Then the King will say to **those on His right hand**, '*Come, you blessed of My Father, inherit the kingdom prepared for you from the foundation of the world:*"

The key points are that; **the way we live in this life has eternal consequences**, and **we will all rise from the dead, whether we were Believers or not.** The Believers will rise unto eternal **life** and the unbelievers unto eternal **damnation**.

Step Six – Eternal Judgment.

The early Church counted it an essential firm foundation to establish in the daily life of every new Believer; to embrace *the consciousness of eternal consequences.* **The reward for our sins should be death on a cross.** Christ made it possible that we could escape that eternal judgment by believing in Him, however, this faith should be reflected in the way in which we value His propitiation for our sins. The life we now live should be consistent with our eternal gratitude.

John 3:16 (NIV 1984)

"16 "For God so loved the world that he gave his one and only Son, that
***whoever believes in him shall not perish but have
eternal life."***

Romans 14:10 (NIV 1984)
*"10 You, then, why do you judge your brother? Or why do you look
down on your brother? For **we will all stand before God's
judgment seat.**"*

As people who will stand before our Lord, every Believer should
embrace the following heart attitude:

**We need to live with a daily awareness that at the end of our
lives we will stand before the Throne of God, and give account
of ourselves, to God.**

Romans 14:12 (NIV 1984)
*"12 So then, **each of us will give an account of himself** to God."*

**Sometimes people forget that we will all give an account of
ourselves to God.** Many people live as if they are beyond having to
give account. Be reminded that it was Christ who forewarned us of this
day of accounting.

When we harness ourselves with this mindfulness of eternal judgment, we will constantly adjust and consider our ways in view of our
appearing before our King.

**We need to live our lives as those who will have to give account
for our actions.**

The fact remains that ***our words and actions are important and
has a bearing on how we will spend eternity***. One of the constant
and consistent messages of the Lord Jesus to His Disciples, and then
from the Apostles to the Believers in the various Churches, was the
message that our faith and walk need to be consistent with the faith
we profess. We are all on public display daily. Our lives tell a story.

Jesus once told His Disciples, and us, that we will give account "*for every idle word*" we speak in "*the day of judgement.*"

Matthew 12:36-37 (NKJV)
"36 But I say to you that *for every idle word men may speak, they will give account of it in the day of judgment*. 37 For by your words you will be justified, and by your words you will be condemned.""

As Believers, our words should be considered before we utter them. May the Lord help us to put aside the language of the world. I have seen, through the years, how the language of new Believers becomes one of the first signs to their unbelieving friends that things have changed. We see that the crudeness and swearing stops, the negativity is replaced with positiveness, and the lying and deceit is replaced with honestly, respect and kindness. May this be your testimony as well.

James 2:21-24 (NIV)
"[21] Was not our ancestor Abraham considered righteous for what he did when he offered his son Isaac on the altar? [22] *You see that his faith and his actions were working together*, and his faith was made complete **by what he did.** [23] And the scripture was fulfilled that says, "Abraham believed God, and it was credited to him as righteousness," and he was called God's friend. [24] *You see that a person is justified by what he does and not by faith alone.*"

James 2:12 (NKJV)
"12 *So speak and so do as those who will be judged* by the law of liberty."

Colossians 4:5-6 (NIV)
"[5] *Be wise in the way you act toward outsiders*; make the most of every opportunity. [6] *Let your conversation be always full of grace*, seasoned with salt, so that you may know how to answer everyone."

Our lives bear witness to the life of Christ in us. May this changed life bear witness unto eternity.

We need to be Faithful Servants doing what God called us to do.

One day Jesus told His Disciples a Parable on stewardship. He told them of a certain master who gave each one of his servants, talents to use. After a long while He returned and required them to give account of the talents they received. When you read this parable in Matthew 25, you quickly notice the message of how Jesus requires us to use our talents and produce a harvest. May the Lord grant that you and I use our talents to full use so that we may produce a multiplied harvest when He returns.

Matthew 25:20-21(NKJV)
"20 "So he who had received five talents came and brought five other talents, saying, 'Lord, you delivered to me five talents; look, I have gained five more talents besides them.' 21 His lord said to him, '***Well done, good and Faithful servant; you were Faithful over a few things, I will make you ruler over many things. Enter into the joy of your lord.***'"

I want to stand before the Lord and hear those wonderful words: "***Well done, good and faithful servant.***"

Ephesians 2:10 (NKJV)
"10 For we are His workmanship, created in Christ Jesus for good works, which God prepared beforehand that we should walk in them."
1 Peter 4:10-11 (NKJV)
"10 As each one has received a gift, minister it to one another, as good stewards of the manifold grace of God.

Conclusion of Step 1

These six foundations were installed and taught to every New Believer. Laying a solid and sound foundation to build one's faith on is essential to build a spiritual house that will withstand the storms of life.

The expanded content description is in the my Book on "**The Process of Discipleship**," however, the full content of this Foundational Series on Discipleship is contained in my Book; "**Discipleship Foundations – Step One – Salvation**."

Step 2 – Establish Spiritual Roots, Values and disciplines.

Once you have a "Born Again" Believer then you can start the investment process of instilling the Values of the Kingdom of God in the Believer. If you build spiritual values and disciplines into people who have never bowed their knees to the Lordship of Christ, you are building on sand. As I mentioned earlier, if you are going to build people up then make sure that you build in those lives that has Christ as their Rock and Foundation.

Values.

I always wondered where to start once people committed their lives to Christ. When I look at how Jesus did it, remembering that He started His Discipleship journey with people who left everything to follow Him, **I find that Jesus started by teaching His Disciples the Values of the Kingdom of God.** One of the biggest challenges we face in our ministries, is that we're sitting with people who are "churched", but never adopted and applied the values of the Kingdom of God in their lives.

The second phase of Discipleship deals with establishing roots from which our faith will grow and mature. Having strong roots are essential to growing a healthy and stable spiritual life.

The Kingdom of God is established on Values. **Values are roots** from which one draws one's strength. This phase marks the Believer's walk as a young man or woman, as they assimilate the values of the

Kingdom of God. Through the teachings of Jesus we learn the values He taught His Disciples.

Humility

*Matthew 5:3 (NIV 1984) 3 **"Blessed are the poor in spirit**, for theirs is the kingdom of heaven."*

1 Peter 5:5-6, 1 Peter 3:8, Philippians 2:3-5, Philippians 2:8.

Humility is the quality of having a modest or subjected view of one's own importance.

Penitence

*Matthew 5:4 (NIV 1984) "4 **Blessed are those who mourn**, for they will be comforted."*

Luke 18:13-14, Psalms 51.

Penitence is the value of reflective living. Penitence is the applied value of humbly and honestly assessing one's actions before God, with a willingness to acknowledge our wrongs and to follow through with repentance and seeking true forgiveness.

Meekness

*Matthew 5:5 (NIV 1984) "5 **Blessed are the meek**, for they will inherit the earth."*

James 3:13, Matthew 6:10, John 4:34, John 6:38, Isaiah 53:7.

Meekness is the consistent characteristic of submissiveness. Meekness is to present oneself in every situation as one who lives under the rule and directive of another.

Spiritual Passion

*Matthew 5:6 (NIV 1984) "6 **Blessed are those who hunger and thirst for righteousness**, for they will be filled."*

1 Timothy 4:12, 15, Romans 12:11.

Spiritual passion is the value of giving, and expressing oneself fully in one's faith.

Merciful

*Matthew 5:7 (NIV 1984) "7 **Blessed are the merciful**, for they will be shown mercy."*

Luke 6:36

To be Merciful is to be filled with grace towards all people, being constantly mindful of how much we've been forgiven of.

Purity

*Matthew 5:8 (NIV 1984) "8 **Blessed are the pure in heart**, for they will see God."*

Psalms 24:3-5, Philippians 4:8, 1 Timothy 1:5, 1 Timothy 4:12, James 4:8, 1 John 3:2-3.

Purity is characterized by freedom from immorality, adultery and sinful contamination, and is a value of the Kingdom of God.

Peacemakers

*Matthew 5:9 (NIV 1984) "9 **Blessed are the peacemakers**, for they will be called sons of God."*

James 3:8, Romans 14:19, Romans 12:18, Psalms 34:14, Acts 7:26, 2
Corinthians 5:19-20, Ephesians 4:3.

A peacemaker is someone who actively steps up in every adversarial situation to work towards a peaceful outcome. Peacemakers are reconciliatory in action. There is Power in Unity. The value of living, as far as is possible from your side, at peace with people around you is actually a Characteristic of Believers.

Patient endurance under suffering.

Matthew 5:10-12 (NIV) "[10] **Blessed are those who are**
persecuted because of righteousness, *for theirs is the*
*kingdom of heaven. [11] "**Blessed are you when people insult***
you, persecute you and falsely say all kinds of evil
***against you because of me.** [12] Rejoice and be glad, because*
great is your reward in heaven, for in the same way they persecuted
the prophets who were before you."

Luke 6:22, 1 Peter 2:19-20, Matthew 5:38-42, Matthew 16:24, James
1:2.

It is the ability to endure through unjust treatment because of your faith, and even go beyond the expected response to such attacks by acting in a non-retaliatory way.

Example

*Matthew 5:13-16 (NIV 1984) "13 **You are the salt of the earth**.*
But if the salt loses its saltiness, how can it be made salty again? It is
no longer good for anything, except to be thrown out and trampled
*by men. 14 **You are the light of the world**. A city on a hill*
cannot be hidden. 15 Neither do people light a lamp and put it under
a bowl. Instead they put it on its stand, and it gives light to everyone
*in the house. 16 In the same way, **let your light shine before***

men, that they may see your good deeds and praise your Father *in heaven."*

Matthew 12:34-37.

Being an example is the expression we give as to how much we value the Lord Jesus, and the extent to which we desire to make His Name known among the people of the earth. Being salt and light.

Custodian.

*Matthew 5:19 (NIV 1984) "19 Anyone who breaks one of the least of these commandments and teaches others to do the same will be called least in the kingdom of heaven, but **whoever practices and teaches these commands will be called great** in the kingdom of heaven."*

A custodian is someone who intentionally obeys and keeps the Word of God. A custodian is a keeper and preserver of the Word of God and seeks in earnest to uphold the Word of God in every situation and circumstance. A custodian is intent on upholding the Word of God. A Custodian is an upholder and advocate for the moral guidelines God set for His people.

Reconciliatory

*Matthew 5:23-24 (NIV 1984) "23 "Therefore, if you are offering your gift at the altar and there remember that your brother has something against you, 24 leave your gift there in front of the altar. **First go and be reconciled to your brother**; then come and offer your gift."*

Matthew 18:15-17.

Being a reconciler is a Kingdom value. We value reconciliation when we take the initiative to sort things out with a brother or sister, and this is what Jesus encourages us to do.

Resoluteness

Matthew 5:37 (NIV 1984) "37 **Simply let your 'Yes' be 'Yes,'** *and your 'No,' 'No'; anything beyond this comes from the evil one."*

Joshua 24:15 "And if it seem evil unto you to serve the LORD, **choose you this day whom ye will serve***; whether the gods which your fathers served that were on the other side of the flood, or the gods of the Amorites, in whose land ye dwell: but as for me and my house, we will serve the LORD."*

Resoluteness describes the value of being a man or woman of your word, even if it hurts.

Loving

Matthew 5:43-48 (NIV 1984) "43 "You have heard that it was said, 'Love your neighbor and hate your enemy.' 44 But I tell you: **Love your enemies and pray for those who persecute you, 45 that you may be sons of your Father in heaven***. He causes his sun to rise on the evil and the good, and sends rain on the righteous and the unrighteous. 46 If you love those who love you, what reward will you get? Are not even the tax collectors doing that? 47 And if you greet only your brothers, what are you doing more than others? Do not even pagans do that? 48 Be perfect, therefore, as your heavenly Father is perfect."*

John 13:34-35, 1 Corinthians 13.

Love is a strong feeling of affection. We value love when we unconditionally show our affection in meaningful ways. All people want to know and feel that they are loved. Love is from God. Love God, love His people, love the Samaritans, and those who hurt, abused and rejected you. Love God's Commandments. We show that we love God by obeying Him.

Discreetness

*Matthew 6:3-4 (NIV 1984) "3 But when you give to the needy, **do not let your left hand know what your right hand is doing,** 4 so that your giving may be in secret. Then your Father, who sees what is done in secret, will reward you."*

Psalms 112:5.

It is the inherent value of doing extra-ordinary things without desiring to be seen and acknowledged for doing them.

Forgiving

*Matthew 6:12 (NIV 1984) "12 Forgive us our debts, **as we also have forgiven our debtors."***

Matthew 6:14-15, Colossians 3:13, Matthew 18:21-22.

Forgiveness is the ability to release those who wronged you, and treat the offenders as if they never did a thing to hurt or harm you.

Kingdom of God Investor.

*Matthew 6:19-21 (NIV 1984) Treasures in Heaven "19 "Do not store up for yourselves treasures on earth, where moth and rust destroy, and where thieves break in and steal. 20 But **store up for yourselves treasures in heaven,** where moth and rust do not destroy, and where thieves do not break in and steal. 21 For **where your treasure is, there your heart will be also."***

Acts 2:44-45, Acts 5:1-10.

A Kingdom of God Investor is someone who values the Kingdom of God above earthly thing and as an expression of that value, puts their treasures into the Kingdom of God.

God-minded

Matthew 6:24 (NIV 1984) "24 **"No one can serve two masters.**
*Either he will hate the one and love the other, or he will be devoted
to the one and despise the other. You cannot serve both God and
Money.*

Colossians 3:1-2.

It is a Kingdom value to be God-minded. Being God-minded
means that you think about God, His Word and the eternal things of
above, all the time.

Kingdom of God prioritizer.

Matthew 6:33 (NIV 1984) 33 But **seek first his kingdom and his
righteousness,** *and all these things will be given to you as well."*

We truly value the Kingdom of God when we seek to put the
Kingdom values above that of our own. We value the Kingdom of God
when it takes precedence over every decision we make.

Introspective

*Matthew 7:1-2 (NIV 1984) "1 "Do not judge, or you too will be judged.
2* **For in the same way you judge others, you will be
judged,** *and with the measure you use, it will be measured to you."*

*Matthew 7:3-5 (NIV) 3 "Why do you look at the speck of sawdust in
your brother's eye and pay no attention to the plank in your own eye?
4 How can you say to your brother, 'Let me take the speck out of
your eye,' when all the time there is a plank in your own eye? 5 You
hypocrite,* **first take the plank out of your own eye**, *and then
you will see clearly to remove the speck from your brother's eye.*

It is the constant self-awareness and assessment of our own

standing before God, and thereby enabling us to be considered in our assessment of others' actions and deeds.

Persistent

*Matthew 7:7-8 (NIV 1984) "7 **Ask** and it will be given to you; **seek** and you will find; **knock** and the door will be opened to you. 8 For **everyone who asks receives**; he who seeks finds; and to him who knocks, the door will be opened."*

Being persistent is living a life in full pursuit without giving up. Keep on asking, seeking and knocking since we have this Promise. Persistence moves you to explore every possibility.

Considerate

*Matthew 7:12 (NIV 1984) 12 So in everything, **do to others what you would have them do to you**, for this sums up the Law and the Prophets.*

Philippians 2:4 "Look not every man on his own things, but every man also on the things of others."

Romans 14:13.

Consideration is the value of thinking beforehand how your preferences, actions, presence at certain places and responses might impact others.

Conservative

*Matthew 7:13-14 (NIV 1984) "13 **Enter through the narrow gate.** For wide is the gate and broad is the road that leads to destruction, and many enter through it. 14 But small is the gate and narrow the road that leads to life, and only a few find it."*

To be conservative is the considered choice of living rather care-fully than liberally. It is the making of careful and conservative choices within the guidelines of the Bible. You would rather err on being too conservative than allowing yourself liberties that might be frowned upon by God.

Fruit-bearing

Matthew 7:16-18 (NIV 1984) 16 By their fruit you will recognize them. Do people pick grapes from thornbushes, or figs from thistles? 17 Likewise every good tree bears good fruit, but a bad tree bears bad fruit. 18 A good tree cannot bear bad fruit, and a bad tree cannot bear good fruit.

Matthew 12:33, Matthew 13:23, Matthew 21:43.

One of the most powerful ways in which we show and proof our legitimacy as Children of God, who turned from our wicked ways unto the living God, is to bear the fruit of a changed life in our lives. It is also the ability to reproduce after our own, renewed, self.

Practitioner

*Matthew 7:24 (NIV 1984) The Wise and Foolish Builders "24 "Therefore **everyone who hears these words of mine and puts them into practice** is like a wise man who built his house on the rock."*

James 1:22, Romans 2:13, Luke 6:47,49, Luke 8:21, Philippians 4:9.

We show that we value the Kingdom of God by being doers of the Word. Jesus values doers, those putting things He teaches into practice in their lives. It is a value in the Kingdom of God to be a practitioner.

Accountability

*Matthew 12:36 (NIV) 12 " But I tell you that **men will have to give account on the day of judgement for every careless word they have spoken.**"*

Romans 14:12, Hebrews 4:13, 1 Peter 4:5, Colossians 4:6.

Accountability is to value living answerable for one's actions, deeds and words, both to man and God. Accountability is expressed by taking responsibility for one's actions and words.

Living by Faith

Matthew 17:20 (NIV 1984) 20 He replied, "Because you have so little faith. I tell you the truth, if you have faith as small as a mustard seed, you can say to this mountain, 'Move from here to there' and it will move. Nothing will be impossible for you.'"

Romans 1:17, Hebrews 11:1.

Faith believes beyond proof. Faith is doing things because of what you belief to be true. Faith is acting purely because God said you should or could. Our actions flow from what we truly belief.

Childlikeness

*Matthew 18:3-5 (NIV 1984) 3 And he said: "I tell you the truth, **unless you change and become like little children**, you will never enter the kingdom of heaven. 4 Therefore, whoever humbles himself like this child is the greatest in the kingdom of heaven. 5 "And whoever welcomes a little child like this in my name welcomes me.*

Childlikeness is the heart attitude of humility towards God, expressed by simple obedience in action. Those who value childlikeness take the Words of the Lord Jesus literally and apply it without trying to dissect or interpret it. They simply do what is asked.

Cooperation

*Matthew 18:19 (NIV 1984) 19 "Again, I tell you **that if two of you
on earth agree about anything** you ask for, it will be done for
you by my Father in heaven.*

Cooperation is expressed by a heart attitude that desires to work
together with others and seek to find mutual agreement for the sake of
Christ.

Servanthood

*Matthew 20:26-28 (NIV 1984) 26 Not so with you. Instead, **whoever
wants to become great among you must be your servant,**
27 and **whoever wants to be first must be your slave**– 28
just as the Son of Man did not come to be served, but to serve, and to
give his life as a ransom for many."*

Servanthood is at the top of the values defining Great Leaders in
the Kingdom of God. Great Leaders in the Kingdom of God are characterised by their serving.

Committed

*Luke 9:62 (KJV) "[62] And Jesus said unto him, **No man, having
put his hand to the plough, and looking back,** is fit for the
kingdom of God."*

John 15:13, Psalm 37:5.

Children of God, Believers, are characterized by their commitment
and loyalty to the Kingdom of God. They start and finish tasks. They
don't give up when things are tough or hard. They stick to the task and
assignment before them. Loyalty is shown by the extent to which one
is prepared to stay committed to someone. Loyalty is the allegiance
one commits to.

Gratefulness

*I Thessalonians 5:18 "**In everything give thanks**: for this is the will of God in Christ Jesus concerning you."*

It is the feeling you have, or express, of appreciation for something you have, or received, or observed.

Stewardship

*Matthew 17:24-27 (NIV) "[24] After Jesus and his disciples arrived in Capernaum, the collectors of the two-drachma tax came to Peter and asked, "Doesn't your teacher pay the temple tax?" [25] "Yes, he does," he replied. When Peter came into the house, Jesus was the first to speak. "What do you think, Simon?" he asked. "From whom do the kings of the earth collect duty and taxes—from their own sons or from others?" [26] "From others," Peter answered. "Then the sons are exempt," Jesus said to him. [27] "But so that we may not offend them, go to the lake and throw out your line. Take the first fish you catch; open its mouth and you will find a four-drachma coin. **Take it and give it to them for my tax and yours.**"*

Matthew 22:21 (NKJV) "21 They said to Him, **"Caesar's."** And He said to them, **"Render therefore to Caesar the things that are Caesar's, and to God the things that are God's."**

Stewardship is proofing oneself faithful as a steward with the Gifts, talents and resources of the King. Embracing the accountability and faithfulness to administer the resources as directed by the Lord is a Kingdom Value.

Obedience

*Luke 11:28 (NIV) "28 He replied, "**Blessed rather are those who hear the word of God and obey it**."*

John 8:55, John 14:23-24, Acts 5:29,32, Romans 6:17, Matthew 28:20, Ephesians 6:1, 5-6, 2 Thessalonians 1:8, Hebrews 5:9, Deuteronomy 28:1-13.

Obedience is expressed by the way we fully comply and execute that which is expected and demanded of us.

Carefulness

*Colossians 4:5-6 (NIV) "5 **Be wise in the way you act toward outsiders**; make the most of every opportunity. 6 Let your conversation be always full of grace, seasoned with salt, so that you may know how to answer everyone."*

Ephesians 5:15

Carefulness is that considered approach we apply to our words, actions, deeds and thoughts, especially as we consider how it might advance or tarnish the Kingdom of God.

Compassion

*1 Peter 3:8 "Finally, be ye all of one mind, **having compassion one of another**, love as brethren, be pitiful, be courteous:"*

Compassion is a feeling of sorrow or pity for someone, and expressed by showing them kindness, mercy, sympathy or tenderness.

Caring

*Galatians 6:2 (NIV) "2 **Carry each other's burdens**, and in this way you will fulfill the law of Christ."*

Romans 14:13

Caring is being thoughtful and sympathetic towards others, especially considering their cares, burdens and concerns.

Confident

*Philippians 1:6 (NIV) "6 **being confident of this**, that he who began a good work in you will carry it on to completion until the day of Christ Jesus."*

*2 Corinthians 3:4 (NIV) "4 **Such confidence we have** through Christ before God."*

2 Corinthians 3:5-6, Ephesians 3:12, 2 Thessalonians 3:4, Hebrews 3:6, 4:16, 10:35, 11:1, 1 John 4:17, 5:14.

Confidence is the trust and faith you have in someone or something. It is a strong belief and feeling of certainty with which you do things. God is the source of confidence, and as we place our indisputable trust and faith in Him, He works this confidence in us to do extra-ordinary things.

Steadfastness

*1 Corinthians 15:58 (NIV) "58 Therefore, my dear brothers and sisters, **stand firm. Let nothing move you. Always give yourselves fully to the work of the Lord**, because you know that your labour in the Lord is not in vain.*

Steadfastness is the inner assertiveness to be firmly fixed and focused on doing what you purposed to do. It is the ability to be constant and unchanging in your course of faith.

Contentment

*1 Timothy 6:6 (NIV) "6 But **godliness with contentment is great** gain."*

1 Timothy 6:7-10, Philippians 4:11.

Contentment is the pre-positioning of being satisfied and pleased regardless of the circumstances you might find yourself in. Contentment is the satisfaction with one's current state.

Transforming

*Romans 12:2 "And be not conformed to this world: but **be ye transformed by the renewing of your mind**, that ye may prove what is that good, and acceptable, and perfect, will of God."*

Colossians 3:10, Ephesians 4:23-24.

Transformation takes places when we renew our mind. Transformation is the process of being changed in condition, character, form or appearance. Only a commitment to being renewed in the spirit of your mind will ensure a lifetime of transformation.

Deferent

*1 Corinthians 9:22 (NIV) "22 To the weak I became weak, to win the weak. **I have become all things to all people so that by all possible means I might save some**."*

1 Corinthians 9:19-23, I Corinthians 10:33, Romans 14:13, Ephesians 5:1.

It is the considered and thoughtful action of living an exemplary life with the expressed purpose of leading others to Christ through my way of living.

Diligence

*Colossians 3:23 "And whatsoever ye do, **do it heartily**, as to the Lord, and not unto men."*

1 Thessalonians 4:11, Ecclesiastes 9:10.

Diligence is the paying of careful and unceasing attention. Diligence is developed in us by paying attention and being conscientious in everything we do.

Trustworthiness

*Matthew 25:21 (NIV) "21 "His master replied, 'Well done, **good and faithful servant**! **You have been faithful** with a few things; I will put you in charge of many things. Come and share your master's happiness!'*

1 Timothy 6:20, 1 Corinthians 4:2.

Trustworthiness is truthfulness and faithfulness combined. This is a rewarded characteristic of Believers. Believers are known for their trustworthiness, truthfulness and faithfulness.

Gentleness

*2 Timothy 2:24 "And the servant of the Lord must not strive; but **be gentle unto all men**, apt to teach, and patient."*

Galatians 5:23, Philippians 4:5, Colossians 3:12, 1 Timothy 6:11, Matthew 11:29.

Gentleness is the ability to be patient and kind, and expressed by a continual compassionate leniency towards all people.

Discernment

*Philippians 1:10 (NIV) "10 so that you may be able **to discern what is best** and may be pure and blameless for the day of Christ,"*

Philippians 1:9-11, Hebrews 5:14, Ezekiel 44:23, Psalms 119:125, Proverbs 28:2.

Discernment is the ability to distinguish between right and wrong, between what is more expedient or not, and what is best. Discernment is also the ability to see the difference between things and to understand clearly the distinction between thoughts, ideas and concepts.

Truthfulness

*Ephesians 4:25 "Wherefore **putting away lying, speak every man truth with his neighbour**: for we are members one of another."*

Truthfulness is the ability to speak and act in an honest, open, just and righteous way.

Generosity

*Acts 20:35 (NIV) "35 In everything I did, I showed you that by this kind of hard work we must help the weak, remembering the words the Lord Jesus himself said: '**It is more blessed to give than to receive**."*

2 Corinthians 8:2, 2 Corinthians 9:6, 11, 13.

Generosity is the ability to be unselfish with a readiness to give freely.

Kindness

*Ephesians 4:32 (NIV) "32 **Be kind and compassionate to one another**, forgiving each other, just as in Christ God forgave you."*

Colossians 3:12, Galatians 5:22.

Kindness is that generally warm-hearted, friendly and well-meaning interaction with others. Kindness is seen in the thoughtfulness and consideration with which we deal with people.

Watchfulness

*Titus 2:12 "Teaching us that, denying ungodliness and worldly lusts, **we should live soberly, righteously, and godly**, in this present world."*

Hebrews 2:1, Mark 14:38, Acts 20:28.

It is the action and activity of paying close attention to one's own, and other's lives, especially as it impacts others positively for Christ's sake.

Perseverance

Galatians 6:9 "And let us not be weary in well doing: for in due season we shall reap, if we faint not."
Hebrews 12:1, Romans 8:25, James 1:4, 12.

Perseverance is the inbred ability to endure through difficult and hard times. It is the continuing in the faith regardless of what challenges might be encountered.

Honoring

*John 5:23 (NIV) "23 that all may **honor the Son just as they honor the Father**. Whoever does not honor the Son does not honor the Father, who sent him."*

Matthew 15:4,

1 Thessalonians 5:12-13 (NIV) "2 Now we ask you, brothers and sisters, to acknowledge those who work hard among you, who care for you

*in the Lord and who admonish you. **13 Hold them in the
highest regard in love because of their work.** Live in peace
with each other."*

To show honour is to be respectful in gesture, words and behavior.
Being respectful is to show honour, reverence and deference to those
you honour.

Submissive

*Hebrews 13:17 **"Obey them that have the rule over you,** and
submit yourselves: for they watch for your souls, as they that
must give account, that they may do it with joy, and not with grief:
for that is unprofitable for you."*

Submission is the self-determined subjection to the will of
another. For us it is our submission to the Will and Word
of God.

Conclusion on Values

In fact I have determined and narrowed the values down to 52
Kingdom Values. In my Book: **"The Values and Disciplines of the
Kingdom of God"** I have outlined and explored these for adoption
and application in our lives.

Of course the **Fruit of the Spirit** are values by which we are often
characterized and determined to be Children of God, however, these
come as a direct result of the Holy Spirit's presence and pre-eminence
in our lives.

Love – the greatest value of all.

The greatest Value that sets us apart as Disciples of the Lord is of
course Love. ***"By this shall all men know that you are My Disciples, if you have love one for another."*** These words, and many
more, from the teachings of Jesus to His Disciples, and us, stand out as

Lighthouses in our journey to assimilate the Values of the Kingdom of God. Our part is to live the values.

Assimilating the Values of the Kingdom of God is one thing, however, maintaining them in our lives is another, and **it is** therefor **equally important to establish spiritual disciplines**, which will ensure that these Values are kept and maintained.

The concurrent area of development in the young Believer's life is Spiritual Disciplines.

Spiritual Disciplines.

Spiritual disciplines are habits, practices, and experiences that are designed to develop, grow, and strengthen our inner man. Spiritual disciplines build the capacity of our character and keep the values we aspire to assimilate into our lives, intact. Spiritual disciplines form the structure within which we train our soul to obey.

 Spiritual disciplines are habits, practices, and experiences that are designed to develop, grow, and strengthen our inner man.

— Dr. Hendrik J. Vorster

The Apostle Paul taught his disciple, Timothy, to train himself to be godly.

> 1 Timothy 4:7 (NIV) "7 Have nothing to do with godless myths and old wives' tales; rather, *train yourself to be godly*."

The New Testament Church practiced spiritual disciplines.

It seems from the impact that the early Church had, that they had a few practices, which positioned them for such a revival atmosphere where people were added to the Church on a daily basis.

We also have a number of examples from that of the spiritual Disciplines of the Apostles. As the Church grew, the complexities of ministry grew, however, what set the Apostles apart was their discipline to keep their Spiritual Disciplines undisturbed. Almost on every occasion the Apostles are mentioned it is connected with them going for prayer, busy praying or as a result of them praying and ministering the Word of God that awesome things happened.

> **Acts 6:4 (NIV)** "4 and *we will give our attention to prayer and the ministry of the word.*"

Acts 2 verses 42-46 highlight some of the spiritual practices of the Believers in the Book of Acts.

> **Acts 2:42-47 (NIV)** "*42 They devoted themselves to the apostles' teaching* and *to fellowship, to the breaking of bread and to prayer.* 43 Everyone was filled with awe at the many wonders and signs performed by the apostles. *44 All the believers were together and had everything in common. 45 They sold property and possessions to give to anyone who had need. 46 Every day they continued to meet together in the temple courts. They broke bread in their homes* and ate together with glad and sincere hearts, *47 praising God* and enjoying the favor of all the people. *And the Lord added to their number daily those who were being saved.*"

In this portion of Scripture we observe at least seven spiritual disciplines, which existed in the early Church. They practiced these disciplines daily. They gave themselves to it wholly. **The Spiritual Disciplines** of devoting yourself to **the Word of God** (*Apostle's Teachings*), **worship** (*fellowship*), **Communion** (*Breaking of Bread*), **Prayer**, **Simplicity** (*had everything in common*), **Stewardship** (*They sold property and possessions to give to anyone who had need*) and **Witnessing** (*enjoying the favor of all the people.*) The amazing thing about this testimony and example is that the Lord crowned their private and corporate devotion, by "*daily adding to their numbers those who were being saved.*"

Kingdom of God Spiritual disciplines.

Along with teaching His Disciples the Values of the Kingdom of God, Jesus taught His Disciples Spiritual Disciplines. He knew that these values would only remain if maintained and undergirded by well-established spiritual disciplines.

Prayer:

Jesus offered us, and His Disciples, advice on *the spiritual discipline of prayer*. He often taught them on this spiritual discipline and He Himself modeled it to them. One of those occasions where He taught them on prayer was in His message on the mountain. Along with teaching His Disciples the values of the Kingdom of God, He also taught them these disciplines.

Matthew 6:6-8 (NIV) "6 But when you pray, go into your room, close the door and pray to your Father, who is unseen. Then your Father, who sees what is done in secret, will reward you. 7 And when you pray, do not keep on babbling like pagans, for they think they will be heard because of their many words. 8 Do not be like them, for your Father knows what you need before you ask him."

Luke 11:2-4 (NKJV) "2 So He said to them, "**When you pray, say**: "Our Father in heaven, Hallowed be Your name. Your kingdom come. Your will be done on earth as it is in heaven. 3 Give us day by day our daily bread. 4 And forgive us our sins, for we also forgive everyone who is indebted to us. And do not lead us into temptation, but deliver us from the evil one."

Fasting:

Jesus also taught us on *the Spiritual Discipline of Fasting* in Matthew 6 verses 16-17. Jesus fasted 40 days prior to His earthly ministry started. We've upheld this practice of Fasting at the beginning of every year, for many years now.

> Matthew 6:16-17 (NIV) 16 "**When you fast**, do not look somber as the hypocrites do, for they disfigure their faces to show others they are fasting. Truly I tell you, they have received their reward in full. 17 But when you fast, put oil on your head and wash your face,

Stewardship:

Jesus taught us on the *Spiritual Discipline of Stewardship* in Matthew 6 verses 2-4, and through the Parable of the Talents in Matthew 25 verses 14 -30. On one occasion He taught them that good stewardship is to pay their taxes in Matthew 22 verses 15 to 22. Through developing and applying this discipline to our lives we also learn to honor the Lord with our Tithes and Free-will offerings. These are of course just a snippet of an in depth study on Stewardship.

> **Matthew 6:2-4 (NIV) 2** "So **when you give** to the needy, do not announce it with trumpets, as the hypocrites do in the synagogues and on the streets, to be honored by others. Truly I tell you, they have received their reward in full. 3 But when you give to the needy, do not let your left hand know what your right hand is doing, 4 so that your giving may be in secret. Then your Father, who sees what is done in secret, will reward you.

> **Matthew 25:14, 20-21 (NKJV) The Parable of the Talents** "**14** "For the kingdom of heaven is like a man traveling to a far country, *who called his own servants* and *delivered his goods to them.*" 20 "So he who had received five talents came and brought five other talents, saying, '*Lord, you delivered to me five talents; look, I have gained five more talents besides them.*' 21 His lord said to him, '*Well done, good and faithful servant; you were*

faithful over a few things, I will make you ruler over many things. Enter into the joy of your lord.'"

Matthew 22:21 (NKJV) "21 They said to Him, **"Caesar's."** And He said to them, **"Render therefore to Caesar the things that are Caesar's, and to God the things that are God's."**

Reading, Meditating and Practicing the Word of God.

Jesus taught us **the Spiritual Discipline of having an intake of the Word of God** on a Daily Basis. During His days of Testing, Jesus used the Word to defend and persevere through the temptations Satan tried on Him. Jesus quoted **Deuteronomy 8 verse 3** that: *"Man shall not live by bread alone, but by every Word that proceeds from the mouth of God."* Jesus presented Himself as the Bread of Life. Every New Testament Book endorses and encourages us to embrace the Words of the Lord on a daily basis.

Luke 4:4 (NKJV) "4 But Jesus answered him, saying, "It is written, *'Man shall not live by bread alone, but by every word of God.'"*

Psalms 1:1-3 NIV "*1 Blessed is the one who* does not walk in step with the wicked or stand in the way that sinners take or sit in the company of mockers, 2 but **whose delight is in the law of the Lord, and who meditates on his law day and night. 3 That person is like a tree planted by streams of water, which yields its fruit in season and whose leaf does not wither— whatever they do prospers.**"

Colossians 3:16 NIV "*16 Let the Word of Christ dwell among you richly* as you teach and admonish one another with all wisdom through psalms, hymns, and songs from the Spirit, singing to God with gratitude in your hearts."

Romans 10:17 ESV *"17 So faith comes from hearing, and hearing through the word of Christ."*

Worship:

Jesus taught His Disciples *the discipline of worship*. The first part of the **"Lord's Prayer"** is devoted to *"Hallowing Our Father in Heaven."* In the Gospel of John He teaches us that the Father is *"looking for worshippers."* On one occasion He even said that if the disciples would cease to shout out His praises that *"these stones would cry out."* God dwells in the praises of His people. The First commandment is to "love the Lord your God with all your heart, with all your soul, with all your mind, and with all your strength." What better way is there to take time to worship Him on a daily basis and to give expression of your love for the Lord.

Luke 19:37-40 (NKJV) 37 Then, as He was now drawing near the descent of the Mount of Olives, *the whole multitude of the disciples began to rejoice and praise God with a loud voice for all the mighty works they had seen*, 38 saying: " *'Blessed is the King who comes in the name of the Lord!' Peace in heaven and glory in the highest!"* 39 And some of the Pharisees called to Him from the crowd, "Teacher, rebuke Your disciples." 40 But He answered and said to them, *"I tell you that if these should keep silent, the stones would immediately cry out."*

John 4:23-24 (NKJV) 23 But the hour is coming, and now is, when the true worshipers will worship the Father in spirit and truth; for *the Father is seeking such to worship Him*. 24 God is Spirit, and *those who worship Him must worship in spirit and truth*.

Mark 12:29-30 (NKJV) 29 Jesus answered him, "The first of all the commandments is: 'Hear, O Israel, the Lord our God, the Lord is one. 30 And *you shall love the Lord your God with all your heart, with all your soul, with all your mind, and with all your strength.*' This is the first commandment.

Simplicity:

Jesus taught His Disciples on **the Spiritual Discipline of Simplicity.** He encouraged His Disciples to live simple lives without pursuing earthly treasures. The early Church lived such simple lives. We see that they sold their lands and houses and had everything in common. They laid their treasures at the feet of the Apostles, thus laying up treasures in Heaven. Their treasures were laid up in Kingdom Advancing pursuits. When He sent out His Disciples He sent them out with a few simple instructions in Matthew 10. They were not to take with them a purse or extra sets of clothing. This is truly living a simple life.

> Matthew 10:9-10 (NKJV) 9 Provide neither gold nor silver nor copper in your money belts, 10 nor bag for your journey, nor two tunics, nor sandals, nor staffs; for a worker is worthy of his food.

When Jesus taught His Disciples on the mountain He encouraged them to rather lay up treasures for themselves in heaven, thus discouraging them to live lives full of treasures here.

> Matthew 6:19-21 (NKJV) 19 "Do not lay up for yourselves treasures on earth, where moth and rust destroy and where thieves break in and steal; 20 but **lay up for yourselves treasures in heaven**, where neither moth nor rust destroys and where thieves do not break in and steal. 21 **For where your treasure is, there your heart will be also**."

The Apostle Paul speaks about contentment.

> 1 Timothy 6:6-8 (NKJV) "6 Now godliness with contentment is

great gain. 7 For we brought nothing into this world, and it is certain we can carry nothing out. 8 And having food and clothing, with these we shall be content."

Servanthood.

Jesus taught His Disciples *the Spiritual Discipline of Servant-hood*. If you have Kingdom advancing aspirations, it is best done along the pathway of service to your fellow man.

> Mark 9:35 (NKJV) "35 And He sat down, called the twelve, and said to them, "If anyone desires to be first, he shall be last of all and servant of all.""

Jesus modeled this in a number of ways. He served humanity by His death and resurrection. He served His Disciples by giving them the Words of Life. He laid His life down for His sheep. Serving is giving yourself wholly for a cause. It is the applying of all your mental, physical and emotional faculties for the cause of advancing the Kingdom of God through our active engagement with people in and out of the Kingdom of God.

Obedience

Jesus taught His Disciples the *Spiritual Discipline of Obedience*. Part of the process of Discipleship is to teach our disciples "to obey everything" Jesus taught us.

> **Matthew 28:20 (NKJV) "20 teaching them to observe all things that I have commanded you;** and lo, I am with you always, even to the end of the age." Amen."

Jesus practiced and modeled obedience unto death. Our disciplines are not just for a season or for a specific event, but it is an inward aptitude of discipline for this life.

Philippians 2:8 (NKJV) "8 And being found in appearance as a man, He humbled Himself and *became obedient to the point of death*, **even the death of the cross."**

Jesus was obedient unto death. It is ours to follow in His footsteps.

John 14:23-24 (NIV) "23 Jesus replied, *"Anyone who loves me will obey my teaching.* **My Father will love them, and we will come to them and make our home with them. 24 Anyone who does not love me will not obey my teaching. These words you hear are not my own; they belong to the Father who sent me."**

Jesus learnt obedience through His suffering. Disciplining ourselves daily towards submission and obedience to the Word, Will and Purpose of God will most certainly unlock great favor and blessing over our lives. The Blessings that will follow those who fully obey are written in Deuteronomy 28 verses 1-13. Learn to obey!

Conclusion on Spiritual Disciplines.

There are many spiritual disciplines to explore and assimilate into our daily lives. *The Spiritual Disciplines of Fasting and Prayer, Stewardship, Simplicity, Servanthood, studying and meditating on the Word of God,* are some of the most valued disciplines to uphold. You can read more on these in my Book on *"The Values and Spiritual Disciplines of the Kingdom of God."* Spiritual disciplines will keep the fire of God burning ablaze inside of you.

This brings us to the Third Step in the Process of Discipleship, and is the discovery and development of the Spiritual Gifts in each Believer.

Step 3 – Discovering and developing our Spiritual Gifts, and developing ministry skills to fulfill God's Purpose on our lives.

The third phase of Discipleship deals with us discovering and developing our spiritual gifts, where we develop ministry skills to fulfill our calling in service of the Lord and we continue to grow strong and healthy roots to ensure that we, both bring forth healthy fruit, as well as, withstand the evil temptation of the enemy.

Character Building happens when we apply the Values of the Word of God on a consistent basis. This is the phase where we become Overcomers by the Confession of our mouths and the application of the Word of God. This stage is marked by developing our skills and gifts. This is a continuation of the "Young men" phase.

1. **Gift Discovery Course. DISC. Weekend.**
2. **Walk through the Bible Course. Weekend.**
3. **Faith sharing Course. Weekend.**
4. **Overcoming Course. Weekend.**
5. **Group Leader Training Course. Weekend.**

These five weekend encounters are designed to help the Disciples develop skills and abilities that would assist them in fulfilling the purpose of God in their lives.

Gift Discovery Course.

Weekend Encounter One. God has gifted each one of us with spiritual gifts for the purpose of building each other up in our faith. This course is designed to help the Disciple discover the Gifts of God upon their lives. These are distinctly different from natural gifts, although there is often some confluence between them. Once they discover their spiritual gifts, they are taught how to develop and avail themselves to be used by God in them to the building up of the Church.

1 Corinthians 7:7 (NIV) "7 I wish that all of you were as I am.

But *each of you has your own gift from God*; one has this
gift, another has that." .

1 Peter 4:10 (NIV) "10 *Each of you should use whatever gift
you have received to serve others*, as faithful stewards of
God's grace in its various forms."

Walk through the Bible Course.

Weekend encounter Two. Since most of our Disciples are new
to the faith, we need to help them understand the message of the Bible
in it's entirety. The best way is to give them a crash course over a
weekend and take them through the **Bruce Wilkerson** course –
"**Walk through the Bible**." I highly recommend this course at this
phase in the discipling process.

Faith Sharing Course.

Weekend encounter Three. We are all witnesses of what God
did in our lives. Our call is to testify of what He has done in our lives,
and continue to do. There are a variety of courses geared to equipping
people to share their faith. The wise Church Planting Leader will
continue to explore new and old ways to equip his or her leaders to
effectively share their faith. The best strategy is always to have a Holy
Spirit inspired strategy.

We have used Evangelism Explosion, The Four Spiritual Laws, The
"*John 3 verse 16*" presentation of Ralph Neighbour, Service Evangelism of Armstrong, and other more known ways like tent evangelistic,
Healing services and Open-air outreaches. Whatever the Lord guides
you to do, do that with all your heart.

Nowadays, more than before, **I am convinced that the most
efficient way of sharing our faith is by living a changed life.**
Nothing impacts other than when they observe the renewal and
transformation Christ brought in our lives. For many people out
there it is a matter of "seeing is believing." When they see, it

confronts them with the miracle working power of God that saves people.

Overcoming Course.

Weekend Encounter Four. This course is designed to uproot lingering roots from our past such as Fear, Unforgiveness, Rejection and Resentment. If there still remains any area in our Disciples' lives where worldliness remains, these are dealt with during this weekend.

The Bible outlines the extent of worldliness in Matthew 13 in the Parable of the Sower. Interestingly, the thorns only became a threat to the growth of the seed when it was due to reproduce. It is therefor fitting that once you've developed spiritual values and disciplines, that you uproot those "cares of the world," and "thorns" that might choke the Word inside of the Believers and keep them from becoming fruitful.

> Matthew 13:22 (NKJV) "22 Now he who received seed among the thorns is he who hears the word, and the cares of this world and the deceitfulness of riches choke the word, and he becomes unfruitful."

Here we advice to use the material of Neil Anderson – "Bondage breaker," or pursue using the "SOZO" material from Bethel – Redding. Both are excellent resources, although the latter would be significantly more intense in helping the person become whole and emotionally and spiritually well-adjusted.

Group Leader Course.

Once you've led two or more people to Christ, you need to gather them, like Jesus did with His Disciples, to teach them. This might be a wonderful experience for your disciples as they meet with you, the experienced one, weekly, but daunting as they contemplate reproducing that with their own.

This course will help them understand that it is really the Holy

Spirit who bring this transformation and life changes in people's lives, and that you and I are simply facilitators in the work of God.

> Acts 20:28 (NIV) "28 Keep watch over yourselves and ***all the flock of which the Holy Spirit has made you overseers.*** Be shepherds of the church of God, which he bought with his own blood."

As this Scripture highlights, being a Shepherd, or group Leader, is an honorable appointment by the Holy Spirit. This is both a huge responsibility and honour to be entrusted with the welfare of God's own Children's lives. This course helps our Disciples learn the skills to do so with excellence.

Here we use the resource material from www.touchusa.org. Dr. Randall Neighbour, along with a few other Cell Church Leaders, put together a wonderful resource in: "Cell Leader Training Course." I've used this resource in many nations with wonderful results.

> Ephesians 4:12 (NIV) "12 to equip his people for works of service, so that the body of Christ may be built up."

Our calling is to equip God's people for their work of ministry, and that is exactly what we do when we lead our Disciples through Step 3 in the Process of Discipleship.

Step 4 – Discipling Fruit-producers.

The fourth phase of Discipleship deals with us bearing Fruit through consistently putting into practice what we've learnt, and by living a life of love, worth following, and shepherding those entrusted to our care.

This Step is all about producing fruit through application of learnt experiences and Gift discovery and use. I am always excited about this phase since it is always great to disciple obedient practitioners.

Jesus taught about the importance of putting the Word into practice on a number of occasions. We should carry that same expectation in our hearts for our Disciples.

> Matthew 7:24 (NIV) "24 "Therefore **everyone who hears these words of mine** and **puts them into practice is like a wise man** who built his house on the rock."

> Luke 8:21 (NIV) "21 He replied, "**My mother and brothers are those who hear God's word and put it into practice**.""

At this stage of the journey your Disciples are more mature and diligent followers of the Lord Jesus. They are accountable in their walk with God and before men. Our role is to lead them to become purposeful Leaders, and we do that by addressing the following areas as we walk with them through as they put God's Word into practice.

Walking with purpose.

Finding one's purpose and living out the Purpose God designed you for, is most fulfilling. Romans 8 verse 28 says that we have been "Called for a purpose." That purpose is to make His Name known and to do the things God planned for us to do.

> *Romans 8:28 (NIV) "28 And we know that in all things God works for the good of those who love him, who have been **called according to his purpose**.*"

> *Ephesians 2:10 (NIV) "10 For we are God's handiwork, **created in Christ Jesus to do good works**, which **God prepared in advance for us to do**.*"

Help those whom you Disciple to understand that God Called them, not just to be Born Again, but for a purpose. The test of maturity is our willingness and obedience to serve the purpose and will of God.

Build purposeful relationships. Finding Worthy Men/Woman
(Matthew 10:11, 2 Timothy 2:2.)

The second area that we focus on is to keep our Disciples focused on building purposeful relationships. It is important to constantly keep your Disciples focused, and one of those key areas is to keep them focused on is souls, and more specifically on finding "worthy men and woman" to advance the Kingdom of God. We need to reach the lost regardless of the cost.

Priesthood. Praying effectively.

During this phase we take our Disciples one step deeper in their walk with God by teaching them to be Priests. Thus far they primarily learned and practiced personal prayer, but that is not all that God planned for them in regards to prayer. God desires them to serve as "Holy Priests."

> *Revelation 1:5-6 (NIV) "5 ...To him who loves us and has freed us from our sins by his blood, 6 and **has made us to be** a kingdom and **priests to serve his God and Father**—to him be glory and power for ever and ever! Amen."*

One of the key functions of a Priest is to make intercession on behalf of those entrusted to their care. We take time to teach our Disciples to pray on behalf of those they trust the Lord to reach, as well as those whom the Lord gave them already. This is the process of developing them in their prayer lives to be Priests.

Caring compassionately.

It is such an honour to be entrusted with one of the precious sheep in God's fold. Our gratitude is shown in the way in which we care for those entrusted to our care. Learn to be a "**Good Shepherd**." Every man of God carries this care in their hearts for God's people. Teach your Disciples to care for those whom the Lord entrusted to them.

Walking worthily.

As we grow in our Faith, and our responsibility and accountability increases, so does our consciousness to walk worthily according to the trust God placed in us. As you increase in fruitfulness and more souls look to you for guidance, directions and an example to follow, you need to think and rethink how you speak, what you say and do, and what example you want others to follow. We constantly consider our ways, actions, whereabouts, especially as to how they might advance the Kingdom of God. We are Christ's Ambassadors!

Walking in the Spirit.

During this phase of Discipleship we teach our Disciples the value of a consistent walk under the direction and guidance of the Holy Spirit since He is our Helper and the most powerful partner in our ministry. Without His work in our lives, no sanctification can take place. Without His work in our ministry we will see no fruit on our labours. He changes hearts. He Heals, delivers and convicts. Walking in fellowship with the Holy Spirit has many providential advantages since He is our ultimate Teacher. It is His Anointing on our lives that make all the difference.

Practicing hospitality.

One of the requirements for an Elder is that he or she needs to be hospitable. Having a clean house that is always open to those who need to come over for a chat, prayer or some ministry is essentials. Keeping your house clean and presentable is always a good indication of one's diligence in discipline. You don't need to necessarily cook every time people come over, but a simple glass of water when they arrive goes a long way in presenting yourself as a good host. Cleanliness and hospitality are two key essentials as an aspiring Christian Leader. Always offer prayer before they leave your house.

This Step really help to groom your Disciple into becoming a World class Leader, fit and prepared to lead from the front. It is an exciting journey, and during this phase you'll see how your Disciples become true spiritual sons and daughters who come of age and desire to learn to carry the values and principles on to the next generation. It is only when your Disciples start putting things into practice that you will find this step of immense value.

Step 5 – Multiplying the Body.

The fifth step of Discipleship deals with our Disciples multiplying themselves through their Disciples, by helping and guiding them to consistently put into practice what they've learnt through their union with Christ.

We model it to them, and they model it to their Disciples, by living a life of love worth following, and shepherding them into their purpose.

> Philippians 4:9 (NIV) "9 Whatever you have learned or
>   received or heard from me, or seen in me—put it into
>   practice. And the God of peace will be with you."

Our example become increasingly important as we honour the Call of God to make Disciples. Fruitfulness and the subsequent multiplication come as a direct result of our union, collaboration and yieldedness to the Holy Spirit. There are countless promises in God's Word to affirm that a life built in and on the Word will be prosperous. We repeatedly read that obedience and submission to the Will of God positions us for Favor.

Fruitfulness and Multiplication.

The fifth step in the process of developing as a disciple is to develop in the gifts and graces upon our lives until we become fruitful and through us the Kingdom of God starts multiplying, disciples.

Fruitfulness refers to the ability of a disciple to win souls for Christ.

Multiplication refers to our disciples making fruit-producing disciples.

Reproducing through others.

The key elements of this step in the process of Discipleship is to reproduce and multiply the Body of Christ through strengthening and encouraging your Disciples to be models and worthy examples to their Disciples, as well as help your disciples to being fruitful and to multiply. Through this step we equip our Disciples to go higher and deeper in their own walk with God.

> Genesis 1:28 (KJV) "[28] And God blessed them, and God said unto them, **Be fruitful, and multiply,** and replenish the earth, and subdue it: and have dominion over the fish of the sea, and over the fowl of the air, and over every living thing that moveth upon the earth."

> Genesis 17:6 (KJV) "[6] And I will make thee exceeding fruitful, and I will make nations of thee, and kings shall come out of thee."

> Genesis 28:3-4 (KJV) "[3] And God Almighty **bless thee, and make thee fruitful, and multiply thee**, that thou mayest be a multitude of people; [4] And **give thee the blessing of Abraham**, to thee, and to thy seed with thee; that thou mayest inherit the land wherein thou art a stranger, which God gave unto Abraham."

> Matthew 3:8 (NIV) "*[8] Produce fruit in keeping with repentance.*"

The art of being a Discipler.

There is this myth out that to be effective in Discipleship, you have to be outgoing and sociable, and most people I speak to don't see themselves as that. I have the privilege of knowing some of the greatest servants of God on this planet, and what I've learnt and observed from them is that some are extreme introverts and some are indeed extreme extroverts, however, most of them tend more towards being introverts. So, how do they build and lead these nation-changing ministries?

Being a Facilitator.

The first skill to develop is to come to learn that being a good Discipler requires you to be a good Facilitator. They acquire simple skills to learn how to facilitate the work of the Holy Spirit. Being a good facilitator requires listening skills, spiritual sensitivity, understand how to ask open-ended questions to learn how to help people to go deeper in their openness with God and with each other. Transformation takes places when we make ourselves vulnerable through our transparency.

Hearing the Voice of the Holy Spirit.

One of key skills in Discipleship, is being a facilitator of what the Holy Spirit desires to develop and grow in the Disciple's life. Developing our Spiritual hearing and understanding the voice of the Holy Spirit is key to being a great Discipler.

Having the heart of a Shepherd.

A Discipler is primarily a Shepherd, an under-shepherd in the Kingdom of God, and most of the times they need to learn how to be a Shepherd.

The Discipler's Characteristics. Living a life worthy to be reproduced in others.

The more we allow the Nature and Life of Christ to shine through the fruit of Kingdom Values, the more reproducible we become. The

"Fruit" people look for in our lives, are the Kingdom Values. The Values of Love, Forgiveness, Mercy, Humility, Servanthood, Gentleness, and Patience, along with the Fruit of the Spirit are some of the most distinguishable Christian Characteristics. When we consistently keep these in operation, we become examples for others to follow.

> Philippians 4:9 (NIV) "9 Whatever you have learned or received or heard from me, or seen in me – put it into practice. And the God of peace will be with you."

The Apostle Paul lived such a life.

The Discipler's meetings.

The meetings with your Disciples should be no more than an hour at a time. Remember, you are their Pastor, and they need constant ministry. Even though some grow very familiar with their Disciples, make it your goal to keep the Shepherd/Sheep relationship.

The meetings should have **time for feedback** where the 3-to-1 principle applies. (Three compliments for every one rebuke or correction.) **Encourage**, encourage, encourage. Also take **time to pray** for their needs and challenges. This could be for their personal life, their ministry life or some of their Disciple's lives. Always **go prepared to minister** to them with a "Rhema" Word in your heart for them. The key ingredient is **encouragement. Affirm their success, calling and gifts**. Affirm their Values and Disciplines. What you value in them is what they will value about themselves.

The Discipler's prayers.

The Prayer of a Discipler is powerful. Affirm God's Call on their lives. Thank God for them and their serving Him. Thank God for what He did in their lives, and through their lives in the lives of others.

Always affirm their calling, God's Purpose, their ministry giftedness, their heart and endurance in prayer. Stand with them in prayer before God for their needs, wants, desires and challenges, as if it was your own. The feeling and sense of you standing with them can never be fathomed.

Pray prophetically into their lives, their family's lives, and into their Disciples lives. Intercessory prayers, prayers of exhortation, prayers of thanksgiving and prophetic prayers will almost always leave your Disciples encouraged and Hopeful for the future. One of the prayers that we often pray is the prayer for Mercy, Grace and Forgiveness.

When you work with people, then you might find yourself disillusioned at ties as they fail and fall. May God grant you the Grace to be Gracious and Compassionate with them in your prayers, as if it was you who did wrong and are pleading for God Grace and Forgiveness.

The Discipler's advice.

Choose to rather be a Facilitator than someone telling them what to do in every situation. Our advice needs to be Biblical, balanced, firm and impartial. Sometimes the best advice might be you simply summing their conversation up, and helping them clarify how God already guided them.

Remember the key ingredient in counseling is listening. Try to understand before you give directive advice. Be sensitive to the Holy Spirit in every meeting. Never make light of things that might be difficult things for them to overcome and deal with. Be attentive to their verbal and non-verbal communication. May the Holy Spirit give you discernment.

The Discipler's encouragement.

As a Discipler you hold a God-given position of authority over your Disciples. Your words, advice, guidance, corrections and teachings have a profound impact on those entrusted to you. You have this privilege because of Christ, and not because of you speaking well, looking well, dressing well or anything you might think, They are with you as your Disciples because God entrusted them to your care.

As much as what each one of us need daily encouragement, give encouragement to your Disciples. I love reading through the Psalms, and I find daily encouragement from my reading and meditation in it. Bring some of your daily encouragement to them as well. It does not need to be a Heaven and Earth moving Word of encouragement, but it needs to come from your heart for them.

The Discipler's focus and legacy.

One of the key characteristics of a great Discipler is their ability to keep their Disciples focused on seeking and saving the lost, on Discipleship and the whole journey it takes to lead Believers to become wholly devoted followers of Jesus Christ. Keep your Disciples focused on fulfilling God's Call on their lives, and constantly remind them of the legacy they wish to leave. The Bible says; *"Without a vision people cast off restraint."* Always keep up the restraint for your Disciples to dream, have visions and reach for goals.

Phase Three of Discipleship – Congregating the Discipleship groups.

Phase Three marks the formalization of the next step in planting a dynamic Church and that is congregating the Discipleship Groups.

Once your Disciples are proving to be putting into practice what you've been teaching them then they will increasingly become fruitful. Once they lead people to Christ, and gather them into groups to disciple them, they will become even more effective.

Once you have at least three discipleship groups going, other than the one you're leading, then you can proceed with Phase Three activities.

Formulating the Church constitution for the Church structure, and office bearers.

Having a soundly formulated Church Constitution will harness you against many harmful false doctrines, which go around. You will be wise to think through and receive wise council before you formalize your church Constitution.

Organizing the Leaders. Appointing Elders.

By this time of the Church Planting journey you would be intimately aware of the strengths and weaknesses of your Leaders. You will also be aware of God's greater purpose on your Disciple's lives and of course you would by now have seen their abilities and capacities to reproduce and how they run under pressure.

Consistent with your pursuit to develop the right DNA in your Church, appoint only Leaders who are fruitful and carry the right heart for the harvest and to making disciples. I choose some of them, after prayer, to be the first elders of the Church.

Organizing Administration and Key staff.

Depending of the size of your Church Planting vision, you might need some key staff to prepare for your public launch. Most Apostolic Leaders need administrative assistance. It is therefor vital that you look for someone who would serve in a volunteer capacity as a Church Secretary. They could assist you with appointment coordination, database formulation and upkeep, simple letters processing, and documentary profiling and processing.

The first staff, volunteer or paid, should be at minimum: a Personal Assistant, a Worship Leader and worship team of at least three people including the Leader, a Tech person to handle the Sound, lights, projection, recording and technical setup and coordination. The tech person will need at least two assistants to help with setup, even if you're in a permanent facility.

You will also need a Children and/or Youth Leader with at least as many assistants as what you have Discipleship groups. This person can serve both leadership roles for a start, however, as the ministry grows you might consider employing a full-time worker to oversee at least one Key Leader over each of these two areas.

Consistent with our vision to continue with a strong emphasis on corporate outreach you might consider employing an Evangelistic Outreach leader to coordinate the Church's outreach programs. Outreach is the ministry of every person, however, to make a maximum impact in your area we coordinate our efforts. These would most certainly fulfill your initial demands for establishing a sound, well-rounded team.

Formulizing the liturgy for the congregational services.

Determining both the order and progression within the services, as well as determining the worship style is of utmost importance prior to launching the church publicly. Thinking through the long-term vision, it is far more expedient to set a liturgical order that would serve the church well for future multiplication into multiple services, than having them run for as long as what it takes. Rather limit these services to around **90 minutes**, than having them too long and to hard to multiply.

Also, determine the kind of **worship style and songs** you will have in your celebration services prior to starting. If you don't set the platform, it might become an unhealthy distraction down the road.

The **key elements** for meeting together "in His Name" are; **Worship, Prayer, The Reading and Ministry of the Word, Communion, pastoral/salvation/care ministry, and notifications**.

Developing a plan for Acts 1 verse 8 witnessing.

God called us to be His **witnesses in Jerusalem, Judea, Samaria, and the ends of the earth**. Be determined to lead your church to touch and engage all four of these areas right from the onset of your ministry launch.

- **Jerusalem** is the sub-culture that you primarily minister to. This is the primary and prominent group your launch discipleship group consist of.
- The **Judean group** is that people group who are the same

is your primary group, but reside far away in another city or town, but in the same country, province or state.

- **Samaria** refers to the people group that is different from your primary group yet live in close vicinity to where the core group live. These might be other cultural or ethnic group.
- **The ends of the earth** is exactly that, mission outreaches to people who are both different and distant from your group. God anointed and called us to be His witnesses to all. Be intentional about having a plan, and most importantly, that you lead it at this point of your church planting journey.

Organizing disciples into body ministry areas.

By this time of your Church Planting process all your Disciples would have completed Phase Three of Discipleship Journeys. They would be familiar with, and developing their Gifts and Skills. Encourage them to operate under the guidance of the Holy Spirit to build up their Disciples, and as they have seen, experienced and received Holy Spirit ministry from you, let them minister under that same anointing. Create opportunities where they are able to minister to the larger, combined groups as well, but in an orderly and edifying way.

Finding the right place to bring everyone together.

Up to this point the ministry primarily took place in your, and your disciple's homes. It is time to look for a suitable place to congregate all the discipleship groups on a regular basis. God desires His people to meet together regularly. Unless you have the resources to buy land and build, or to buy a suitable facility, you might have to start in a temporary meeting place. I have started churches like this in rented places many times in my life. I know some churches that grew to tens of thousands before they ever ventured into buying land.

What is important to look for? Since this will become the

secondary "window" into the "church," is your location, and the way you present yourself to the world. One of the many advantages of planting a church in this way is that after six to nine months you should have some funds saved up to do the things that need to be done for taking the church public.

The right location would be a place that is normally used for gathering people like a School Hall, Hotel Conference facility or Community Hall, provided that they present well and have a "safe" feel to them. Avoid using clubs or facilities that are close or associated with Bars, Clubs or Sports facilities. These don't carry the right atmosphere and are often used for functions that might leave you running around on Sunday mornings to get the place cleaned out and prepared as a place of worship. Ask God to direct you to the right place and choose wisely.

Organizing Diaconia.

Organize the rest of your disciples, and their disciples to serve as deacons during the first phase of the church's public launch. You need people to assist with set up and preparation for your joint services. You need a **Set up and Pack up team**, a **Welcoming team**, an **Ushering team** to receive, count and bank the tithes and offerings, and if you're in an urban area you might need **Carpark attendants** to direct traffic and people before and after services. The rule of thumb is to have one Carpark attendant for every 12 discipleship groups. You will need a **Hospitality team** to serve refreshments like water, coffee and tea. You will need a **Follow-up Team** to get in contact with visitors, and connect them with their closest Elder to direct them to the best new Discipleship group. You need a **Clean-up Team** to leave the facilities in a better condition as what you've found it each week.

Formulizing Systems.

Our bodies function with coordinated systems like a digestive system, cardio-vascular system, respiratory system, and neurological system. Each one of these function independently from each other yet if any one of them fail, our whole body fail. It is the same in planting a dynamic church; you need all the systems in place for it to function in a healthy and progressive way.

The systems that are essential to planting a dynamic church are; **Administrative System, Financial System, Care System, Outreach System, Worship System, Prayer and Devotions System, Missions System, and Welfare System**.

You can explore more on the systems in my Book: "**Systems for growing a Dynamic Churches.**"

PHASE THREE OF CHURCH PLANTING - CONGREGATING THE DISCIPLESHIP GROUPS

Phase **Three marks the formalisation of the next step in planting a dynamic Church and that is congregating the Discipleship Groups.** Once your Disciples are proving to be putting into practice what you've been teaching them then they will increasingly become fruitful. Once they lead people to Christ, and gather them into groups to disciple them, they will become even more effective.

Once you have at least three discipleship groups going, other than the one you're leading, then you can proceed with Phase Three activities.

a) Formulating the Church constitution for the Church structure, and office bearers.

Having a soundly formulated Church Constitution will harness you against many harmful false doctrines, which go around. You will be wise to think through and receive wise council before you formalise your church Constitution.

. . .

b) Organizing the Leaders. Appointing Elders.

By this time of the Church Planting journey you would be intimately aware of the strengths and weaknesses of your Leaders. You will also be aware of God's greater purpose on your Disciple's lives and of course you would by now have seen their abilities and capacities to reproduce and how they run under pressure.

Consistent with your pursuit to develop the right DNA in your Church, appoint only Leaders who are fruitful and carry the right heart for the harvest and to making disciples. I choose some of them, after prayer, to be the first elders of the Church.

c) Organizing Administration and Key staff.

Depending of the size of your Church Planting vision, you might need some key staff to prepare for your public launch. Most Apostolic Leaders need administrative assistance. It is therefor vital that you look for someone who would serve in a volunteer capacity as a Church Secretary. They could assist you with appointment coordination, database formulation and upkeep, simple letters processing, and documentary profiling and processing.

The first staff, volunteer or paid, should be at minimum: a Personal Assistant, a Worship Leader and worship team of at least three people including the Leader, a Tech person to handle the Sound, lights, projection, recording and technical setup and coordination. The tech person will need at least two assistants to help with setup, even if you're in a permanent facility.

You will also need a Children and/or Youth Leader with at least as many assistants as what you have Discipleship groups. This person can serve both leadership roles for a start, however, as the ministry grows you might consider employing a fulltime worker to oversee at least one Key Leader over each of these two areas.

Consistent with our vision to continue with a strong emphasis on corporate outreach you might consider employing an Evangelistic Outreach leader to coordinate the Church's outreach programs. Outreach is the ministry of every person, however, to make a maximum impact in your area we coordinate our efforts. These would most certainly fulfill your initial demands for establishing a sound, well-rounded team.

d) Formulizing the liturgy for the congregational services.

Determining both the order and progression within the services, as well as determining the worship style is of utmost importance prior to launching the church publicly. Thinking through the long-term vision, it is far more expedient to set a liturgical order that would serve the church well for future multiplication into multiple services, than having them run for as long as what it takes. Rather limit these services to around **90 minutes**, than having them too long and to hard to multiply.

Also, determine the kind of **worship style and songs** you will have in your celebration services prior to starting. If you don't set the platform, it might become an unhealthy distraction down the road.

The **key elements** for meeting together "in His Name" are; **Worship, Prayer, The Reading and Ministry of the Word, Communion, pastoral/salvation/care ministry, and notifications**.

e) Developing a plan for Acts 1 verse 8 witnessing.

God called us to be His **witnesses in Jerusalem, Judea, Samaria, and the ends of the earth**. Be determined to lead your church to touch and engage all four of these areas right from the onset of your ministry launch. **Jerusalem** is the sub-culture that you primarily minister to. This is the primary and prominent group your launch discipleship group consist of. The **Judean group** is that people group who are the same is your primary group, but reside far away in another city or town, but in the same country, province or state. **Samaria** refers to the people group that is different from your primary group yet live in close vicinity to where the core group live. These might be other cultural or ethnic group. **The ends of the earth** is exactly that, mission outreaches to people who are both different and distant from your group. God anointed and called us to be His witnesses to all. Be intentional about having a plan, and most importantly, that you lead it at this point of your church planting journey.

f) Organizing disciples into body ministry areas.

By this time of your Church Planting process all your Disciples would have completed Phase Three of Discipleship Journeys. They would be familiar with, and developing their Gifts and Skills. Encourage them to operate under the guidance of the Holy Spirit to build up their Disciples, and as they have seen, experienced and received Holy Spirit ministry from you, let them minister under that same anointing. Create opportunities where they are able to minister to the larger, combined groups as well, but in an orderly and edifying way.

g) Finding the right place to bring everyone together.

Up to this point the ministry primarily took place in your, and your disciple's homes. It is time to look for a suitable place to congregate all the discipleship groups on a regular basis. God desires His people to meet together regularly. Unless you have the resources to buy land and build, or to buy a suitable facility, you might have to start in a temporary meeting place. I have started churches like this in rented places many times in my life. I know some churches that grew to tens of thousands before they ever ventured into buying land.

What is important to look for? Since this will become the secondary "window" into the "church," is your location, and the way you present yourself to the world. One of the many advantages of planting a church in this way is that after six to nine months you should have some funds saved up to do the things that need to be done for taking the church public.

The right location would be a place that is normally used for gathering people like a School Hall, Hotel Conference facility or Community Hall, provided that they present well and have a "safe" feel to them. Avoid using clubs or facilities that are close or associated with

Bars, Clubs or Sports facilities. These don't carry the right atmosphere and are often used for functions that might leave you running around on Sunday mornings to get the place cleaned out and prepared as a place of worship. Ask God to direct you to the right place and choose wisely.

h) Organizing Diaconia.

Organize the rest of your disciples, and their disciples to serve as deacons during the first phase of the church's public launch. You need people to assist with set up and preparation for your joint services. You need a **Set up and Pack up team**, a **Welcoming team**, an **Ushering team** to receive, count and bank the tithes and offerings, and if you're in an urban area you might need **Carpark attendants** to direct traffic and people before and after services. The rule of thumb is to have one Carpark attendant for every 12 discipleship groups. You will need a **Hospitality team** to serve refreshments like water, coffee and tea. You will need a **Follow-up Team** to get in contact with visitors, and connect them with their closest Elder to direct them to the best new Discipleship group. You need a **Clean-up Team** to leave the facilities in a better condition as what you've found it each week.

i) Formulizing Systems.

Our bodies function with coordinated systems like a digestive system, cardio-vascular system, respiratory system, and neurological system. Each one of these function independently from each other yet if any one of them fail, our whole body fail. It is the same in planting a dynamic church; you need all the systems in place for it to function in a healthy and progressive way.

The systems that are essential to planting a dynamic church are; **Administrative System, Financial System, Care System, Outreach System, Worship System, Prayer and Devotions System, Missions System, and Welfare System**.

You can explore more on the systems in my Book: "**Systems for growing a Dynamic Churches.**"

10

UNDERSTANDING CHURCH PLANTING FINANCES

O ne of the first things that come up in Church Planting conversations around the world is the need for finances to fulfill the vision God placed inside the Pastors and Church Planting Leaders. I think that God is also concerned about it, and therefor devised a plan for Church Planters to be well resourced.

I once heard a saying that said: "*God will provide for what He commands,*" Or "*His Vision, His Budget.*" I also learned that "*the Provision is in the Harvest.*" All of these might be true, so let us explore "How" God provided for His work in the Bible.

Tabernacle.

When God commissioned Moses to build a Tabernacle where He could meet with His people, He simply commissioned Moses to "tell the Israelites to bring" Him an offering. The condition was that it be a freewill offering from their hearts. He did provide a list of what He wanted. What is important to observe from this example is that: 1. God initiated and commission the building of a Place of Worship, 2. He gave His Servant Moses the design and instructions, and 3, He instructed Moses to tell the Israelites to bring freewill offerings. The

Provision came from the People of God, and this while they were in the desert.

> Exodus 25:1-3 (NIV) 1 The Lord said to Moses, 2 *"Tell the Israelites to bring me an offering. You are to receive the offering for me from everyone whose heart prompts them to give.* 3 *These are the offerings you are to receive from them*: gold, silver and bronze;

The Builders received from Moses daily freewill offerings, and at one point stopped the work to request that the giving stop since they were amply supplied.

> Exodus 36:3 (NIV)
> 3 They received from Moses all the offerings the Israelites had brought to carry out the work of constructing the sanctuary. And *the people continued to bring freewill offerings morning after morning*.

> Exodus 36:5-7 (NIV) 5 and said to Moses, *"The people are bringing more than enough for doing the work the Lord commanded to be done."* 6 **Then Moses gave an order** and they sent this word throughout the camp: *"No man or woman is to make anything else as an offering for the sanctuary."* And *so the people were restrained from bringing more*, 7 because *what they already had was more than enough to do all the work."*

How awesome is that? The people of God supplied so much towards the building of the Tabernacle that the Builders had to request Moses to ask them to stop giving.

> Exodus 25:8-9 (NIV) 8 *"Then have them make a sanctuary for me, and I will dwell among them*. 9 Make this

tabernacle ***and all its furnishings*** exactly ***like the pattern I will show you.***"

I was actually intrigued when I read this portion, in that the design actually came from the Lord, and the Lord made provision from the onset of the project for all the furnishings as well. So often I hear Pastors build a place of worship and only trust the Lord for the basic building and not include the furnishings as well.

Well, in the end we have an example of God providing the Vision for a Place of Worship to be built, and stirring the heart of His people to give towards the vision. We can conclude to say that "the provision is in the harvest."

Start up funding.

When you pioneer a new work in a new area you will need funding to support yourself and what you believe God called you to do. So how do you do that?

The provision is in the harvest!

Start your ministry by supporting yourself.

You supported yourself to here. Prepare yourself to support yourself for at least the next 9 to 12 months still. The provision is in the harvest! I believe, and have seen it over and over, that if you follow our strategy of a.) ensuring that God called you, and that He empowered you to be where He wants you to be, and b.) you focus your attention on finding "worthy" men and woman, and c.) you effectively Disciple them through the Process of Discipleship, then there will be more than enough funds coming in on a consistent basis to support you and the work that God commissioned you to do.

Let's take for example if God called you to "Karamatatoet" – wherever that is – and you find at least five "Worthy" men there who support this new work that you started. You will find that, through their stewardship, their tithes would cover more than what your stipend would have been if you surrounded yourself with poor people.

If your "Worthy" men tithe $100 each per month, then you could be earning $400 per month and $100 could be saved for future expenses. These figures would be relative and proportional to the area you work in. Conversely, if your "Worthy" men tithe $1000 each per month, you could be earning $4000 per month and save $1000 towards future expenses.

Always work with a margin for unexpected or even planned future expenses. "Worthy" men love hearing that you have a budget, and they love hearing that you are saving. What poor people don't know is that it builds more confidence and unlocks more funds for expansion and ministry when the "Worthy" people around you hear "budget," "Savings," and "Margin." It unlocks more funds when your "worthy" men see you purchase things like projectors, musical instruments, printed materials and advertising materials out of the surplus funds, than asking and begging them to help you to make things happen.

If you build the right margin in your mind from the beginning, then you will always have more available funds than what you need. I've seen so often that this strategy moves your "worthy" men to reimburse you for those incurred expenses and slowly but surely you build up funds to do bigger and better things.

If you build with poor people, then they will demand account of you for every penny, and you will never be able to purchase great things since they will always have holes and demands for the available funds. I pray that the Holy Spirit will give you insight in what I am sharing.

How to prepare a Budget.

So, I've been speaking about a Budget, so, let's look at what a budget looks like. A ministry budget needs to have a few developmental aspects so that as your grow and expand that you can adjust your budget projections accordingly. A budget is a faith statement, which is reduced in writing, to know what you trust God to provide for you in the coming year.

This section does not provide guidance for those who are totally cashed up and are able to employ multiple staff, with facilities from the start. This is really to assist the 99% of Church Planters who start their ministries in their lounge rooms.

A budget consists of an income and an expenditure column. The projected income should be more than the projected expenses. As we learnt earlier, make provision for all the insurances, registrations and statutory expenses right from the start.

Phase One – Pioneering Budget

The pioneering budget requires you to trust God for at least five "worthy" men and woman whose hearts will be stirred to support the work of God. How do I do it? I never ask for money, or speak about money at the beginning. I support myself and trust God to come to a place of raising enough support to not work outside any longer as soon as possible.

 Forming a group with your "worthy" men, unlocks support quicker.

Minister to your newly found "worthy" men, in a group, as soon as possible, be that at your house or in one of their homes, but bring them together as soon as possible. I found that if you minister effectively to them then almost immediately their hearts will be stirred to give something towards the "expenses." It seems to be a thing, that when you minister to them one by one, then they don't get it that you need support, but, when you meet and minister to them in a group, they suddenly realize that they need to do something.

Pareto Principle.

Use the Pareto 20/80 Principle in your budgeting in this phase. Only use 80% of what you receive from your "worthy" men, for yourself, even though they, at this point, will give it to you personally. Take 20% and put it away, even though you would want to use it for yourself.

Tithe.

Take half of it, which equates to 10% (tithe) of what you actually received, and sow it into your Discipler – the one who is Discipling you. If you don't have such a person yet, then get one, since you will need a Discipler to help you get to where you want to go. If you lay the foundation of good stewardship in your life, and in your ministry, from the very first time you receive any kind of honoring gifts, then you open up the doors to God's supply over your ministry. Tithing starts with you and me. If we tithe, and model it to our Disciples (worthy men) then they will follow in our footsteps, and the DNA for tithing will be established right from the onset of your ministry. Tithe!

 10% makes a big difference.

The remaining 10% that you put away will become the funds for you to use to put into a Bank Account for your ministry when the time is right. Somehow, once you open up a Bank Account in the Name of the ministry, you will see a further unlocking of funds coming in. It somehow just puts the funds at arms length away from you and then the funds remain. Jesus used Judas to carry the purse. Entrusting someone else to be a co-signatory and steward of the funds, even if it is a little, will both give people more faith in your stewardship as well as give "worthy" people a buy-in into the ministry.

Please, just don't start by begging for money. Trust God, and make Him your source. Believe me, He will supply in all your needs.

Phase Two – Congregating Budget.

Once you've established your pioneering group, and they in turn starts reproducing by having their own Discipleship groups, then the things change with the budget.

One of the first things you should do is register your church with the authorities, if allowed in your nation. The statutory documents for such registration varies from country to country. My advice is that you ask someone you trust to help you to register your ministry. The Senior Pastor of a similar kind of ministry might be a helpful resource. You will find that the "10%" comes in handy now. It will provide for paying for the registration process, as well as give you funds to open up a Ministry Bank Account.

Elders and Board members.

The appointment of Elders and the nomination of Board members for the registration of the Church go hand in hand. This marks a major milestone in the planting of a Dynamic Church. As far as is possible, after much prayer, only involve those Disciples (worthy men) whom you intend appointing as your first Elders, in this process. Only involve as many as what you might need to register the ministry as a Charitable organization. If you trust them enough to appoint them as Elders, then you should have enough trust in them to appoint them as Board members, to, alongside you, govern the ministry into it's future.

Do not make any appointments based on people's status or potential in society, make it based on their fruit in bringing people to Christ as well as in if they honour the Word of God in their lives by bringing their tithes to you, and your newly found ministry. Do not let people decide over your ministry funds who do not contribute and support the work, in the hope that if they're involved that they might be motivated to give, they won't. Jesus said; " where their treasure is there their heart shall be also."

How much salary? Hendrik's Rule

How much salary should you receive if you're the pioneering Church Planting Pastor, is sometimes hotly debated. I suggest that you receive 80% of all the funds that come into the treasury, until you receive tithes from all twelve of your "worthy" men. If you have 12 Disciples who each give $100 per month as tithe, then 80% of the

$1200 per month income will bring you on par with the people you Disciple. It will give you $1000. This general rule of thumb will keep the mouths closed of those ready grumblers who might join your church at a later stage. If you keep this rule – **Hendrik's Rule**, then the ones you Disciple, will protect and support you. This is another reason, not the main one, why it is important to plant a church with "worthy" men and woman. If you surround yourself with less fortunate people they will always question and grumble about what you receive. I believe God wants to bless you.

In this way, whatever comes in beyond the remaining $200 per month, will assist you to start attending to paying for Discipling materials, and within a few months, paying for a place of Worship, where you can congregate the Discipleship groups. It will even put you in a position to have enough funds to put down a deposit on a building or property. You will need a deposit when you Rent a Hall, and saving your money in liue of those expenses will be helpful.

A word of caution!

As far as what is possible, don't increase your personal income, from the church you are pastoring, beyond the Hendrik's Rule. Keep it as your guideline. This will encourage you to surround yourself with the most "Worthy" of men and woman to fulfill the High Calling God has for you.

Phase Three – Public Church Launching Budget.

The real budgeting exercise starts when you plan going public. There are a whole lot of equipment that needs to be purchased, basic printing work prepared, Signs made, and purchases made for hosting, and educating children and youth.

At this stage you should have a relatively good indication of what comes in per month, both from your Discipleship group as well as from your Disciple's groups, into the ministry account. This will form the base from which you could project your income and expenditure for your first year's budget. You should see, at the end of this first year, at least a 20% over budget surplus from the growth income.

General Considerations.

A healthy pioneering group will make for a healthy launching church. The quality of people you start your ministry with will directly determine the welfare of the ministry you lead. My assumption is made from my research and experience in some third world countries. These assumptions are also simply hypothetical. In some countries and rural regions these figures might be halved or even quartered, and in some developed countries these figures might be multiplied by 10.

Income considerations.

My assumption is that you will take at least 6 to 9 months to reach your Twelve Disciples, and a further 3 to 6 months for your Disciples to be fruitful and to start their Discipleship groups. From my experience this should bring you to a minimum place of having 12 Disciples, and each one of them leading a group of at least 6 disciples. I've seen this entire scenario take place in less than 6 months in some first and third world countries. As a direct result, and a combination of the Solid Foundation that is laid in the Disciples and the follow up with Values and Spiritual Discipline equipping, you should see this pioneering group grow to around 50 to 80 adults before going public.

| Budget for 2018 | | | |
Income		Expenditure	
Tithes – Worthy men (12 x 100) x 12 months	14400	Pastor wages ($1000 x 12 months	12000
Tithes – Disciples of worthy men (12 *WM x 6 **D x 80 x 12)	69120	Secretary/Bookkeeper ($250 x 12)	3000
Offerings (10% of tithe income usually)	6912	Children and Youth worker ($250 x 12)	3000
Special Gifts and donations 10% of above amount	9043	Hall Rent ($500 x 12)	6000
		Ministry Tithe	9947
		Registration Fees	250
		Licence Fees	250
		Insurance	1000
		Health cover	3000
		Transport Costs ($400 X 12)	4800
		Banners and Signage	1000
		Sunday School Curriculum	3000
		Youth Curriculum and equipment	3000
		Sound Equipment	12000
		Projector and screen	3000
		Chairs (100 x $20)	2000
		Musical Instruments	10000
		Welcome and Visitor Cards, and Stationary	500
		Hospitality ($50 x 12)	600
		Outreach Budget	12000
Total Income	99475	Total Expenditure	90347

*WM – Worthy men, **D – Disciples

My assumption is that you will truly find "worthy" men and woman to pioneer the vision and work God assigned for you. The more serious we are about seeing fruitfulness and multiplication in the Body of Christ, the more serious and intentional we will be to find the highest quality of "worthy" men and woman to start with.

Expenditure Considerations.

You might be surprised when you look at this simplified budget, to see how much can be accomplished if you just work on a budget. Most of the "would love to have" list is covered in this budget, yet most Church Planters do not accomplishing, and can't show anything with what they got in.

Stick to the budget.

The key is to budget and to stick with the budget for at least the first and second year. By the third year you will both be accustomed working with a budget, you will see the impact on your income as it becomes known that you work with a budget and not at the whim of every person who things they can make a demand on what the church should be doing with their finances.

25% of budget towards assets.

You will also notice that you were able to purchase equipment and movable assets with about 25% of your income budget, without making any please for it. If you keep this trend during the first three you should have all the Sound, musical and Information Tech. equipment you will need to last you at least the first 10 or more years of ministry.

After 3 years you should be able to have an increased amount to work with, and one of the key things to apply this to is for the purchase of land or a building. This 25% towards assets will always keep you ahead in terms of what your increased needs might become for the Church. It might be applied towards a Youth Hall, a Kitchen, a Parsonage, or extension facilities.

Inclusions after second year of working with a Budget.

- **Outreach budget to consist of two parts: evangelism and welfare.**

The first would be to split the Outreach budget into two parts. One part will remain for Outreach – for all your corporate evangelistic harvesting events, and one part will be assigned towards Welfare – looking after Widows, Orphans and the poor.

- **Missions.**

The second inclusion will be to challenge the congregation to sow into Missions – our work beyond the borders of our locally assigned work. Mission work is that what we get engaged in, in other countries, with different people groups and cultures. The strength and health of a church is always measured by it's sending and multiplying capacity. My only advice at this point would be to support your own mission endeavours, unless you partner with others. Don't just give to sooth your conscience without being involved personally. There is so much need and cry for help in the world. Pioneer a new work in a foreign nation and cast the vision in your church for those who sense the Call of God to go and serve in the Mission field.

- **Associate Staff**

The third inclusion for expansion is the appointment of an associate Pastor, or Pastors to assist with the future care of the larger flock. Right from the start, it would be advantageous to always cast the vision for ministry among your Disciples. Almost, without fail, you will find people who have a true sense of the Call of God to ministry on their lives. Get them enrolled in a Bible Seminary to engage in Part-time studies, unless they are resourced to go and complete a Full-time Bible College Degree. My suggestion is that you make this a budget item and pay for their Bible College preparation. It is far more expedient to employ those who grew up under your Leadership, than finding people from the outside who do not carry the same DNA or Vision that you have and that is well instilled in the life of your church.

- **Future Church Planting**

The fourth inclusion is an apportionment towards future church plants. Start assigning a 5% budget towards future church plants. Within 5 years you will be amazed to see how that amount grew and what you are able to assist with in planting a Daughter Church.

Things to remember in your Budget.

There are a number of non-negotiable items in a budget.

- **The first** is the **tithe**.
- **The second** is the honoring of **the Man of God**.
- **The third** is **the staff**.
- **The fourth** is your **Governmental and Statutory requirements**, such as taxes, reports, which needs to be met in full compliance with the law.
- **The fifth** is the on time payments of **utility bills** like telephones, water and electricity, and gas.
- **The sixth** is the **Core ministry** activities of the Church.

When difficult times come revert back to the basics, honour God, honour the Man of God, and honour your staff as far as is reasonable, unless their areas of responsibility does not justify a Full-time worker any longer.

Making decisions in difficult times.

Hard financial difficult times can impact a Church due to internal influences or external influences.

Internal influences could be that of an unexpected break away from the Church, the death of a key contributor, the infidelity of key staff or volunteer workers, or any other internal conflict. These events, activities or actions of people could have devastating effects on the Church's financial stability.

We one time had a key worship leader fall into adultery and had to remove him from leading worship. This had a huge impact on our young church since few people actually knew of his extra-marital affair, and because of some of the laws in my Nation, we were prevented to speak about it publically without opening ourselves up for major lawsuits. This was an internal action of a key leader that had a devastating effect on our church. Many people simply left since they did not know the facts and we were not at liberty to discuss it, and he played the game without being honest with those who wanted to know why he was not there anymore. His "I have no idea" answers didn't help us either.

If I could give one bit of advice: **Time tells**. It wasn't too long before people started seeing him out and about with his girlfriend. Unfortunately not all people who had much to say about our handling of the situations came back. It did have an impact on our finances.

External Factors could be major Environmental Catastrophes like floods, fires and hurricanes or tornadoes. It could also be the shutdown of major industries that leaves droves of people destitute. These factors could have major implications for the vitality of the any local church and it requires true Leadership to navigate a Church through the difficult decisions during such a time.

We were pastoring a church in a Gold mining town in South Africa during the early 1990's. During that time the Gold Index price dropped to around $270/oz and it became too unprofitable to mine and hence most of the shafts got shut down and almost half of our small town of 5000 inhabitants found themselves jobless and homeless. It had a huge impact on our community, but also on our church since most of our congregants were mine workers. Through a series of miraculous events at that time, God opened a door for us to accommodate around 150 families in one of the mine's old single quarters. God made a way where there seemed to be no way.

Be prayerful when making decisions in difficult times. Pray and obey. You will see the Lord performing mighty miracles. Be encouraged!

Financial policies and procedures.

Financial policies and procedures will help you communicate clear and precise steps to be good stewards of the funds coming into the ministry, especially on Sundays.

It is essential to establish clearly defined policies to address every instance where funds are handled, be that physically or in book form. We should always remember that we are working with God's money and therefor are accountable to Him first for how we work with this entrustment.

It is far better to have too much policy to ensure that you cover every eventuality, than having too little and leaving too much open for self-interpretation and thereby giving the enemy an opportunity to tempt the weaker souls among us.

Policies provide guidelines as to how you think best that the funds should be handled. Procedures provide guidelines as to the steps that needs to be taken when handling the funds.

I have attached a brief general guideline to assist you in drafting your own policy and procedure statement. Ensure that you print these out and make sure that you take each and every person who might ever handle funds, through it, and let them sign acceptance of receiving and understanding it.

Here is a brief outline to assist you as you draft your own:

General

1. The CHURCH Board is charged with the responsibility of administering and overseeing the financial affairs of the church and setting an annual budget in collaboration with the Campuses and Various Ministries under its jurisdiction.
2. The CHURCH Board has authority to open and close Bank Accounts within the CHURCH network of Churches.
3. The CHURCH Board will make use of reputable financial processing programs such as MYOB or Pastel Accounting to keep their books.

4. The CHURCH Board will comply with all financial and statutory regulatory authority requirements.

5. The CHURCH Board will ensure financial records are kept and audited annually. All financial records and audited materials shall be kept in safe keeping for at least 10 years, before it may be shredded and burnt.

6. The CHURCH Board will ensure financial policies are upheld and kept throughout its Campuses and Affiliated Churches.

7. Since the CHURCH will make all pastoral staff appointments, the full remuneration liabilities will be invoiced through to the specific Campus or Affiliated Churches.

8. Each Campus and Affiliated Church shall pay a Tithe of their general tithes and offerings to CHURCH for general oversight and administrative purposes.

9. The personal Tithes of all Campus and Affiliated Church Pastors will be paid into the CHURCH Pastoral Development Account.

10. **Pastoral Staff Tithes**

All Pastoral Staff shall pay a tithe of their gross income, meaning the combination of Fringe Benefit payments and Salary, and all other expenses that might be paid on their behalf such as Super and Health Fund payments, into the CHURCH Pastoral Development Account.

The Tithes of Pastoral Staff shall be paid in arrears upon receipt of their salaries, without a delay of more than 7 days.

Where the Tithe of a Pastoral Staff member is overdue for two pay periods or more, the CHURCH Board will seek an explanation from the Campus Pastor or Campus Church Eldership. If agreeable, the CHURCH BOARD may grant an extension to the Pastor or Campus Church to pay their Tithes. Where there is a refusal to cooperate in such circumstances the Pastor's credentials may be withdrawn, if found to be in violation of their commitment to upheld the constitution, or until compliance is ensured.

The Pastoral Tithe does not include any insurance fees, license fees or any legal liability costs.

Expenditure Policy

All expenditures must be in accordance with the approved budget, unless approved otherwise by the Senior Pastor, up to an authorised value of $2,000.00, or CHURCH Board approval. (Note: The budget is a guideline and not an authorization to spend.)

Associate and Campus Pastors have authority to approve expenditures up to $1,000.00, however it still has to be ratified by the CHURCH Board, in arrears. The same accountability procedures are to be adhered to.

Treasurers have authority to pay all regular operational expenses, regardless of the amount, as well as incidental payments up to $500.00 per transaction. All payments need to done with either EFT (electronic funds transfer) or the a CHURCH Debit Card.

Expenditure authorization is to be obtained "before" an expense is incurred. E-mail authorisation is acceptable, but a copy must be attached to the expenditure form. An exception is made for regular monthly expenditures.

An Honorarium of $500 can be paid to visiting Ministers, by taking up a second offering for that purpose. If the amount taken up, for that purpose is more, then give them the full amount. If the amount taken up is less, then retain the full amount, bank it, and then get the CHURCH Treasurer transfer the agreed honorarium.

All EFT payments will require the Senior Pastor to sign off on.

All expenditures are to be supported by a tax invoice on an expenditure form. The expenditure cannot be reimbursed if a tax invoice is not produced. Such expenses, unaccompanied by the appropriate documentation will be regarded as personal expense. Signature, date and bank details are required on the expenditure form when submitting. Be certain that the expense description is clear enough for a third party to understand (e.g. an auditor).

All expenditure forms with relevant supporting documentation should be submitted within 7 days of purchase.

The appropriate authority is to approve the expenditure by signing and dating the expenditure form. If within budget, this would be the ministry leader.

If in doubt about church expenditures, please ask for clarification from the church treasurer or the Senior Pastor.

Authorization Policy

All expenditures must be in accordance with the following general authorization:

The Associate Pastor, Campus Pastor or Campus Ministry leader may approve expenditure within budget.

The Senior Pastor may approve all other expenditures in the amount of $5,000 or less.

The CHURCH BOARD must approve expenditures in excess of $5,000.

Cash Handling Policy

Tithes and offering should be collected in every public service for the furtherance of the ministry.

All cash or cheques takings should be recorded on a CHURCH Teller Sheet.

All cash or cheques offerings should be counted by no less than two people on the day of taking, and given to the local Treasurer for verification and banking.

Treasurers should ensure that collections be kept in safe keeping until banked into the CHURCH's Operating Account.

Treasurers, or their CHURCH authorised delegates, should bank collections within 7 days of collections being received.

Treasurers should keep all the Teller Sheets and banking books in a safe place and submit them on a regular basis, not exceeding 30 days, to the CHURCH Treasurer and Accountant.

Treasurers should keep and provide all Tax receipts on a monthly basis to the CHURCH in preparation for the relevant TAX refund process.

The only exception of the cash handling policy is when a love offering is taken up for some cause. In such events, the cash shall be counted by two people, recorded along with the rest of the normal tithes and offerings, and then sent or given for the specific cause. This will ensure that we have on record what amounts were received and for what purpose it was given.

Terminology

CHURCH – refers to your local registered Church organization.

CHURCH Board – refers to the Board of Directors of your church.

Treasurer – refers to those who are appointed from time to time to assist with bookkeeping and financial administrative matters.

Teller Sheets – refers to those forms, provided by the church, to record all monies received.

Tithes – refers to the Biblically defined income.

Offerings – refers to cash and or cheques received during Church Services and functions.

Collections – refers to either or both tithes and offerings.

11

UNDERSTANDING CHURCH STAFFING

Who to get on staff first.

Depending on the size of your Church Planting vision, you might need some key staff to prepare for your public launch.

Administrative Assistant.

Most Apostolic Leaders need administrative assistance. It is therefor vital that you look for someone who will be willing to serve in a volunteer capacity as a Church Secretary, in the beginning. They could assist you with appointment coordination, database formulation and upkeep, simple letters processing, and documentary profiling and processing.

The first staff member, voluntary or paid, should be at minimum be a Personal Assistant.

Worship Leader.

Worship have become such an integral part of the Church over the past century that it is almost impossible to congregate God's people without dedicating time in Worship of God. a Worship Leader would be the next most important appointment you will have to make. Trust God for someone who is one of your Disciples, or at most, one of your Disciple's Disciples.

Along with the Worship Leader, trust God for a worship team of at least three people, including the Leader, and a Tech person to handle the Sound, lights, projection, recording and technical setup and coordination. The tech person will need at least two assistants to help with setup, even if you're in a permanent facility. The Technical Staff will always fall under the jurisdiction of the Worship Leader or Pastor.

Children and Youth Leader.

You will need a Children and/or Youth Leader with at least as many assistants as what you have Discipleship groups, at the public launch of your Church. This person can serve both leadership roles at the beginning; however, as the ministry grows you might consider employing a full-time worker to oversee both these primary areas of ministry, with at least one Key Leader over each of these two areas.

Evangelistic Outreach leader.

Consistent with our vision to continue with a strong emphasis on corporate outreach you might consider employing an Evangelistic Outreach leader to coordinate the Church's outreach programs. Outreach is the ministry of every person, however, to make a maximum impact in your area we coordinate our efforts.

Pastoral Assistant.

Ministry can be demanding, especially when you have a rapid growing Church. It is therefor important to consider employing an Associate Pastor soon after your public launch to assist you with the sudden increase and demand for ministry and assimilation of souls into Discipleship groups for care and discipleship. Remember, the central work of the Church is to seek and save lost people, and then to make them wholly devoted Disciples (Followers) of the Lord Jesus Christ.

These would most certainly fulfill your initial demands for establishing a sound, well-rounded team.

Things to think about before you hire staff.

It is so important to think through the engagement of staff prior to even discussing anything with them. It is much easier to contemplate scenarios beforehand that trying to think of ways to remove them if they don't fit the expectation.

The following are areas to consider prior to considering a person:

1. Why do need a person to fill a position? Is it absolutely necessary?
2. What would the person look like (personality, gift mix, work ethic, devotion, age, and experience) to best fit the position?
3. What would my expectation be of him/her in that position?
4. How will I gauge their success?
5. How much am I prepared to budget for their remuneration?
6. What will I tolerate, and what will be intolerable?

Once you've answered these questions to yourself, then, and only then consider whom God might have for you to fill the position.

In contemplating a person, make sure you are completely satisfied that they are the best fit for the position before engaging them, or even before you indicate your intention of appointing them. You must have complete peace when you make appointments. If you don't have peace, wait and continue your search until you have complete peace. Never be pressured by circumstances to make appointments.

In consideration of a person, consider the following carefully:

1. Consider their qualifications.

They must have suitable or compatible qualifications, or be absolutely committed to receiving such qualifications. In the latter instance it would only be a consideration if the person shows exceptional passion and commitment for the role or position.

2. Consider their Personality.

If possible, let them complete an Aptitude, Personality Profile Test such as the DISC profiling test. This will assist you to know whether the person is suited for the specific position.

3. Consider their Passion.

Does the person have passion, and what drives their passion? You can teach someone skills, but you can't give people passion. Passion is the fire that drives them beyond assignments and commitments.

4. Consider their age.

My advice to Church Planters is to "go young." Almost a quarter of the people on the planet are under the age of 25. We also know from well-researched statistics that people more often give their lives to the Lord in their Teens, than in any other stage of their lives. Make age appropriate appointments.

5. Consider their health and welfare.

It helps to submit short-listed candidates to a thorough health check-up and assessment. The candidates might look well at face value but a thorough health check-up might reveal underlying health issues that might impede on their performance and durability. They might not last the pace and endurance you require. Carefully consider their health condition.

6. Consider their criminal record.

Ask the hard questions. Have they been sequestrated before? Have they been summoned for outstanding debts? Have they satisfactory resolved it? Have they been in prison? If so, for what offense have they been imprisoned? Have they been ever been charged for sexual misconduct, fraud, theft, or any other offense? If so, for what offense have they been charged for? I would advice that the applicants should provide you with a current Police clearance certificate, prior to offering them a contract for employment.

7. Consider their financial situation.

Of course some people come from less fortunate situations, however, be sure to know that they will be able to act responsibly with the entrustment you will give them. There should simply not be any unresolved mark against them, or else it might embarrass them, as well the Church for employing them. May I encourage you to give people a chance if you have a clear check in your spirit and you have complete peace about employing them.

8. Consider their family and living situation.

If they are married, please ensure that they have the blessing and support of their spouse in taking up this Church position. The Bible gives us some guidance, and I think it is of great value to see that their children serve the Lord alongside them. If their house and living arrangements is not suitable, re-consider such an appointment. Ministry is hard, and the enemy of our souls will use every opportunity to derail, discourage and use dysfunctional family and home situations to stop the work of God. Be careful, since an unhealthy home situation might become a bigger problem for you to solve than the blessing of having someone step up and filling a desperately needed area of ministry.

9. Consider their walk with God.

Regardless of the position you need to fill, make sure that whoever you employ are saved and in full alignment with your Church' doctrine. Make sure they support you and the entire program of the Church. Be sure of their commitment to have daily times of prayer and studying the Word of God. Be sure that they have a good reputation with outsiders. If something bothers you before the time, it will just get worse once you've employed them, so, rather look for someone else, than employ a potential problem. Once people are in the Church's employment, they are Ambassadors of the Church and we need to keep our good Name as far as is possible.

Well, I pray that you will find some wisdom and sound advice from this deliberation to make wise appointments.

Who not to hire.

Never hire people who have a history of stirring up strife. If they did it before they will most likely do it with you. Never hire people who slam their previous employers, especially if it relates to their work ethics, behavior or cleanliness. Never hire problems or potential problems. Don't think that by employing them that they will have a change in behavior.

What not to tolerate in staff.

Never tolerate rebellion. The moment you become aware that one of your staff complaints to congregants or even people outside the Church, you dismiss them immediately. You should never tolerate paid dissension. The moment you become aware that a staff member hosted a meeting with disgruntled people to muster up support for his grievances, dismiss them with immediate effect.

You are going to have a fall out anyway, and those who are disgruntled are going to go anyway, so get rid of the yeast and the source of it quickly. It might be a painful experience, but the pain will be much less than dealing with a mass exodus later. Be decisive and firm. It will only happen once or at most twice, and then it will never happen again. People are like sheep, they need to be taught how to deal with disputes or disagreements in a God-honoring way.

How to release staff.

Releasing staff is never easy, especially if the circumstances are challenging, for instance if there was a matter of sexual misconduct, or if they committed fraud, or if they embrace a false doctrine and remain unwilling to turn from their error. These are difficult cases, and of course there are many more examples like these.

My advice is to remember that it was not you who transgressed, but they. Make every attempt to keep your emotions under control in dealing with the facts. Make every attempt to bring them to their sense before releasing them from their position. Always have a trusted Elder sit in with you when you deal with the matter. If it is a lady, let your wife or a respected and trustworthy sister sit in. This is just for your protection. They are not there to gang up with you, no, they are simply there to observe and to be reliable witnesses. If it is clear that there is no repentance, regret or remorse, then be decisive and remove him or her from his or her position with immediate effect.

Never negotiate a peaceful exits with traitors, sexually immoral, fraudsters or people who made themselves guilty of causing dissension, embracing false doctrines or any other reason. Do not allow them to have your platform in any event. It always causes more strife than clarify reasons.

Dismiss them in writing, and at the next main service of the Church make a short statement to inform the Church of their dismissal as well as the reason for their dismissal. Do not go into the gory details and open yourself up for potential lawsuits. Simply state the indisputable facts. Never withhold outstanding dues to the dismissed, unless it for fraudulent misconduct to see if you can recover some of the swindled funds.

How to build a team spirit.

Now that we've dealt with all the difficulties of staff employments and dismissals, let us take a few moments to consider how to build a healthy team spirit among your employed and volunteer staff.

Building a team spirit is an exciting journey and requires a whole lot of intention to make it happen, and to maintain it. As the pioneering Leader this is sometimes an extremely difficult task, since you might be, like many of us, a Goal-oriented person, rather than a natural people-oriented person, even though we might think we are.

So, how do we do it?

There are a number of things that builds a team spirit.

1. Eat together.

Take time to eat together as a team and be intentional to not talk about ministry or work related matters. Focus conversations on their Family, their children, school, hobbies, and where would they love to go on vacation. We all have to eat, so, use this as a time of letting people getting to know you as well.

2. Exercise together.

A great way of building a team spirit is to do some sporting activities together with your team. Meet for an early morning run together. Go and play tennis or squash with two or three people of your team. Go and attend a gym class together with your entire team where they do aerobics or pilates, where you are all led by someone outside of the team. It will sure bring a few smiles to your faces.

3. Take time to celebrate what God has been doing. At the beginning of each week, before anyone gets into doing anything, dedicate a morning, with your team to bring testimonies of what God's been doing in their lives, in the Church, or of something incredible that God did for someone else.

This is a time dedicated to ONLY share of the Goodness and Greatness of our God. It might be small things or big things, but let everyone commit to sharing one good and great thing during this time, and then thank God together for what He has and is doing, and then dismiss everyone for morning tea, before your business meeting of the week starts. Separate the two so that there will be a clear distinction between the two.

4. Encourage your team.

Take time every day to encourage each other by sharing some good thing you like or observed that they are doing. Use words of affirmation to affirm one another's gifts and value to the team. If you model it, and encourage your team to do it on a daily basis, then, before you know it, your whole team will do it end be encouraged, and a great team spirit will grow and develop.

5. Go camping together.

Go on a midweek staff retreat for a team building exercise. Employ the services of Team-building experts. These exercises are great for developing your team, and to build collaboration in the team. Do at least one a year, however, as the team grows and the church grows, you might need at least two team building exercises per year. They defuse tense situations, and help rebuild trust and appreciation.

6. Do an in-house specialized training to up-skill all your staff.

Hire the services of a Psychologist, or specialising professional to come and do a two day staff enrichment course, which will broaden their understanding and insight into something they have never thought off. Schedule the time on the calendar, but let it come as a surprise who and what they will learn and experience. You could get someone to do a training on First Aid, or Microsoft Office upskilling. These are great team building exercises.

7. Go with your team to Conferences.

Attend a Church Conference with your team. Sit together and discuss the sessions together. Learning together sometimes help develop a great team spirit.

Afterword

Team spirits are not developed over a weekend or in a day. It develops over time and by consistent effort and intentional focus on developing it. It grows and develops primarily through the effort and intention you, as the primary leader, puts into it. I encourage you to put your Goal orientation aside for a few moments each week and build your team.

12

PHASE FOUR OF CHURCH PLANTING - MINISTRY DEVELOPMENT AND CHURCH LAUNCHING PHASE

This phase is landmarked by the Discipleship Groups congregating for Weekly Worship, observing the Sacraments and Celebration. During this phase we start seeing this body of Believers going public as a unified Body where each one does his or her part to build the Church up. During this phase the Church mobilizes herself into a corporate harvesting machine. By maintaining the DNA of Discipleship and keeping her focus on seeking and saving the lost, the church will traject herself on a pathway of continued growth. You will find Timothy's raised, Paul's released, and the Kingdom of God expanding in various and wonderful ways.

Phase Four – Church launching phase.

The following ministries are essential to develop when you launch the church. This list of ministries could be much larger, however, for the purpose of this book it will suffice to at least develop these ministries as you lead the various Discipleship groups to form a unified body of Believers.

Evangelism.

Every Church needs a ministry to coordinate the corporate outreach efforts. Evangelism is the lifeblood of every new church. Evangelism should be an intentionally driven ministry. Trust God for an Evangelist to head up this ministry within the Church Body. The purpose of this ministry is specifically focused on corporate outreach events, since most of the evangelism takes place through personal evangelism within the Discipleship groups. These corporately driven outreach events are really harvesting events to *"making His Name known among the Nations."*

Corporate harvesting events are those outreach events, which enable the Church Body to be highly visible, and to bring in masses of new believers. These corporate harvesting events could be tent campaigns where the focus is on healing, or where music and song is used to bring the message of Christ. The Church have two major opportunities every year to draw the attention of their communities to Christ, and that is during Easter and during the Christmas Season. Every Church will use these two widely known seasons, and celebrated to some extent in most countries globally, to mobilize their people to invite their friends, family and colleagues to their harvesting events.

Fellowship.

Every church needs a coordinated ministry to help the church to connect beyond the Discipleship groups and Sunday Worship services. Some of the best ways to encourage fellowship among the church body is to set up, at minimum, a table where coffee, tea and water is available for people to enjoy some fellowship over a cup of coffee, before or after corporate gatherings.

Some churches set up a designated area to promote church interaction and fellowship. This ministry could be called a hospitality ministry, and in many cases provide an opportunity to connect with those who randomly came to worship services. Beyond creating a space and opportunity for fellowship, this ministry will encourage the church body to share a "potluck" meal together, at regular intervals. The Leadership could provide the non-alcoholic drinks and even maybe dessert for such corporate fellowship events.

Take time to intentionally plan and develop this corporate unifying ministry. It develops a sense of corporate identity as a friendly and homely place to be. There is an ever-increasing amount of lonely people on earth, and very few places where it is truly safe to develop wholesome relationships and build relationship with people who share the same values. The church should be that place where people can find and build such good and sound relationships.

Worship.

Every Church needs a Worship Team. It is essential to develop a ministry where those who have a passion, skill and gifts, can live themselves out, and serve as encourager to lead the church into worship. Worship is an integral part of our ministry to the Lord. Worship is the time we dedicate during our corporate gathering to love and adore our Saviour. It is a time where we praise Him for His Goodness and Greatness. It is a time of Thanksgiving and Celebration.

The Worship ministry is a broad ministry and could involve singers, musicians, dancers, but also those in creative arts and technology. Thought the first few are easy to understand that they be involved in the worship team, the last two (creative arts and technology) are becoming an increasing important part of the worship team. This ministry has at its core the desire to use whatever means to encourage people to connect with God through worship.

Nowadays, with the incredible opportunity of technology and mobile applications like Facebook, Instagram, Twitter, and such communication tools, the church needs people who could maximize this opportunity to help and encourage the church to communicate and to connect with God through devotional interaction applications. There are incredibly gifted people, who love the Lord dearly, who could play a major role in developing a website, a church App, or multi-media presentations that will encourage and promote worship.

Use whatever skills and gifts are available to build this ministry in your local church. In fact, this is one of the primary areas that you need to invest in, in full-time staff. Getting a full-time worship Leader or Pastor will most certainly help the Church greatly to advance their worship of God.

Preaching.

Preaching is an important part of our corporate gatherings as a church body. Along with Worship and the ministration of the sacraments, the preaching of God's Word stands central to every corporate gathering of the church. Preaching is that ministry whereby God speaks, through His Word, and His Spirit to encourage, admonish and instruct His people.

Preaching should be Biblical.

Scripture should be the main source of our message. Preaching is delivering a message, from God, and on God's behalf, to His people. It should therefor be from Scripture.

> 2 Timothy 4:2 (NIV) "2 Preach the word; be prepared in season and out of season; correct, rebuke and encourage—with great patience and careful instruction.

Preaching should encourage and bring guidance.

Preaching should bring encouragement to the child of God. It should bring guidance on how to live your life in a godly way. Preaching should provide us with a reminder of what God desires and of His Will for us. Encouragement and guidance should be present in each and every delivery of God's Word to His people.

Children and Youth.

Every church will actively engage the children and youth as an integral part of their ministry focus. One of the essential considerations in ministry is that we should recognize that the way we connect effectively with children and youth differ significantly than how we communicate with adults and the elderly. Care will be taken to minister to children and youth in a way in which they will hear and understand God's Word.

It is therefor essential to trust God, right from the beginning, for people who have a heart, and understanding, for ministering to children, young people and young adults. I believe they should, for efficiency sake, be ministered to separately during our corporate services. They enjoy different emphasis in the songs they sing. Children and youth enjoy more upbeat rhythms in the songs they sing. Multi-media plays an increasing role in keeping them engaged. There are efficient ways to communicate messages to children, and youth.

There should be a coordinated system of communicating the same message throughout the different genres within a church. As the primary leader, you should know and understand the Will and Guidance of the Lord, well in advance, so as to prepare your various ministries accordingly.

Nowadays, especially when your church grows and you lead a church of 250 and more, the demand to provide, and lead, such coordinated guidance is prized highly. A ministry can so quickly develop into an uncoordinated, dysfunctional gathering, especially if you don't balance the strengths within the various ministries we've discussed thus far. You might have a strong children's ministry leader, but who slants towards only one aspect of the nature of God, like grace, and at the same time have someone leading the youth who thinks everything is just about being free, and you actually sense that God desire your church to embrace His love and care more during this season, then suddenly, without a coordinated system, you might find the ministry, at large fraying. I encourage that you, as the primary leader, lead and ensure collaboration between all the ministries within the church.

Make provision for a dedicated space for both the children and the youth. The less you value them, the less you will be thoughtful of their integral importance of being part of the church body entrusted to your care. I encourage you to always look for a space where you have dedicated areas for ministry for the children and the youth, even if that means that you minister to the children during a separate time in the same facility, and to the youth during another dedicated time.

I grew up in a church where we had Sunday School from 8am to 9am on Sunday mornings, and afterwards we had our Main Adult service from 9am onwards. We shared the same facility, and it worked well. We had Friday evening dedicated youth services and later, because of the increase of our youth contingency, we also dedicated Sunday evenings to a youth oriented styled service.

Remember children go to school and are disciplined enough to sit in classrooms from around 8am till at least 1pm to learn and listen. We have to be smart at reaching and ministering to all our people in as appropriate way as what we are able and as what our culture and circumstances allow.

Missions.

Every church is on a mission and should be intentional about being in mission with people in their *"Jerusalem, Judea, Samaria, and the ends of the earth."* Missions refer to that engagement and spreading of the gospel message outside of our naturally aligned sphere of connections, like our family, friends and colleagues. Take your people on a mission trip to a neighboring neighborhood for a special outreach program. Lead them on a mission's trip to another town or village to share the gospel there. Take your people to a foreign country to come alongside a foreign missionary to share the gospel of Jesus Christ. One of the things Jesus expressly desires is that we be His witnesses wherever we go.

> Acts 1:8 (NIV) "8 But you will receive power when the Holy
> Spirit comes on you; and you will be my witnesses in
> Jerusalem, and in all Judea and Samaria, and to the ends of
> the earth.""

Taking and leading your people into foreign territories will impact their lives, and especially their faith walk, incredibly. I have always watched and saw the increase in devotion and dedication in those who go on mission outreached. The result of participating in a mission outreach event most certainly brings a greater anointing and engagement with God's people.

Welfare.

Every church should engage herself with the care of the welfare of Orphans, Widows, the Elderly and the Poor. Although it is not the primary engagement, and should never be, the care for those in less fortunate circumstance should harness our attention. Looking after orphans and widows in their distress validates our faith. The Apostle James draws our attention to this important area of ministry.

> James 1:27 (NIV) "27 Religion that God our Father accepts as
> pure and faultless is this: to look after orphans and widows
> in their distress and to keep oneself from being polluted by
> the world."

I have to caution you, the Primary Leader, here. Do not let this important and valued part of ministry become the primary focus of your ministry, unless the Lord directs you specifically into it.

For the Apostles, their main calling and engagement was the preaching of God's Word and prayer. For most of us, that main calling is to preach the Word and lead our disciples into a living, fruit-producing relationship with the Lord. The Apostles assigned this welfare ministry over to Deacons to take care of the Widows. This principle could possibly be extended to take care of the orphans and less fortunate as well.

> Acts 6:1-4 (NIV) In those days when the number of disciples
> was increasing, the Hellenistic Jews among them
> complained against the Hebraic Jews because their widows
> were being overlooked in the daily distribution of food. 2 So
> the Twelve gathered all the disciples together and said, "It
> would not be right for us to neglect the ministry of the
> word of God in order to wait on tables. 3 Brothers and

sisters, choose seven men from among you who are known
to be full of the Spirit and wisdom. We will turn this
responsibility over to them 4 and will give our attention to
prayer and the ministry of the word."

The two considerations we need to consider are: 1. Where God
desires us to provide care and assistance, and 2. Who to release to lead
it? Jesus said that the "poor will be with you always." The sound guidance Scripture gives us is to first provide for the needs in your own
midst.

Galatians 6:10 (NIV) "10 Therefore, as we have opportunity, let
us do good to all people, especially to those who belong to
the family of believers."

Through the years, we founded a "Place of Refuge," feeding
schemes, soup kitchens, low cost food assistance outlets, among some
of the welfare activities we've been involved in. During these care and
welfare undertakings we were able to provide hundreds of people with
newly found skills through our skill development centers. We were
able to provide much needed food assistance to over 5000 people on a
monthly basis, and we were able to help those who loose everything in
life, to have a roof over their heads, food to eat, and most of all, a place
where they would receive love and care in a dignified environment.
May the Lord guide you as you venture into the world of providing for
those in need around you.

Pastoral.

As part of our care of the people entrusted to our care, every
church will employ resources and people to pastorally care for her
people. Frequently we read that the Lord sees us as "sheep" and He
being our "Great Shepherd." We are seen as "under Shepherds" caring
for His sheep on His behalf. We could be mistaken to think that if we
have a strong Discipleship focus, where people are led and cared for in
a small group that they are all well cared for. Being a great Discipler or

small group leader does not necessarily mean that you're a great Pastor. Christ is our Great Shepherd and under His assignment we care for His people.

> Hebrews 13:20-21 (NIV) 20 Now may the God of peace, who through the blood of the eternal covenant brought back from the dead our Lord Jesus, that **great Shepherd of the sheep**, 21 equip you with everything good for doing his will, and may he work in us what is pleasing to him, through Jesus Christ, to whom be glory for ever and ever. Amen.

> 1 Peter 5:2-3 (NIV) 2 ***Be shepherds of God's flock that is under your care,*** watching over them—not because you must, but because you are willing, as ***God wants you to be***; not pursuing dishonest gain, but eager to serve; 3 not lording it over those entrusted to you, but ***being examples to the flock***.

I believe that God actually anoints us with the ability to provide spiritual care for those entrusted to our care. Somehow through His anointing on our lives we are able to find the right words and encouragement to provide care and guidance to those in need.

> Ephesians 4:11 (NIV) "11 So **Christ himself gave** the apostles, the prophets, the evangelists, the **pastors** and teachers,"

Be prepared to employ professionally trained and spiritually equipped pastors on staff as your church grows. It is a myth that you can simply raise up "pastors" to efficiently care for the people of God. If God, in His Wisdom, anointed and appointed some to be "Pastors," then we need to rethink such illusions.

Be on the search for those upon whose lives rest the "Pastoral" anointing, to employ as your church grows. Small group leaders and Discipleship group leaders are great, however, the God-designed way of providing ultimate Pastoral Care for His people is by those whom God anointed and appointed for that purpose. Be wise and appoint

"Pastors" to provide that care beyond the incredible efforts and work of the Body of Believers who share and care for one another.

Administration.

Administration and organization are essentials parts in leading a well-run and coordinated church body. We live in an increasingly more structured and legally structured world where legislation and laws demand greater compliance and accountability of the church. Unfortunately many pastors are not administratively inclined and therefor do not spend appropriate time to attending to this vitally important aspect to growing a dynamic church. The administration matters that requires our attendance, changes, as the church grows and develops.

When you start a new church take time to attend to these essentials: (of course this list changes and the requirements are different in different nations.)

Prior to registering the Church, determine who your first Board members will be. You will be required to have a chairman, vice-chairman, secretary, treasurer, and at least one additional member. In some nations some of these positions could be combined and therefor less people required serving on your Board. Many founding Pastors ask their spouses to serve on their founding Board. If necessary, appoint your Discipler as one of your first board members.

Ask other Pastors to serve as your founding Board members. They will both provide great confidence to those enquiring about your Board, as well as, they might even assist you in your process of establishing the new church. If you founded your church with "worthy" men and woman, you might ask some of them to serve in this capacity. My advice is that you always keep the Board as small as possible. Some people turn into funny beings when they become Board members, so, take care and prayerfully consider those whom you desire to serve in this capacity.

Another requirement is that of providing a Constitution and Statement of Faith to register your church. As many Church Planting Pastors do not think structure and organization, may I encourage you to, either employ professionals like attorneys, or align yourself with an established church movement for this registration process. The basic documentation you might need for the registration process are:

Constitution.

A Constitution consists of:

1. Name of Church or Ministry.
2. Vision. (What you believe God Called you to do. Your dream.)
3. Mission Statement. (How you will do what you want to achieve.)
4. Statement of Faith. (What you believe.)
5. Structure. (What offices you will have both statutory - (legally, where will the power of decisions lie) and organizationally – (how will these positions inter-relate to each other.
6. Policies. (Consisting of Staff recruitment, employment and dismissal policies to volunteer recruitment, deployment and dismissal. Also broad financial control mechanisms. Also concluding procedures in the event that the ministry closes down.)
7. Office Bearers. (Define the Office Bearer positions.)
8. Definition of terminology.

In the beginning, this should get you of the ground and at least get you registered. This is not conclusive and you will definitely have to spend some money down the road to get a professional Attorney assist you with redrafting and submitting a more expanded and tailor-made constitution.

Statement of Faith.

A good guide will be the Apostles Creed, the Nicene Creed and those readily available "Statements of Faith" from Churches and Denominations like the church you dream of starting.

Here is an example of our Cornerstone Church's Statement of Faith.

The Church has adopted the following Declaration of Faith as its standard and official expression of its doctrine.

We Believe:

1. In the divine inspiration of the Bible, as the revelation of the mind and will of God.

2. In one God eternally existing in three persons; namely, the Father, Son, and Holy Ghost.

3. That Jesus Christ is the only begotten Son of the Father, conceived of the Holy Ghost, and born of the Virgin Mary.

4. That Jesus was crucified, buried, and raised from the dead. That He ascended to heaven and is today at the right hand of the Father as the Intercessor.

5. In the Holy Spirit: (the third person of the trinity), proceeds from the Father and the Son and is of one substance, majesty and glory with the Father and the Son.

6. In the personality of the devil who, originally a created angelic being, exercised authority in the presence of god and who as a result of his transgression was cast down.

7. That sin is any lack of conformity in a free moral agent to the character, nature and will of God; whether it be in act, disposition, state, thought or will.

8. That repentance is a godly sorrow for sin brought about in the heart of the individual by the Holy Spirit resulting in a turning about in submission to God and His will.

9. That all have sinned and come short of the glory of God and that repentance is commanded of God for all and necessary for forgiveness of sins.

10. That God fully restores those who believe, accept and confess Jesus Christ as their Lord and Saviour to His family and bestows His grace and righteousness upon them.

11. That justification, regeneration, and the new birth are wrought by faith in the blood of Jesus Christ.

12. In sanctification, subsequent to the new birth, through faith

in the blood of Christ; through the Word, and by the Holy Ghost

13. Holiness to be God's standard of living for His people.
14. In water baptism by single immersion, and all who repent should be baptised in the name of the Father, and of the Son, and of the Holy Ghost.
15. In the baptism with the power of the Holy Ghost subsequent to a clean heart.
16. In speaking in tongues, witnessing, gladness and prophecy, as the Spirit gives utterance, as some of the evidences of the baptism in the power of Holy Ghost.
17. Divine healing is provided for all in the atonement.
18. In the Lord's Supper and washing of the saints' feet.
19. In the premillennial second coming of Jesus. First, to resurrect the righteous dead and to catch away the living saints to Him in the air. Second, to reign on the earth a thousand years.
20. In the bodily resurrection; eternal life for the righteous, and eternal punishment for the wicked.

Procedures and Policies.

Policies and Procedures are essential since they provide sound guidance in the operation of the church. Attending to these policies will most certainly protect and keep your church operationally sound and possibly clear of unnecessary mistrust and smear campaigns.

Financial policy.

(How to work with the funds that is given to you and to the church during services. It also covers the "how to" of what to do with the funds until it is used. Basically it deals with accountability procedures.)

Health and safety policy.

(If someone get themselves hurt at your church, or during one of your services, or if some calamity strikes like a bomb attack, a fire, or something catastrophic happens; What will you do? Who will do what? Where will they do it? Who will report it? How will they report it? Etc.)

Child protection policy.

(Check in procedures, checkout procedures, hygiene and toilet procedures and protocol's, police check approval for all child workers, age appropriate programs, training requirements.)

Evacuation policy and procedures.

(In the event of a fire or any other catastrophe you need to have an evacuation plan, outlining the steps you will take to ensure the safety of the people, and or, the remaining people.)

Job descriptions.

Job descriptions sounds like an overkill when you just start out on your church planting journey, however, if you believe the Visions and Dreams God placed in your heart, for the assignment He placed before you, then there is no better time than right now to work on job descriptions.

These job descriptions should at minimum include:

- Job Position (Pastor, evangelist, Youth Worker, Secretary, Accountant, etc.)
- Fulltime or Part-time position
- Wage
- Accountability (to whom will the person be accountable and reportable?)
- Job description (describe your expectation of what you want them to do in this job.)
- Leave (Define the periods for annual holiday (21 days), public holidays and compassionate leave (12 days.))
- Termination of employment (Set out the terms to define 1. When you want to dismiss an employee: ie. The grounds for dismissal, the period of notice for dismissal consistent with the offence, and the procedures for exiting, and what you expect of them once they have left your employment, and 2. When they employee wants to leave your employment. Set out agreeable terms that would be mutually agreeable.)

Employment in the Church is significantly different than working in the secular world. Even thought we are subject to the same labour laws, we do have a higher standard of expectation on the moral and ethic standard of our employees than what the world demands. It is therefor important that we outline these to our best ability beforehand.

Version One is always better than version none!

These are best defined beforehand since we do not have a specific person in mind for the job, and therefor much easier to produce a sound, well thought through document. **Version One is always better than version none!** You can always edit these documents later. At least you have a good departure point to work from. Before you know it, you might find yourself needing these documents. So, sit down, set time aside over the coming week or two, and work on these for each position, whether it is a volunteering position, or full-time position, write out a job description.

Then, when you've compiled all this documentation then you are ready to register your new church. Basic documentation to guide you, or to build your documentation from, is available from www. churchplantingdoctor.com.

The Registration Process:

The registration process looks something like this:

1. Register your Church as a Not for Profit organization with the Registrar of companies.

2. Register your Church with the Tax Authorities for Tax deductible status.

3. Arrange for a dedicated Postal Address for your church.

4. Arrange for a dedicated telephone line for the church.

5. Bank Accounts. Once you've received your registration certificates, both from the Registration Authorities, as well as from the Taxation Authorities, then go to the Bank to open up a few Bank Accounts under the Church registration. Open at least one Operating (Cheque) Account, and as many saving accounts as what you have resources to

distribute to various key ministries, and one Main Saving Account where all tithes, offerings and special gifts will be deposited. The reason for the latter is to gain maximum interest before you transfer it through your Operating account to pay accounts.

Remember these are legally accountable positions and require our attendance for the completion of forms, and the submitting of yearly reports to Authorities such as Financial Statements or Auditor reports. You will also be required to convene regular board meetings to account for the progress of the church and various ministries, as well as accounting for the use of finances, or for the Board approval for expenditures. These have been designed as accountability measures as well as protection to us.

I pray that God will find in you a good and faithful steward over all of His Household.

Governance.

Leading and governing under God is a huge and rewarding responsibility. As one of the gifts of God, the Holy Spirit anoints some of us to lead and govern in His church.

> Romans 12:6-8 (NIV) 6 *We have different gifts, according to the grace given to each of us.* If your gift is prophesying, then prophesy in accordance with your faith; 7 if it is serving, then serve; if it is teaching, then teach; 8 if it is to encourage, then give encouragement; if it is giving, then give generously; *if it is to lead, do it diligently;* if it is to show mercy, do it cheerfully.

We are encouraged to do this with diligence. As the Primary Leader whom God called to lead the Planting of a Dynamic Church, I encourage you to lead with Courage and Diligence. Attend to matters swiftly yet thoughtfully. Guard yourself against "lording it over" those entrusted to your care.

Acts 20:28 (NIV) "28 Keep watch over yourselves and all the

flock of which the Holy Spirit has made you overseers. Be
shepherds of the church of God, which he bought with his
own blood."

1 Peter 5:2-3 (NIV) 2 Be shepherds of God's flock that is under
your care, watching over them—not because you must, but
because you are willing, as God wants you to be; not
pursuing dishonest gain, but eager to serve; 3 not lording it
over those entrusted to you, but being examples to the
flock.

Leading and governing in God's church requires us to always
remember that we do so under Christ, and over those purchased with
His precious Blood.

13

UNDERSTANDING AND IMPLEMENTING SYSTEMS

S ystems form the backbone of every well functioning organization. These systems will help you to lead a progressively healthy church body. Like in our own body's, when any one system falters, it affects the entire well-being of the body. The same is true about a church body, if one or more of these systems are lacking, it has a definite effect on the well-being of the congregation.

Let us take a moment to look at some of these Systems:

Assimilation System

The assimilation system is the ministry by which we engage and integrate new believers into fellowship with the church body. The good start will always be to make visitor cards, which visitors to your church could fill in their personal details for follow-up. They have the choice to give these details to you. If they do, then you need to have someone to call them within 24 hours, to thank them for coming to your church' gathering, offer to visit them, ask them if there was anything they could pray with them, and then set up a time and place to visit.

It is always a great sign if they welcome you to their home, however, nowadays many people live in compromised or shared accommodation and it is therefor not always convenient for you to visit with them where they live. You could either invite them to your place for some coffee or tea, or suggest that you meet them in a more neutral place like a café.

The bottom line is that the best way to connect with people is within 24 hours and face to face. These are never simply for a catch-up, pray, pray, pray. People go to churches because they are seeking the Lord, our responsibility is to firstly connect with them on behalf of God before connecting with them on behalf of ourselves.

People welcome prayer. Pray with them for their needs and challenges. Ask them why they came to church if they don't offer that information at first. Connect them with a Discipleship group leader as soon as possible. The more people they are introduced to, the quicker they will feel welcomed and valued. Try and set up a second meeting as soon as possible for that purpose. Connect people.

One of the best connecting ways I've heard of over the years is to flood your foyer or entrance with people whom you want the church to be associated with. If you want a church of young adults then get the young adults to welcome people at the doors and entrance area. If you want families, then flood the doors and entrances with families to welcome the people.

Another great idea is to have connecters welcome the people. A connecter is someone who introduces people to like-minded people. They greet new comers and quickly move in their conversation to know what they do and where they come from, and then connect them with others from the same area or profession. People love to attend a church where like-minded people fellowship.

Care System

There is a saying that says: ***"People don't care how much you know until they know how much you care for them."*** All people have a need and desire to be noticed and cared for. A church will do well to orchestrate a variety of ministries and opportunities to provide care for their people. This could be done through a ***house visitation***

program, Hospital visitation and care program, community chaplaincy, or youth ministry engagement programs. The more I look at the ministry of Jesus, and the Disciple's, I see how much they valued visiting and ministering people in their homes.

A church could engage those, with counseling and care specialties, to provide more formal, structured and professional care such as marriage counseling. The care system provide both an opportunity to skilled people within the church body to use their skills and gifts to build the Body of Christ up, as well as, provide a gateway into the church through the care of wandering and lost souls. We live in a world where there are many lost and emotionally needy people. Taking care of those who come into fellowship with the church is what God called us to do. Let us do that well through our Discipleship and Care groups.

Financial System

Every church needs to have good accountability stewardship structures. One of those structures relate to our stewardship over the finances flowing in and out of our church accounts.

A good financial system will require you to have a few faithful and reliable people to handle the finances. Good things to consider are:

1. Once the tithes and offerings have been received, safely store it in a secure place until it could be counted, and

2. Have two people count and record the finances.

3. The record sheet and the correlating funds then needs to be given to a third person to bank the funds. This is a necessary step for accountability.

4. Submit both the record sheets and correlating banking receipt to the treasurer. Neither the Chairman, nor Treasurer should preferably be engaged in this process.

The Treasurer needs to provide the board with monthly statements of the income and expenditures. It will serve the church well if there are good policies and procedures in place. Samples of these policies and procedures could be purchased from www. churchplantingdoctor.com

Worship System

Worship is quite a comprehensive ministry. In it's simplest form it is about singing Psalms and spiritual songs unto the Lord. In a developing form it could mean having multiple instruments and singers leading a congregation in songs of Worship, with the support of a Sound man, Projection operator and a Worship Leader. In a developed form this could be expanded to include a choir, a full orchestra, a Lighting and effects team, Projection operators of Multimedia Screens, Videographers, a Studio Manager, a Production Manager, and a Full-time Worship Pastor.

Though some of this might be way beyond what you ever dream or thought of, may I suggest that you have a developmental system to use to expand this ministry in accordance with the way your church grows.

Initially, a Worship Leader who leads with an instrument could lead the coordination and lead the singing of known songs. As soon as what you are able, expand this to include multiple singers and musicians. Music is a wonderful ministry and many people join churches initially because of their worship. To recap: start with a Worship Leader, and add musicians and four or five singers as they become available. Once you are able to purchase a Sound system, also trust God for a Sound man to operate the Sound desk. Don't save on sound. Buy the biggest system that you can afford, not what you think might just do it. You will regret it for the rest of your life. One rule of thumb is that for every one person that is represented on stage, 3 people will attend church.

Once you have an initial team of musicians and singers, rotate the leading with the singers you have to develop variety, and to up skill the team since there will be times that the Worship Leader might not be available and then you have a drop in your worship. Develop the team. A good size worship team has a positive effect on a congregation. The Worship Leader or Pastor should dictate the program and what he/she wants to see happen, and not the creative arts guys nor the sound guys. The Worship Leader needs to take his lead from his weekly meetings with the Senior Pastor to follow his lead in where they need to go with the worship.

Welfare System

Having a care ministry is important for every growing church. At minimum you could ask families to bring tin foods and basic toiletries in bags to church. These could be stored for those initial incidents where you might find people on your doorstep who request assistance. This gathering of food should be kept in a dry and secure place. As the church grows a percentage of the income could be allocated towards such supplies and assistance. Assign the overseeing of this task to a hardworking, tithing person who is of a stable character and exhibits a good and sound judgement of circumstances and people's naïve ways of scheming for "free" food. Never allow a less fortunate, even though they might be passionate, person have charge of this ministry. Their judgement is always marred by their own circumstances and moods.

Beyond this basic food and toiletries assistance, you need a clear Word of the Lord as to how and where He wants your church's efforts to go. As a church grows, so do the people who will table all kinds of suggestions and areas where your church should help. If you have a pre-determined plan then you could shield those suggestions. The typical areas are orphanages, places of safety for abused woman, soup kitchens for the destitute and care for the elderly. These are in many cases consistent where the Lord would ask you to plant a church. Seek the Lord as to what He would like you to do. If it is the Lord's Call then it is also His Bill. He will provide for whatever He directs you to do, otherwise you might find it to be one big bottomless pit where money and resources disappear without any reward.

Global Missions System

Every church should, right from the start, encourage the support of global missions. Connect with leaders like me through www.churchplantingdoctor.com or other mission organizations and encourage a mission trip to some foreign country every year. The impact on those who go to foreign mission fields is profound. It encourages them to share their faith, and in most cases give them perspective on their lives and those who are less fortunate and yet worship God with joy.

Take time during every service to pray for the nations. Pray for those who serve God and work for Him full-time in rural and remote places. Pray for their families. Pray for those working in countries where there is a lot of persecution. Pray for their provision and protection. There is nothing as hard for missionaries who serve in foreign countries as when their support, emotional, prayer or financial, stops. May God use you and your church to partner with those who are going to the nations.

Afterword

Implementing these Systems will ensure that your church will grow in a healthy way, but also ensure Growth and Health.

14

PHASE FIVE OF CHURCH PLANTING - MULTIPLICATION

One of the greatest and most rewarding moments in ministry is when you see your disciples becoming fruitful and when they start multiplying. The intention of was always to make us fruitful and to multiply us through our faith lineage as children of Abraham.

> *Galatians 3:7 (NIV) "7 Understand, then, that those who have faith are children of Abraham."*

> *Galatians 3:9 (NIV) "9 So those who rely on faith are blessed along with Abraham, the man of faith."*

> *Galatians 3:14 (NIV) "14 He redeemed us in order that the blessing given to Abraham might come to the Gentiles through Christ Jesus, so that by faith we might receive the promise of the Spirit."*

> *Galatians 3:8 (NIV) "8 Scripture foresaw that God would justify the Gentiles by faith, and announced the gospel in advance to Abraham:* ***"All nations will be blessed through you."***

These few Scriptures encourage us, as Believers to that it is God's

Will to bless us along with our spiritual ancestor Abraham. His desire always has been that "**all nations would be blessed**" through us. This is our spiritual heritage; to be fruitful and to multiply.

In our preparation for multiplication, we may prepare ourselves that God might have entrusted to us some that might stay with and under our Leadership, and others, who like the Apostle Paul, might leave the local church and go out on their own mission from God. Being prepared makes it easier to deal with than when it suddenly happens. Be prepared for Timothy's to bring multiplication, yet stay with you as one of your spiritual sons, and be prepared for Apostle Paul's whom God might raise up under your ministry, and yet they go out with the Call of God to go out on their own ministry.

- **Mobilising Timothy's.**

Some of those whom God will give you as Disciples will be Timothy's. They will be spiritual sons to you and even though you will send them out to plant new churches, they will always remain with you. These spiritual sons are huge blessings in one's life. As a Father of five daughters, I have a dream of seeing my children succeed and accomplish bigger and better things than I did. As a Spiritual Father, I have the same vision and dream for my Spiritual Sons and daughters. Mobilize to see that vision become a reality.

- **Releasing Paul's.**

Some of the Disciples God raised up under your ministry will leave you to go on to lead their own ministries. Thank God in advance for the privilege that you had to play a role in their growth and development. Releasing the "Paul's" could be a very painful experience. Rather prepare yourself in advance that some of the people you pour your life into might leave you at an unexpected point to start their own ministries. Rather expect it than be surprised by it. Release the Paul's!

- **Multiplication strategies.**

The best multiplication strategies are those that are prayerfully planned and prepared. I pray that God will guide you into multiplying His church where you are and around the world. Church planting is the most effective method of evangelism and though every church you plant many new people will come into the Kingdom of God.

15

UNDERSTANDING THE CHALLENGES IN CHURCH PLANTING

C hurch planting is exciting, but costly. To see visions fulfilled will cost you. There is a price to pay to see successful churches planted. Committing to be a Church Planter, or engaging in the ministry of Planting Churches, is committing to a life of great sacrifices, however, the cost of being a Church Planter is outweighed by the eternal treasures stored up for us who faithfully follow the dream of God for our lives.

Jesus, in His first teaching of His Disciples laid this Foundation. He equipped them; to be prepared to for all kinds of persecutions, abuse, slander, evil speaking, mistreatment and even death. He prepared them, with a reminder that, *"the prophets were persecuted in the same way."*

> **Matthew 5:10-12 (NIV)** "**10** *Blessed are those* **who are** *persecuted* **because of righteousness, for theirs is the kingdom of heaven. 11 "Blessed are you when** *people insult you, persecute you* **and** *falsely say all kinds of evil against you* because of me. **12 Rejoice and be glad, because great is your reward in heaven, for** *in the same way they persecuted the prophets who were before you.*"

In this session, I will focus my attention to the **challenges and sacrifices** to be considered by every Church Planter. I just want you to be better prepared for the journey you're about to undertake. Beyond the excitement of being involved in something great, there is the sobering reality of the dual natural and spiritual oppositions we will face in seeing these wonderful visions fulfilled.

Successful Church planting requires monetary resources, people resources, skill resources and equipment resources, and sometimes some of these are simply lacking. These are some of the things that might cost you money, but then there are the time, relationship and energy commitment costs, which are not always clearly outlined and defined. Beyond the monetary challenges lies a spiritual and emotional battle. I pray that you will find yourself equipped and better prepared for some of the challenges you might face in days and years to come.

1. Loneliness and isolation.

One of the challenges, which many, if not most of us, will face, is that of loneliness and isolation. Since the call of God often takes most of us out of our "Father's land" to a place where God wants to use us for His Glory, it unfortunately also bring alongside this separation, the feeling of loneliness and isolation.

For Abraham it was leaving his country, his family and his Father's house. The cost for Abraham to see the promise of God fulfilled meant that he had to leave his heritage, his country and family.

When God called me, and my family, out of Africa to Australia, God used the same Scripture to call us out of our nation, our culture, our comfort, our family and friends. Following His Call almost always will cost us something that is dear and precious to us.

> Genesis 12:1-4 (NIV) 1 The Lord had said to Abram, "**Go from your country, your people and your father's household to the land I will show you**. 2 "I will make you into a great nation, and I will bless you; I will make your name great, and you will be a blessing. 3 I will bless those who bless you, and whoever curses you I will curse; and all peoples on earth

will be blessed through you." 4 ***So Abram went, as the Lord had told him***; and Lot went with him. Abram was seventy-five years old when he set out from Harran."

I remember the adjustments we had to make when we migrated to Australia, a new country, far away from the known environment we grew up in, the familiar faces, knowing you could drop in at lifelong friends, and suddenly they are miles away in a different country and time zone.

Church Planting and following the Call of God can be a difficult experience and in many ways leave you, and the members of your family, feeling lonely and isolated. For us, it is sometimes easier since we have a sense of purpose in obeying the Call of God, but for our loved ones, it is sometimes a different experience. Take time to take care of their needs as they come to terms with their new country or environment.

2. Desertion.

One of the toughest challenges in Church Planting is when key staff or people you love, trusted and invested in, suddenly leave the fellowship. This could be for known or unknown reasons. People leave for all kinds of reasons. It still hurts when they decide to leave, and often we find that it causes an unsettling within the fellowship, especially if they occupied key leadership positions.

The Apostle Paul had such an encounter once, just as they set out on a Holy Spirit inspired mission in Acts 13. They just encountered a major demonic spiritual attack with Simon the Sorcerer, but God gave them success and salvations followed. This was such an amazing encounter, yet as soon as they left Paphos and arrived in Perga, one of the team members left the team. This was such a set back for Paul that later when Barnabas wanted to bring John Mark back, he refused.

Acts 13:13 (NIV) "13 From Paphos, Paul and his companions sailed to Perga in Pamphylia, ***where John left them to return to Jerusalem***."

Acts 15:37-40 (NIV) "37 Barnabas wanted to take John, also called Mark, with them, 38 but ***Paul did not think it wise to take him, because he had deserted them in Pamphylia*** and had not continued with them in the work. 39 They had such a sharp disagreement that they parted company. ***Barnabas took Mark and sailed for Cyprus***, 40 but Paul chose Silas and left, commended by the believers to the grace of the Lord."

Paul did not want John Mark back on the team since he deserted them back in Pamphylia. Sometimes it hurts so much when someone deserts the team that it is hard to let him or her come back and act as if things are fine. This is something you and I need to prepare ourselves for. We too might have people deserting our mission. I can tell you, it's hard, I've had dear friends simply desert us while we stepped out in faith to pursue what God called us to do. The worst part is that it is done without explanation. I pray that you too will find comfort from the Lord, as you pour your pain and heartache out before Him.

3. Plots and divisions.

When Paul and Barnabas went to Iconium they had tremendous success, however, some of the Jews did not believe the Message they preached and they started poisoning the minds of the people and plotted to have Paul and Barnabas stoned. It never ceases to amaze me that in the midst of God doing incredible miracles through the lives of His servants, that the enemy would come in through so-called "Believers" and stir up strive, form plots and intentionally cause divisions to harm the works of God.

Acts 14:1-5 (NIV) "At Iconium Paul and Barnabas went as usual into the Jewish synagogue. There *they spoke so effectively that a great number of Jews and Greeks believed*. 2 But *the Jews who refused to believe stirred up the other Gentiles and poisoned their minds against the brothers*. 3 So Paul and

> **Barnabas spent considerable time there, speaking boldly for** *the Lord, who confirmed the message* **of his grace** *by enabling them to perform signs and wonders.* **4 The people of** *the city were divided;* **some sided with the Jews, others with the apostles. 5** *There was a plot* **afoot among both Gentiles and Jews, together with their leaders,** *to mistreat them and stone them.*"

The key is to release those who hurt you by forgiving them like Jesus forgave those who harmed Him. When they stoned Stephen his last words echo in my heart: *"Please forgive them for they don't know what they are doing."* The sooner you bring yourself to a place of releasing those who hurt you, the quicker you can move on. Do not get entrenched by the evil deeds and actions of others, rather, let our resolve be that God will bring vindication for us.

4. Persecution.

On another occasion it was the Jewish Leaders who incited the woman of high standing in Pisidian Antioch to persecute Paul and Barnabas.

> **Acts 13:49-50 (NIV) 9** *The word of the Lord spread through the whole region.* **50 But the Jewish leaders incited the God-fearing women of high standing and the leading men of the city.** *They stirred up persecution against Paul and Barnabas,* **and expelled them from their region.**

Jesus warned us about being persecuted for doing good and doing His will in Matthew chapter 5. He called us blessed who endure such evil treatment.

> Matthew 5:10-12 (NIV) "10 Blessed are those who are persecuted because of righteousness, for theirs is the kingdom of heaven. 11 "Blessed are you when people insult you, persecute you and falsely say all kinds of evil against you because of me. 12 Rejoice and be glad, because great is

your reward in heaven, for in the same way they persecuted the prophets who were before you."

I recently listened to a dear friend of mine telling me of the persecution he and his family have endured in Vietnam for preaching the Good News of Jesus Christ. Even though they have endured so much physical and emotional persecution, their spirits are up and they continue steadfastly in preaching the Gospel. They have endured physical beatings, long periods of strenuous imprisonments where they were malnourished, left for dead, yet God is faithful and He continues to help them. May our spirits be strong to endure such persecutions as well.

5. Imprisonment.

One of the hardest things is to find yourself behind bars, in prison, for your stand for the cause of Christ. The Apostles Paul and Peter were no strangers to finding themselves flogged and imprisoned. On no occasion do we read that they bemoaned their situation, rather the opposite. We frequently read of them worshipping the Lord and witnessing even when they have good reason to be downcast. The Apostle Paul even counted it a privilege. On a few occasions we read of how God sent His Angels to deliver His Apostles from prison. We have record of at least two occasions where God delivered Peter from prison. Once in Acts chapter five, and once in chapter twelve, and then we read about Paul and Silas' experience in prison.

> Acts 5:18-20 (NIV) 18 They arrested the apostles and put them in the public jail. 19 But during the night an angel of the Lord opened the doors of the jail and brought them out. 20 "Go, stand in the temple courts," he said, "and tell the people all about this new life."

> Acts 12:5-9 (NIV) "5 So Peter was kept in prison, but the church was earnestly praying to God for him. 6 The night before Herod was to bring him to trial, Peter was sleeping between

two soldiers, bound with two chains, and sentries stood guard at the entrance. 7 Suddenly an angel of the Lord appeared and a light shone in the cell. He struck Peter on the side and woke him up. "Quick, get up!" he said, and the chains fell off Peter's wrists. 8 Then the angel said to him, "Put on your clothes and sandals." And Peter did so. "Wrap your cloak around you and follow me," the angel told him. 9 Peter followed him out of the prison, but he had no idea that what the angel was doing was really happening; he thought he was seeing a vision."

Acts 16:23-26 (NIV) 23 After they had been severely flogged, they were thrown into prison, and the jailer was commanded to guard them carefully. 24 When he received these orders, he put them in the inner cell and fastened their feet in the stocks.

25 About midnight Paul and Silas were praying and singing hymns to God, and the other prisoners were listening to them. 26 Suddenly there was such a violent earthquake that the foundations of the prison were shaken. At once all the prison doors flew open, and everyone's chains came loose.

Things have not changed much since Joseph was put into prison for the Integrity he upheld. During the ages Prophets and Apostles alike endured this kind of hostile treatment from opposing forces. There are thousands of Christian Leaders behind prison bars today for the faith they upheld. May we who share some kind of a freedom where we share our faith never forget that others pay a high price for the faith they profess.

6. Killing and flogging.

John the Baptist, a Great Man of God, lost his live in a show-off charade by a king. The senseless murdering of Men of God is quite outrageous. Many have lost their lives as a result of their stand in faith. Abel was one of the first one's to loose his life over an offering that was acceptable to God. They tried to kill Joseph. In the New Testament we read about the beheading of John the Baptist. King Herod had James, the Brother of James Killed. Stephen, a man full of the Holy Spirit, was stoned to death.

> Acts 7:59-60 (NIV) "59 While they were stoning him, Stephen prayed, "Lord Jesus, receive my spirit." 60 Then he fell on his knees and cried out, "Lord, do not hold this sin against them." When he had said this, he fell asleep."
> Acts 12:1-2 (NIV) "1 It was about this time that King Herod arrested some who belonged to the church, intending to persecute them. 2 He had James, the brother of John, put to death with the sword."

These kind of brutalities are recorded in Hebrews:

> Hebrews 11:35-40 (NIV) 35 Women received back their dead, raised to life again. There were others who were tortured, refusing to be released so that they might gain an even better resurrection. 36 Some faced jeers and flogging, and even chains and imprisonment. 37 They were put to death by stoning; they were sawed in two; they were killed by the sword. They went about in sheepskins and goatskins, destitute, persecuted and mistreated— 38 the world was not worthy of them. They wandered in deserts and mountains, living in caves and in holes in the ground. 39 These were all commended for their faith, yet none of them received what had been promised, 40 since God had planned something better for us so that only together with us would they be made perfect.

It seems, from this account, that life will be hard and persecution guaranteed if you're an ardent follower of Jesus. May our journey along the pathways of history bring both an appreciation for when we are able to share our faith without the potential of such escalated persecutions, as well as a preparedness that, if we had to face such tribulations, that we will be ready to embrace it, not as if something unique and strange has come on us, but rather that we too have been found worthy of following the Lord in this kind of severe persecutions.

7. Hardships.

We frequently read how the Apostle Paul exhorts the Believers, and his Disciples, to endure hardship. Hardship can come in many forms. Hardship could be the adversity one faces, for doing what God called you to do, or by those who oppose the Message you bring. Some hardships come through people and some through the fall-out with people or institutional problems. It might lead us into poverty, destitution, suffering, difficulty and discomfort. Hardships are those hard to comprehend; "*I don't know what is happening*" times in our ministries. Hardships are those troublesome times when all we need to do is keep on walking even if we don't understand.

Paul exhorts Timothy to keep his head in all circumstances and to endure the hardships he will face. One of the things about hardships is that they make you question yourself, your teachings, your actions and words. It is so important to keep a sound mind during those times of serious reflections, hence Paul's advice to "*keep your head in all situations.*"

2 Timothy 4:5 (NIV)
5 But you, keep your head in all situations, endure hardship, do the work of an evangelist, discharge all the duties of your ministry.

The writer to the Hebrews connects hardships, at times, to the discipline of God. Since hardships pushes us into reflective living, may we also reflect on what the Lord might want to teach us through the hardships we face.

Hebrews 12:7-8 (NIV) 7 Endure hardship as discipline; God is treating you as his children. For what children are not disciplined by their father? 8 If you are not disciplined—and everyone undergoes discipline—then you are not legitimate, not true sons and daughters at all.

Facing hardships is not always the result of us being under God's discipline, it might also come when we in earnest pursue the vision God gave us, such as was the case with Nehemiah. He was a godly man with a heart to see the walls of Jerusalem rebuilt and restored. It was during this pursuit of the vision God placed in his heart that he encountered unparalleled hardship.

> Nehemiah 9:32 (NIV) "32 "Now therefore, our God, the great
> God, mighty and awesome, who keeps his covenant of love,
> do not let all this hardship seem trifling in your eyes—the
> hardship that has come on us, on our kings and leaders, on
> our priests and prophets, on our ancestors and all your
> people, from the days of the kings of Assyria until today.

Another example of hardship comes from Genesis 31 when Jacob recounts the hardships he endured under Laban. His hardship came from mistreatment, unfair working circumstances, sleepless nights, hunger, cold, the heat of day, and many more. When he finally left, God gave him a rich reward for all the hardships and ill-treatment he endured from his Father-in-law.

> Genesis 31:42 (NIV) "42 If the God of my father, the God of
> Abraham and the Fear of Isaac, had not been with me, you
> would surely have sent me away empty-handed. But God
> has seen my hardship and the toil of my hands, and last
> night he rebuked you."

I pray that when you face hardships in ministry that the hardships that these men of God endured will serve as encouragement for you to endure.

8. Hunger, starvation and famine.

Some of the hardships we might face can be compared with those that the Apostle Paul faced. In his letter to the Church in Corinth Paul mentioned some of the hardships he endured for the sake of the advancement of the Gospel.

> 2 Corinthians 6:3-10 (NIV) We put no stumbling block in anyone's path, so that our ministry will not be discredited. 4 Rather, as servants of God we commend ourselves in every way: in great endurance; **in troubles, hardships and distresses**; 5 **in beatings, imprisonments and riots**; in hard work, sleepless nights and **hunger**; 6 in purity, understanding, patience and kindness; in the Holy Spirit and in sincere love; 7 in truthful speech and in the power of God; with weapons of righteousness in the right hand and in the left; 8 through glory and dishonor, bad report and good report; genuine, yet regarded as impostors; 9 known, yet regarded as unknown; **dying**, and yet we live on; **beaten**, and yet not killed; 10 sorrowful, yet always rejoicing; **poor,** yet making many rich; having nothing, and yet possessing everything.

Many of us share this same report as if it was ours. My encouragement to you today is – endure. Stand strong in your faith and the calling with which God called you.

9. Spiritual and demonic attacks.

Sometimes we experience spiritual opposition in our work. These could be observed in the natural, but sometimes we are not able to discern exactly where the problem is. The Apostle Paul wrote about this spiritual dimension on a number of occasions.

> Ephesians 6:12-13 (NIV) 12 For our struggle is not against flesh and blood, but against the rulers, against the authorities,

against the powers of this dark world and against the
spiritual forces of evil in the heavenly realms. 13 Therefore
put on the full armor of God, so that when the day of evil
comes, you may be able to stand your ground, and after you
have done everything, to stand.

This spiritual warfare cannot be fought by natural means. The only
way to win this spiritual battle is by putting on the whole armour of
God and by using the spiritual weapons of prayer, obedience and
declaration.

2 Corinthians 10:3-4 (NIV) 3 For though we live in the world,
we do not wage war as the world does. 4 The weapons we
fight with are not the weapons of the world. On the
contrary, they have divine power to demolish strongholds.

When you have a sense that you're not succeeding and you can
honestly not lay your finger on what the cause might be, remember
that our wrestle is not against flesh or blood, but against the rulers, the
principalities, the spiritual forces of darkness in the air.

This might not always be the enemy either who causes us to find
ourselves up against a brick wall, sometimes it could be the Lord
Himself. May I remind you of Balaam when he was contracted by a
hostile King to curse Israel. It was the Lord who sent His Angel to
block Balaam on his path.

In the New Testament we find the Apostles Paul and Barnabas on
their first Missionary journey in Acts chapter 16.

Acts 16:6-7 (NIV) 6 Paul and his companions travelled
throughout the region of Phrygia and Galatia, having been
kept by the Holy Spirit from preaching the word in the
province of Asia. 7 When they came to the border of Mysia,
they tried to enter Bithynia, but the Spirit of Jesus would
not allow them to.

On both of these occasions it was the Holy Spirit who kept them from preaching the Word in those regions. The Holy Spirit spiritually challenged them to not preach the Word in those regions at that time. We need to be spiritually discerning as to the source of our spiritual opposition. Of course we face spiritual challenges, and mostly from our great Adversary – Satan.

Paul stepped out to preach the Gospel in the region of Paphos to a certain proconsul, Sergius Paulus. It was here that Paul encountered a spiritual challenge in the person of Elymas the sorcerer who opposed them (v.8) and tried to turn the proconsul from believing. Now this is spiritual warfare. Paul was full of the Holy Spirit (v.9) and dealt decisively with this evil man. We too should always keep ourselves "full of the Holy Spirit" so that we will be able to deal in the same way with those opposing spiritual attacks.

> Acts 13:6-11 (NIV) 6 They traveled through the whole island until they came to Paphos. There they met a Jewish sorcerer and false prophet named Bar-Jesus, 7 who was an attendant of the proconsul, Sergius Paulus. The proconsul, an intelligent man, sent for Barnabas and Saul because he wanted to hear the word of God. 8 But Elymas the sorcerer (for that is what his name means) opposed them and tried to turn the proconsul from the faith. 9 Then Saul, who was also called Paul, filled with the Holy Spirit, looked straight at Elymas and said, 10 "You are a child of the devil and an enemy of everything that is right! You are full of all kinds of deceit and trickery. Will you never stop perverting the right ways of the Lord? 11 Now the hand of the Lord is against you. You are going to be blind for a time, not even able to see the light of the sun." Immediately mist and darkness came over him, and he groped about, seeking someone to lead him by the hand.

This might be an extreme example, however, this is most certainly one of the challenges we might face in our pursuits of sharing the Gospel of Jesus Christ.

10. Physical and emotional challenges.

Our challenges are not always spiritual. Sometimes it is very much physical. A few years ago a certain Mafia Leader made numerous attempts to bring harm to our growing church and since I did not give way to his manipulation and intimidation he ensued more direct physical assaults. On a few occasions he came to my office with his bodyguard and got him to physically assault me to use this as a means to persuade me to give in to his demands. This was one of the most demanding times of my ministry.

I always remind myself that I am not the first to endure this kind of hostile treatment from people who oppose the advancement of the Gospel, and most certainly won't be the last. The Apostles endured such physical assaults many times.

> 2 Corinthians 6:3-5, 9 (NIV) We put no stumbling block in anyone's path, so that our ministry will not be discredited. 4 Rather, as servants of God we commend ourselves in every way: in great endurance; **in troubles, hardships and distresses**; 5 **in beatings, imprisonments and riots**; in hard work, sleepless nights and **hunger**; 9 known, yet regarded as unknown; **dying**, and yet we live on; **beaten**, and yet not killed;"

In reading some biographies of some great Missionaries I learnt of a number of them left their missionary assignments due to depression. We should always assess our mental wellbeing as we pursue the work set before us. There are a few things that most certainly helped me keep some kind of sanity when things did not make sense, and reading these biographies most certainly helped and encouraged me greatly.

I frequently travel to some countries where they still persecute preachers, and once I listen to their stories I thank God for these faithful servants who advance the work of God despite being troubled, beaten, imprisoned, and facing hardships. May you too be encouraged that this has been the practice throughout history. May the Lord strengthen you to endure!

11. Evil speaking.

In preparing His Disciples, Jesus forewarned His Disciples that people would speak evil of them. Matthew gives us an account of this fore-warning.

> Matthew 5:10-12 (NIV) "10 Blessed are those who are persecuted because of righteousness, for theirs is the kingdom of heaven. 11 **Blessed are you when people insult you**, persecute you and **falsely say all kinds of evil against you** because of me. 12 Rejoice and be glad, because great is your reward in heaven, for in the same way they persecuted the prophets who were before you."

Jesus endured this kind of treatment from the religious leaders of his day. The Apostles Peter and Paul endured this kind of treatment many times as they continued to share the Word of God.

> Mark 15:29-32 (NIV) 29 **Those who passed by hurled insults at him**, shaking their heads and saying, "So! You who are going to destroy the temple and build it in three days, 30 come down from the cross and save yourself!" 31 In the same way the chief priests and the teachers of the law mocked him among themselves. "He saved others," they said, "but he can't save himself! 32 Let this Messiah, this king of Israel, come down now from the cross, that we may see and believe." Those crucified with him **also heaped insults on him**."
> 1 Peter 2:21,23 (NIV) "21 To this you were called, because **Christ suffered for you, leaving you an example, that you should follow in his steps.** 23 **When they hurled their insults at him, he did not retaliate**; when he suffered, he made no threats. Instead, he entrusted himself to him who judges justly."

In both his letters to the Church in Corinth Paul wrote about his persecutions and the things he endures to advance the Gospel.

> 1 Corinthians 4:11-13 (NIV) 11 To this very hour we go hungry and thirsty, we are in rags, we are brutally treated, we are homeless. 12 We work hard with our own hands. **When we are cursed, we bless; when we are persecuted, we endure it;** 13 when **we are slandered, we answer kindly.** We have become the scum of the earth, the garbage of the world—right up to this moment.

In ministry you will endure this kind of treatment as well. Brace and prepare yourself that when it happens that you are not taken by surprise as if something strange has happened to you. I pray that you will learn during these challenging times to lean into God as your Protector, Guide and Shield. May the example of our Lord and that of the Apostle Paul serve as guidance and encouragement in how t deal with such personal and abusive assaults.

12. Transitioning and waiting challenges.

Sometimes we don't have the full picture revealed to us and a simple wait from the Lord has to suffice. How many times don't we receive that Word from the Lord, to wait?

> Psalms 27:14 (NKJV) "14 Wait on the Lord; Be of good courage, And He shall strengthen your heart; Wait, I say, on the Lord!"
> Isaiah 40:31 (NKJV) "31 But those who wait on the Lord Shall renew their strength; They shall mount up with wings like eagles, They shall run and not be weary, They shall walk and not faint."

A time of waiting could be for our development and maturing in preparation for what God has in store for us. It might also be that the place where God wants us to go is not yet ready for our arrival. God is never late. He is always on time. He is not slow in answering. He is simply patient with us.

> Isaiah 64:4 (NIV) "4 Since ancient times no one has heard, no
> ear has perceived, no eye has seen any God besides you, who
> acts on behalf of those who wait for him.

Never make decisions in haste or when the answers don't seem to be at a time as you expect. Remember that God always has our best interest at heart. Whenever He makes us wait, He clearly has our welfare at heart. Be patient and wait for the Lord.

> Acts 1:4 (NIV) "4 On one occasion, while he was eating with
> them, he gave them this command: "Do not leave Jerusalem,
> but wait for the gift my Father promised, which you have
> heard me speak about."

One time Israel became insolent about entering into the Promised Land and simply wanted to go in on their own, but it was Moses' wisdom that prevailed with: "Unless the Lord Himself goes up with us, we don't go." Never leave the place where you are now until the Lord tells you to move and when He goes out with you. The advice in Lamentations serves as strong guidance to us to wait on the Lord before we do anything.

> Lamentations 3:25-26 (AMPC) "25 The Lord is good to those
> who wait hopefully and expectantly for Him, to those who
> seek Him [inquire of and for Him and require Him by right
> of necessity and on the authority of God's word]. 26 It is
> good that one should hope in and wait quietly for the
> salvation (the safety and ease) of the Lord."

There are many blessings that God desires to bring to us as His Servants, so I encourage you to wait for His Guidance, Directives and empowerment. It was definitely worth the wait for the Disciples, when Jesus asked them to wait in Jerusalem for the Promise of the Father.

Those 10 days made the difference between a global impacting ministry and not going anywhere. May you be encouraged to wait, every time when God says "Wait" that you will patiently wait on Him.

13. Family and relational challenges.

One of the areas where I see that the enemy severely attack the Servants of God is the area of attacking their family and marriage relationships. Satan will use whatever avenue he can find to challenge your obedience and consistency in fulfilling the Call of God. In Jesus' teaching of His Disciples, He advised them that they needed to prepare themselves to even leave their family to fulfill the Call and Purpose of God.

> Matthew 19:27-30 (NIV) 27 Peter answered him, "We have left
> everything to follow you! What then will there be for us?"
> 28 Jesus said to them, "Truly I tell you, at the renewal of all
> things, when the Son of Man sits on his glorious throne, you
> who have followed me will also sit on twelve thrones,
> judging the twelve tribes of Israel. 29 And everyone who has
> left houses or brothers or sisters or father or mother or wife
> or children or fields for my sake will receive a hundred times
> as much and will inherit eternal life. 30 But many who are
> first will be last, and many who are last will be first.

Abraham's wife, Sarah, laughed at him and the faith He held on to that God would give him a son. David's wife, Michal, despised him for his great rejoicing as the Ark of God was brought back into Jerusalem.

> 2 Samuel 6:16 (NIV) "16 As the ark of the Lord was entering the
> City of David, Michal daughter of Saul watched from a
> window. And when she saw King David leaping and dancing
> before the Lord, she despised him in her heart."

Job faced many challenges, but surely one of the greatest was that his own wife would challenge him to "curse God and die." The closest companion of Job was his wife. She is the one who would stand with her husband through everything, but when she challenges him, he makes a choice to maintain his integrity. This must have been so hard. I have heard of many Great Men of God whose spouses left them since the challenges they faced were simply to much for them.

> Job 2:9-10 (NIV) "9 His wife said to him, "Are you still maintaining your integrity? Curse God and die!" 10 He replied, "You are talking like a foolish woman. Shall we accept good from God, and not trouble?" In all this, Job did not sin in what he said."

I don't know the challenges that you might face with your spouse or family, but all I can pray is that God would protect you and keep you and your family safe.

14. Financial challenges.

Another area where Pastors and Church Planters face challenges is with their finances. I daily receive requests for financial assistance, or for prayer regarding financial struggles, from Church Leaders around the world. Everywhere I go to speak on Church Planting I find that the interchangeable top requests for assistance I receive is that for Understanding Discipleship and for financial assistance. Strangely this is hardly expressed as being such a huge challenge by those Leaders in the Bible. Apart of the Apostle Paul mentioning his hardships of enduring "Hunger and Thirst" and "going without food," there is very little emphasis given to the financial struggles the Servants of God faced throughout history.

We live in a different age, and whereas their struggles might have been more on staying alive in the midst of severe persecutions and hostile treatment, and therefor their own welfare was of less importance than what we experience today. Most places where the church is growing and advancing nowadays has some kind of protection systems to secure their safety, and therefor the next area that then demands their care and concern is their physical welfare. The

Apostle Paul mentioned the things he endured, and one of them was hunger.

> 2 Corinthians 6:4-5 (NIV) "4 Rather, **as servants of God we commend ourselves in every way**: in great endurance; in troubles, hardships and distresses; 5 in beatings, imprisonments and riots; in hard work, sleepless nights **and hunger**;"

> 2 Corinthians 11:27 (NIV) "27 I have labored and toiled and have often gone without sleep; **I have known hunger and thirst and have often gone without food**; I have been cold and naked."

His resolve was to learn to be content in whatever circumstances he lived. Through the years we faced many uncertain times. Most churches I know are solely dependent on the weekly offering and tithes of their members or coherants to support their Pastoral Staff. The average church size, around the world is about 85 people per congregation, and therefor the financial stability is highly susceptible to the coming and goings of those who attend and support the work. When an industry closes which impacts on a number of congregants losing their jobs, or if an internal feud between some members causes some families to leave, these have devastating effects on the local Church, but more so on the welfare of the Pastor and staff. In the early years of my ministry we lived from hand to mouth many months. Many months we never received a salary and had to survive on the alms and generosity of some who took pity on us, or at least that is how it felt. I know this is how many of you, reading this book feel, or even felt. The Apostle Paul helped me deal with this constant tension of living in the ups and downs of Sunday incomes. He said that the resolution is to learn to be content in whatever circumstance you find yourself in.

> Philippians 4:11-12 (NIV) 1 I am not saying this because I am in need, for I have learned to be content whatever the circumstances. 12 I know what it is to be in need, and I

know what it is to have plenty. I have learned the secret of being content in any and every situation, whether well fed or hungry, whether living in plenty or in want.

Another thing that helped me succeed and endure through financial difficulties was learning to make the Lord my source and to take personal responsibility for the welfare of my family.

> 1 Timothy 3:5 (NIV) "5 (If anyone does not know how to manage his own family, how can he take care of God's church?)"

This meant that at times I had to become a bi-vocational pastor. I took on part-time work to take care of my family's needs. It is not the church's responsibility to take care of you and your family. It is your and my responsibility. Unless we take responsibility for our families, how can we take care of God's Church? The Apostle Paul worked as a tentmaker on a number of occasions to provide for his own personal needs. I do however believe that if you follow the strategy that I outlined in this book, that you will soon become a Servant of God who will live off the fruit of your labour in a full-time capacity.

15. Vision and Focus challenges.

Mother Theresa apparently once said: "It is a sad sight when people have eyes to see and have no vision." The Bible teaches this principle in a few places.

> Proverbs 29:18 (KJV) "18 Where there is no vision, the people perish: but he that keepeth the law, happy is he."

Most of what we read about in the Bible came as a result of receiving a vision or dream from the Lord. For Noah it was the design and life purpose of building an Ark. For Abraham it was the vision of having a son and taking possession of a foreign country. For Moses it was that Vision in the desert that propelled him into his destiny. David lived by the frequent visions and dreams he received from God. For the prophets of old, or "Seers" as they were often termed and referred to, they wrote these messages down from visions they had.

In ministry it is so vitally important that we always live within the parameters of the visions and dreams we received from God. Fulfilling the assignments we receive through visions is what ministry is all about. If you've become uncertain about what you're supposed to be doing, then it's time for you to take a prayer and fasting retreat to go and seek the Lord for a fresh vision. A vision is a God-given vision, dream or instruction you receive through prayer that clearly assigns you to work to a determined goal or purpose.

16. Authority challenges.

Another challenge we face in ministry is that of our Authority being challenged. Your position and your anointing will be challenged. People will question your Calling, your Authority and the decisions you make. This first happened to Joseph, when he shared the dreams God gave him, with his Brothers and Parents. They immediately questioned him envisioning having authority over them. They hated him, because they possibly knew that God revealed His plan for Joseph's life and they were not pleased about God's Choice. In most instances it is exactly that same spirit that is in operation. People don't like the choice God made of who should have authority and rule over them.

> Genesis 37:8 (NIV) "8 His brothers said to him, "**Do you intend to reign over us? Will you actually rule us?**"
> And they hated him all the more because of his dream and what he had said."

The same thing happened to Moses when he led the Israelites out of Egypt to the promised land. Right from when Moses realised God's purpose for his life, his authority was questioned.

> Exodus 2:14 (NIV) "14 The man said, "**Who made you ruler and judge over us?** Are you thinking of killing me as you

killed the Egyptian?" Then Moses was afraid and thought, "What I did must have become known.""

During their trek through the wilderness en route to the Promised land, a few leaders rebelled against Moses and against Aaron. When Moses summoned them to come, they refused. Their refusal was a clear sign of their rebellion against the Authority God placed over them.

> Numbers 16:12-14 (NIV) 12 Then Moses summoned Dathan and
> Abiram, the sons of Eliab. But they said, "We will not come!
> 13 Isn't it enough that you have brought us up out of a land
> flowing with milk and honey to kill us in the wilderness?
> And now you also want to lord it over us! 14 Moreover, you
> haven't brought us into a land flowing with milk and honey
> or given us an inheritance of fields and vineyards. Do you
> want to treat these men like slaves? No, we will not come!"

We know that God dealt with these rebellious people, and their families in a decisive way and opened the earth and swallowed them up. This should be a lesson to all, however, sadly, few people, especially nowadays, give any respect to those whom God called and anointed for Holy Service. If it happened to Moses and Aaron, it will happen to you, they will question your authority. As long as what you continue in making Holy Spirit inspired decisions and earnestly pursue the guidance and directives of the Holy Spirit on a daily basis, you should be fine. You too will endure through faith, prayer and perseverance.

The last Judge that ruled Israel was the Prophet Samuel. He was a true man of God! However, when the spirit of the world got hold of the people, they insisted that they wanted a King just like the other nations. Samuel felt strong rejection, but even after pleading with the people and with God, God directed him to appoint a king as per their request.

> 1 Samuel 8:6-7 (NIV) 6 But when they said, "Give us a king to
> lead us," **this displeased Samuel; so he prayed to the**

Lord. 7 And the Lord told him: "Listen to all that the people are saying to you; **it is not you they have rejected, but they have rejected me as their king**."

1 Samuel 8:19-22 (NIV) 19 But **the people refused to listen to Samuel**. "No!" they said. "We want a king over us. 20 Then we will be like all the other nations, with a king to lead us and to go out before us and fight our battles." 21 When Samuel heard all that the people said, **he repeated it before the Lord**. 22 The Lord answered, "**Listen to them and give them a king**."

It is a sad day when God tell us to do what the people want. That day brings famine, destitution and sorrow. In ministry, our only resolve when people continue in their persistence to not listen to the Word of the Lord, is for us to pray and do what God would have us do. Sometimes it will feel as if you're the only person on the planet who is still holding on to principles of the Word of God, stand strong, hold fast onto your faith and pray. Prayer solidifies our faith but also brings much needed guidance when our authority and leading is questioned.

Even Jesus' authority was questioned by the high priest a religious leaders of His day.

Mark 11:27-28 (NIV) "27 They arrived again in Jerusalem, and while Jesus was walking in the temple courts, the chief priests, the teachers of the law and the elders came to him. 28 "By what authority are you doing these things?" they asked. "And who gave you authority to do this?""

Just in case you've become confused and unsure: God placed anointing and authority on each one of His Called Servants. You are anointed for a purpose and God anoints you with authority.

Hebrews 13:17 (NIV) "17 Have confidence in your leaders and submit to their authority, because they keep watch over you as those who must give an account. Do this so that their work will be a joy, not a burden, for that would be of no benefit to you."

Finally, may I remind you that one of the only three elements that God instructed to be kept in the Ark of the Covenant is the budded rod of Aaron, an eternal reminder of God's choosing and appointment from among men.

> Hebrews 9:3-5 (KJV) "3 And after the second veil, the
> tabernacle which is called the Holiest of all; 4 Which had
> the golden censer, and the ark of the covenant overlaid
> round about with gold, wherein was the golden pot that had
> manna, and **Aaron's rod that budded**, and the tables of
> the covenant; 5 And over it the Cherubim's of glory
> shadowing the Mercy-seat; of which we cannot now speak
> particularly."

It is never a pleasant experience when people challenge your authority. I pray that these few references, among many, will serve as an encouragement for you when you face this challenge.

How do we prepare ourselves to meet these challenges?

I learned a few lessons about the sacrifices we might have to make as we go through the challenges. I pray that these brief observations might be helpful to you as well. The first is a lesson that I learned from a couple of articles on men and woman who succeeded in doing extra-ordinary things in their lives is that of being mentally and spiritually prepared.

Be Mentally and Spiritually prepared.

The story of Sir Edmund Hillary, and his incredible moun-taineering success, by becoming the first person to summit Mount Everest in Nepal in 1953, taught us incredible lessons on succeeding through the most extreme and strenuous circumstances. One of the key aspects of his incredible success is that he prepared himself spiritually and mentally. We will do ourselves a great favour if we too will prepare ourselves beforehand that we will encounter and experience these kind of hostilities against us and our ministry.

The writer of the Book to the Hebrews, in chapter 11, records the names of those who paid a high price for the advancement of the message of Hope. It seems from the Bible that they encouraged each other by that which was known so that they would endure the harness of the challenges they faced.

It might cost you your business, job or vocation.

One of the essential preparations we need to embrace ourselves with before we embark on our pursuit of planting Dynamic Churches is that it will come at a price, a high price, and at most it might cost you everything you have. This was true for the Apostles and it will be true for us.

> Matthew 4:18-22 (NIV) " [18] As Jesus was walking beside the Sea of Galilee, he saw two brothers, Simon called Peter and his brother Andrew. They were casting a net into the lake, for they were fishermen. [19] **"Come, follow me,"** Jesus said, "and I will make you fishers of men." [20] **At once they left their nets and followed him.** [21] Going on from there, he saw two other brothers, James son of Zebedee and his brother John. They were in a boat with their father Zebedee, preparing their nets. Jesus called them, [22] and **immediately they left the boat and their father and followed him.** "

These Disciples left their boats, their businesses and vocations to follow the Call of Jesus. It might cost you your business, vocation and possessions. This is most certainly what it cost the Disciples as they followed the Lord Jesus.

When Jesus encountered the rich young man He challenged him to sell all his possessions

Matthew 19:21 (NIV) "21 Jesus answered, "If you want to be perfect, go, **sell your possessions and give to the poor, and you will have treasure in heaven**. Then come, follow me.""

When Christ taught His Disciples of the cost of being His follower, He went on to tell them the full extent of what this might mean. In His answer to Peter's plea that they already "left everything," Jesus actually encouraged him with the "reward" that awaits those who "left" everything for Him.

Matthew 19:27-29 (NIV) "27 Peter answered him, "**We have left everything to follow you!** What then will there be for us?" 28 Jesus said to them, "Truly **I tell you**, at the renewal of all things, when the Son of Man sits on his glorious throne, you who have followed me will also sit on twelve thrones, judging the twelve tribes of Israel. 29 And **everyone who has left houses or brothers or sisters or father or mother or wife or children or fields for my sake will receive a hundred times as much** and will inherit eternal life."

It will cost you to deny yourself often.

Mark 8:34-38 (KJV)
"[34] And when he had called the people unto him with his disciples also, he said unto them, **Whosoever will come after me, let him deny himself, and take up his cross, and follow me**."

16

HOW TO SUCCEED IN CHURCH PLANTING

I believe God desire to give us success in our ministries. Success is never guaranteed, however, the following commitments on our part will most certainly increase our chances of succeeding.

A research study on the achievement and paralleled preparation of elite Olympic athletes highlighted a number of areas on which they concentrated which, in turn, added to their ultimate success According to Orlick (2000), there are seven critical elements of excellence that guide the pursuit of performance excellence on a consistent basis: commitment, focus, confidence, positive images, mental readiness, distraction control, and ongoing learning.

It will take a Full Commitment.

Church Planting requires a full commitment. We cannot pursue Church Planting with a Hireling attitude or commitment. To succeed, you will have to lay down your life for the sheep. It is not a job, where you just work for a wage and once you don't receive a wage, then you look for another job that can pay you a wage. In the words of Jesus, you need the commitment of being a Shepherd.

John 10:11-13 (NIV) "[11] I am the good shepherd. The good
shepherd lays down his life for the sheep. [12] The hired
hand is not the shepherd who owns the sheep. So when he
sees the wolf coming, he abandons the sheep and runs away.
Then the wolf attacks the flock and scatters it. [13] The man
runs away because he is a hired hand and cares nothing for
the sheep."

Make a commitment before you enter that you will stand,
regardless.

It will require Focus.

As Church Planters we need to be focused and engaged. As important
as vision is to keep us from perishing, focus is to keep us engaged to
see those visions fulfilled.

It will require Confidence.

Confidence is the feeling you have that you can trust and rely on
someone or something. As a Church Planter you need confidence in
God, the vision He has given you, His anointing upon your life and
that of your team. Confidence in yourself, your abilities and skills are
essential to successful church planting. The writer to the Hebrews tells
us that we should not throw away our confidence since it will be richly
rewarded if we persevere and continue to complete what God assigned
for us to do.

Hebrews 10:35-36 (NIV) [35] So do not throw away your
confidence; it will be richly rewarded. [36] You need to
persevere so that when you have done the will of God, you
will receive what he has promised.

Ephesians 3:12 (KJV) [12] In whom we have boldness and access
with confidence by the faith of him.

You need to develop and keep Positive images.

Since there are so many things that we encounter in Church Planting that might try to distort our image of God, His Church and His Purpose. Keep your eyes on the Lord Jesus. Keep reminding yourself of the Good things God has done.

> Colossians 3:2 (AMPC) "2 And set your minds and keep them set on what is above (the higher things), not on the things that are on the earth.

> Hebrews 12:2 (NIV 1984) 2 Let us fix our eyes on Jesus, the author and perfecter of our faith, who for the joy set before him endured the cross, scorning its shame, and sat down at the right hand of the throne of God.

By Keeping our eyes focused on Jesus, and all that He has done for us, along with a grateful heart, it will both keep us protected, and help us keep positive images and visions alive in our hearts.

You need to have Mental readiness.

Most of our preparedness happens in our minds. Joyce Meyer speaks of "The Battlefield of the Mind." As applicable as what it is for athletes to be mentally prepared during their solitary times of practice and exercise, and when they get on the track to race, it is important for us to constantly keep our minds actively prepared for action, either in our times of devotion or when we step out in the world.

> 1 Peter 1:13 (NIV 1984) 13 Therefore, **prepare your minds for action**; be self-controlled; set your hope fully on the grace to be given you when Jesus Christ is revealed.

> Luke 21:14 (AMPC) 14 **Resolve and settle it in your minds** not to meditate and prepare beforehand how you are to make your defence and how you will answer.

You will need Distraction control.

Many Church Planters struggle with distraction control. We get distracted by unnecessary things like doing things others could do. It might be doing the banking, or taking out post, mowing the lawn or cleaning the Place of Worship. Don't let menial tasks keep you from doing what God Called and Anointed you for.

What we learn from Jesus and His Disciples was their ability to keep focused and not to be distracted by task, that might have importance, but not being primary to what God wants us to do. For the Apostles they practiced "Distraction Control" when there arose a feud among the widows, they determined that it was more expedient to continue on prayer and preaching than to serve the table. This is a great example of one area where many Pastors get distracted.

Acts 6:2-4 (NIV) "2 So the Twelve gathered all the disciples together and said, "**It would not be right for us to neglect the ministry of the word of God in order to wait on tables**. 3 Brothers and sisters, choose seven men from among you who are known to be full of the Spirit and wisdom. We will turn this responsibility over to them 4 and **will give our attention to prayer and the ministry of the word**."

You need to make a commitment to Ongoing learning.

There is a saying: "Leaders are Readers." One of the characteristics of successful Leaders is their ability to always remain teachable and to be open to learn new things. Study is good. I pray that you too will embrace the advice Paul gave his spiritual son, Timothy, to study. I read a lot and I learn a lot. Even though I had the privilege of equipping Church Planters and Leaders in over 70 nations (by 2017) I still learn new things and ways in which we can advance the cause of Church Planting.

2 Timothy 2:15 (AMPC) "15 **Study and be eager and do your**

utmost to present yourself to God approved (tested by trial), a workman who has no cause to be ashamed, correctly analyzing and accurately dividing [**rightly handling and skillfully teaching**] **the Word of Truth**."

It will require absolute Obedience.

Obedience is an essential characteristic and value in the Kingdom of God. Our obedience to God, His Will as defined to us through His Word, and to those whom He placed over us, will most certainly increase our chances for success. Many Church Planters are great at being focused and intentional in execution of their assignment, however, come undone when they remain stubborn and closed to receive wise counsel from those who have gone before them. As mentioned earlier, a Discipler, a Pastor, a Counsellor, to whom we submit for guidance and sound advice will only serve their God-given role when we submit to, and obey, their advice, instruction and directives.

> 1 John 2:3 (NIV 1984) "3 We know that we have come to know him **if we obey his commands**.

It stems from our heartfelt obedience to the Lordship of Christ in our lives. May we fully obey the Lord, in everything He asks or demands of us. Finally, God is a Rewarder, and if nothing else motivates you or keeps you focused and enduring, then let the Holy Spirit remind you of the Reward of the Lord.

Our Reward is with the Lord.

The Word of God, repeatedly, tells us of the Reward of God. This Reward is held for those who persevere and succeed.

> Hebrews 11:6 (NIV) 6 And without faith it is impossible to please God, because anyone who comes to him must believe

that he exists and that **he rewards those who earnestly seek him**.

Revelation 22:12 (NIV 1984) "12 Behold, I am coming soon! **My reward is with me, and I will give to everyone according to what he has done**."

Colossians 3:23-24 (NIV 1984) "23 Whatever you do, work at it with all your heart, as working for the Lord, not for men, 24 since you know that **you will receive an inheritance from the Lord as a reward**. It is the Lord Christ you are serving.

I pray that you will be counted among those who endured, persevered and succeeded.

17

HOW TO PLANT A HOUSE CHURCH

In conclusion of this book, may I encourage you to start where you are right now. Start in your house! If you sense the Call of God upon your life then start with yourself and then with those in your house, and then with those in your sphere of influence.

The early church started in a house. The house is the place where our values are measured and scrutinised more than anywhere else. I pray that your life in Christ would experience such a transformation that those close to you will see and recognize the impact of the Holy Spirit's work in you.

Many Pastors tell me that they have a dream of seeing an Acts Church planted where people will be added to the Church on a daily basis and where signs and wonders will be in the order of every day. Well, it is possible when we apply ourselves with the same diligence to the teachings of the Lord Jesus and His Apostles, and apply the same spiritual disciplines and Kingdom values in our lives.

I have jotted down a few simple guidelines as a reminder of our time together, as well as a quick guide or overview at the task before you:

Before you start.

Count the cost.

During our last session we looked at the "Cost of Church Planting." I pray that you will take the time to consider the path that lies before you. Even though I, and many others know what lies before us, we would still do what we do now because we are "dead men working." Christ set us this example.

Affirm God's Call to plant this Cell Church.

Before you even start dreaming about possibilities, make sure that you have been Called by God to be a Church Planter. All of us have been called to advance the Kingdom of God as part of the Body of Christ, however, only some have been Called to lead the planting of a Dynamic Church. You definitely need that Call and Grace of God on your life. Be sure to affirm the Call of God, as explored in the Chapter on "the Call to Church Planting" session.

Ensure the Elementary Foundations are laid and Spiritual Disciplines established.

Hebrews 6 verses 1-2 points us to six Elementary Foundations to establish in our faith. Through Jesus' Teachings on the Mountain and throughout the Gospels, we learned that the Kingdom of God has Values and demands Spiritual Disciplines to keep those Values in place in our lives.

52 Values of the Kingdom of God.

Matthew 5 from verse 3 shares with us the Values of the Kingdom of God. Nothing impacts people more than a Transformed life. Embracing and living the Values impacts people much more than words, without a demonstration of a changed life. Jesus taught over 80 values to His Disciples. Learn the Values as Jesus taught them, and apply them in willing obedience.

Spiritual Disciplines.

Jesus taught His Disciples Spiritual Disciplines; "When you pray," "When you fast," "When you give." There are many spiritual disciplines to explore and assimilate into our daily lives. *The Spiritual Disciplines of Fasting and Prayer, Stewardship, Simplicity, Servanthood, studying and meditating on the Word of God,* are some of the most valued disciplines to uphold.

You can read more on these in my Book on *"The Values of the Kingdom of God."* Spiritual disciplines will keep the fire of God burning ablaze inside of you.

Wait until you're empowered from on High.

We need the Power of the Holy Spirit in our lives. Do not proceed any further unless you had a dedicated time of Fasting and Prayer for the empowerment of the Holy Spirit upon your life.

Steps to start:

- **Seek a Worthy Man of Peace.**

  1. Look for a lost person who has a good reputation with outsiders.
  2. Look for owners of businesses, leaders in industry and professional people.
  3. Look for people who will follow you.

- **Seek and save lost people.**

  1. Build relationships with people in the Church.
  2. Build relationships with those outside the Church.
  3. Build relationships for a Kingdom purpose.

Baptize those who accept Jesus as Lord and make a firm commitment to Christ.

Gather those whom you sense God has given you to start your first discipleship group.

Transition from individual ministry to discipleship group formation.

Up to this point your ministry centered on you and your personal development as a Disciple of Christ. It also focused on you reaching out to lost people, but specifically to "**Worthy People**" who will be your first Disciples and through whom you will lead the planting of a Dynamic Church.

Stage One – Group formation to take place at least weekly.

This is a Highly directive process where you Disciple the "Worthy men" God gave you. **Meet weekly** and **teach them** the following Foundational Principles, Kingdom Values, Spiritual Disciplines, and Kingdom Identities:

1. Foundational Principles of following Christ. Hebrews 6:1-2.
2. Kingdom Values. 52 Kingdom of God values and the Apostles Teachings.
3. Kingdom Identity:
4. Household of God,
5. Priesthood,
6. Bride of Christ,
7. Temple of the Holy Spirit.
8. Kingdom of God spiritual disciplines.
9. Minister through the Power of the Holy Spirit.

Each time you meet, prepare yourself to minister to them in the Power of the Holy Spirit. What you do at the beginning is what they will do at the beginning. Never be intimidated with numbers. "***Where two or three gather together.***" The Church will only be as strong as what it is strong in groups of two or three. If the Church runs on all cylinders with "two's and three's" then it will run well when everyone congregates together.

If you value each one, and each opportunity to minister, whether there be two or many, your disciples will place the same value on the opportunities and the people, God gives them. Remember, you are building Value and are developing DNA of the Church you dream to have and lead. Do so with patient endurance. Your efforts and diligence will soon be well rewarded.

1. Pray for them, each other, and for souls to be saved.
2. Establish them in Spiritual Disciplines so that they will get to know the voice of the Holy Spirit through prayer and the reading of the Word of God.
3. Teach them to obey everything Jesus taught us.

Stage Two – Teach them to Disciple others. (Balance between being Directive and Facilitating.)

The second stage is the phase of moving from individual ministry to group formation. Discipleship is to equip your disciples to fulfill the purpose God has for them.

Counting the Cost of Discipleship.

Teach them that it will cost them everything, and that they are required to lay down their lives for the sake of Christ.

Stewardship.

Teach them about Stewardship; that everything we have belongs to God and we are mere Stewards entrusted with His possessions. We need to use it in a way that would bring glory and honour to Him. Teach them about "***laying up treasures in Heaven***" and honoring. God with the *"first fruits"* of their labors. Teach them about sowing and reaping, and the giving to the poor.

Witnessing.

Teach them how to share their faith. Learning and Sharing. (Go make...)

Caring with Compassion.

People learn better when they know that you care for them. Learning and Caring.

Accountability.

We all have to give account of our lives: what we do, and how we do it in fulfillment of our assignment. We show our humility by being accountable.

Stage Three – Fruitfulness (High facilitation)

1. Disciples reach their first souls.
2. Disciples gather their first disciples in a group to start their stage one.
3. Disciples take their disciples through stages.

Stage Four – Multiplication (Encouragement.)

1. Disciple's disciples reach their first souls.
2. Disciple's disciples gather their first disciples in a group to start stage one.
3. Disciple's Disciples take their disciples through stages.

Afterword

I pray that these brief outlines might assist you as you pursue the Call of God on your life. Godspeed.

AFTERWORD

Pioneering new Churches is a noble work and calling. Those who sense the Call to pioneer the planting of new churches engage in a pathway of advancing the Kingdom of God in new frontiers.

Calling

To be effective in planting new, dynamic churches, one has to be called by God. As you affirm this Calling by understanding where He wants to use you, and to whom He wants you to minister to, and what strategy He desires you to use to reach them, you will work with greater effectiveness and purpose.

Preparation

Once you understand this purpose, you need to engage in a season of preparation to effective fulfill that Calling. This will demand the establishment of the **Values** of the Kingdom of God in your live. It will also require the earnest development of **Spiritual Disciplines** that will both sustain the Anointing of God on your life and ministry, as well as maintain the Values in your life so that you will always be a good example for others to follow.

Strategy

The Strategy Jesus taught and modelled to us is that of first finding a Worthy Man or Woman in the place where He sends us. Worthy men and woman holds the keys both to ensuring you build a solid support structure around yourself, as well as ensuring that your work is multiplied through these *"reliable people who will be able to teach others."*

Make Disciples, not Members.

Jesus called each one of us to make Disciples. The way in which we systematically and purposefully do this will ensure that we make Disciples who will make Disciples. We build people in their faith by ensuring that they are saved. We build Kingdom values into their lives, and establish them in Spiritual disciplines. We help them to discover the Gifts of God, and teach them to use these Gifts in a God-honoring way to build others up. We also equip them for their work of ministry by teaching them skills to share their faith and to effectively care for those entrusted to them.

Discipleship is Caught more than taught.

Discipleship is more about the commitment you make to be an example for others to follow than about teaching other what to do and what not to do. Effective Discipleship stands central to the Calling and Activity of every Church Planter. The intentional focus to pioneer a new Church by starting to find "Worthy people" to lead to Christ, and committing to Disciple them will ensure a solid life-long dynamic ministry. Even though this might seem like a slow and inefficient start at the beginning, it will soon prove to be dynamic as your Disciples become fruitful and multiply.

Function before Form

Before you attend to establishing structures and Systems to maintain the growth of the new church, first ensure that you focus on functioning as an organically growing Body of Believers. Too many struggling congregations think that if their structure is right that it will produce growth. This is a myth. Keeping the winning of the lost and discipling them as the top priority of the congregation will keep it growing, and that will require astute leadership to structure the growth in a disciplined way.

Systems manage and maintain Church Growth

There are many systems which greatly help us maintain the health and growth of the new church. These should be introduced in a systematic and disciplined way. Systems are the disciplined ways in which a church functions to keep it organized and structured.

Finally

I pray that God will use the contents of this book to help you understand the requirements and the process of leading the planting of many dynamic new churches. God Bless you!

2 Timothy 2:2 (NIV)

2 And the things you have heard me say in the presence of many witnesses **entrust to reliable people who will also be qualified to teach others**.

OTHER BOOKS BY DR. HENDRIK J. VORSTER

Discipleship Foundations -
Step One - Salvation Disciple
Manual

Step One - Salvation

This Course explores the "How to" be Born Again and to establish a solid Foundation for your faith in Jesus Christ. It is based on Hebrews chapter 6 verses 1 and 2, and explores:

Repentance of dead works,

Faith in God,

Baptisms,

Laying on of hands,

Resurrection of the dead, and

Eternal Judgement

Teacher Manuals and Video Teaching material are available through our website: www.churchplantinginstitute.com or at www.amazon.com

Discipleship Foundations
Step Two - Values and
Spiritual Disciplines Disciple
Manual

Step Two - Values and Spiritual Disciplines Disciple Manual

This Course explores the "How to" develop spiritual disciplines as well as 52 Values Jesus taught. It is based on the teachings of Jesus to His Disciples, and explores:

Spiritual Disciplines

The disciplines we explore are: Reading, meditating on the Word of God, Prayer, Stewardship, Fasting, Servanthood, Simplicity, Worship, and Witnessing.

Values of the Kingdom of God

Humility, Mournfulness, meekness, Spiritual Passion, Mercifulness, Purity, Peacemaker, Patient endurance, Example, Custodian, Reconciliatory, Resoluteness, Loving, Discreetness, Forgiving, Kingdom of God Investor, God-minded, Kingdom of God prioritiser, Introspective, Persistent, Considerate, Conservative, Fruit-bearing, Practitioner, Accountability, Faithful, Childlikeness, Unity, Servanthood, Loyalty, Gratefulness, Stewardship, Obedience, Carefulness, Compassion, Caring, Confidence, Steadfastness, Contentment, Teachable, Deference, Diligence, Trustworthiness, Gentleness, Discernment, Truthfulness, Generous, Kindness, Watchfulness, Perseverance, Honouring and Submissive.

Teacher Manuals and Video Teaching material are available through our website: www.churchplantinginstitute.com or at www.amazon.com

Discipleship Foundations
Step Three - Developing Gifts
and Skills

Step Three - Developing Gifts and Skills

This course is run through five weekend encounters. These weekend encounters have been designed to help Disciples discover their spiritual gifts, as well as learn skills to use their gifts, and to serve the Lord for the extension of His Kingdom. The Weekend Encounters are:

Gifts Discovery Weekend Encounter

We learn about Ministerial Office gifts, Service gifts, and Supernatural Spiritual Gifts. We discover our own, and then learn How we may use them to build up the local Church.

Survey of the Bible Weekend Encounter

During this weekend we do a survey of the Bible, from Genesis to Revelation. We also learn about the History of the Bible as well as How we can make most of our time in the Word.

Sharing your Faith Weekend Encounter

During this weekend we learn about the Gospel message, and How to share our faith effectively.

Overcoming Weekend Encounter

During this weekend we deal with those thistles and thorns that smother the growth and harvest of the good seed sown into our lives. We address How to overcome fear, unforgiveness, lust and the cares of the world with faith and obedience.

Shepherd Leader Weekend Encounter

During this weekend encounter we learn about being a Good Shepherd, and How to best disciple in a small group.

Teacher Manuals and Video Teaching material are available from our website: www.churchplantinginstitute.com or at www.amazon.com

Discipleship Foundations
Step Four - Fruitfulness

Step Four - Discipling Fruit-Producers

We were saved to serve. This course has been designed to mobilise Believers, from Learners to Practitioners. These sessions have been prepared for individual use, with those who are bearing fruit, and want to produce more fruit. Developing these areas in a sustained and systematic manner will ensure both fruitfulness and multiplication. Attending to these areas will ensure that you bear lasting fruit.

We explore:

1. Introduction.
2. Walking with purpose.
3. Build purposeful relationships. Finding Worthy Men
4. Priesthood. Praying effectively for those entrusted to you.
5. Caring compassionately.
6. Walking worthily.
7. Walking in the Spirit.
8. Practicing hospitality.

Teacher Manuals and Video Teaching material are available from our COURSES link from our website at:

www.churchplantinginstitute.com or at www.amazon.com

Discipleship Foundations
Step Five - Multiplication

Step Five - Multiplication

This course was designed to assist fruit-producing disciples to live a life that will encourage a lifetime of fruitfulness. It will also give our disciples skills and guidelines to navigate their disciples through seasons of challenge and growth. This course is packed with Leadership advancing principles. The more these areas are addressed and encouraged, the more we will experience growth and multiplication. We explore:

1. Vision and dreams.
2. Set Godly Goals.
3. Character development
4. Gifts development - Impartation and Activation
5. Fruitfulness comes through constant challenge.
6. Relationships - Family, Children and Friends
7. The Power of encouragement
8. Finances - Personal and Ministry finances
9. Dealing with setbacks

- How to deal with failure?
- How to deal with betrayal?
- How to deal with rejection?
- How to deal with trials?
- How to deal with despondency?

10. Eternal rewards

Teacher Manuals and Video Teaching material are available from our website: www.churchplantinginstitute.com or at www.amazon.com

Values
of the
Kingdom
of
God

Dr. Hendrik J. Vorster

SPIRITUAL
DISCIPLINES
OF THE
KINGDOM
OF
GOD

www.amazon.com

Values of the Kingdom of God
By Dr. Hendrik J Vorster

Everyone desires to be known as a pleasant to be around with kind of person. This book helps you develop values towards such a godly character. This book explores 52 Values of the Kingdom of God.

Books are available from our website: www. churchplantinginstitute.com or at www.amazon.com

Spiritual Disciplines of the Kingdom of God
By Dr. Hendrik J Vorster

Every Believer desires to be a Fruit-producing branch in the Vine-yard of our Lord. Developing spiritual disciplines is to develop spiritual roots from which our faith can draw sap to grow strong and fruit-bearing branches. This Book explores Nine Spiritual Disciplines of the Kingdom of God.

Books are available from our website: www. churchplantinginstitute.com or at

Church Planting
How to plant a dynamic church

Dr. Hendrik J. Vorster
Foreword by: Dr. Yonggi Cho

Church Planting - by Dr
Hendrik J Vorster

Church Planting - How to plant a dynamic, disciple-making church

By Dr Hendrik J Vorster

This is a handbook for those who wish to plant a disciple-making church. This book explores every aspect of church planting, and is widely used in over 70 Nations on 6 Continents. Here is a list of the areas that are explored:

1. The challenge to plant New Churches
2. Phases of Church Planting
3. Phase One of Church Planting - The Calling, Vision and Preparation Phase
4. The Call to Church Planting
5. Twelve Characteristics of Church Planting Leaders
6. Church Planting Terminology
7. Phase Two of Church Planting - Discipleship
8. The Process of Discipleship
9. Phase Three of Church Planting - Congregating the Discipleship Groups
10. Understanding Church Planting Finances
11. Understanding Church staff
12. Phase Four of Church Planting - Ministry development and Church Launching Phase
13. Understanding and Implementing Systems
14. Phase Five of Church Planting - Multiplication
15. Understanding the challenges in Church Planting
16. How to succeed in Church Planting
17. How to plant a House Church

Student Manuals and Video Teaching material are available from our website: www.churchplantinginstitute.com or at www.amazon.com